Voice of Gold, Mr. Ybarra neglects neither Verdi's private life nor his interesting personality. He tells of Verdi's early marriage, which ended tragically with the death of his wife and their two children; he tells of the period of despair which followed; and he tells of Verdi's awakening love for Giuseppina Strepponi, first his mistress, later his wife. This book, with its vigor and gusto, will take its place beside T. R. Ybarra's many previous successes.

T. R. YBARRA has served as foreign correspondent for *The New York Times* and *Collier's* Magazine and has spent a good part of his life in Latin America. His autobiographical volume, *Young Man of Caracas*, was a Book-of-the-Mo.   Club selection.

VERDI

Also by T. R. Ybarra

YOUNG MAN OF CARACAS

YOUNG MAN OF THE WORLD

CARUSO: THE MAN OF NAPLES AND THE VOICE OF GOLD

Verdi

MIRACLE MAN OF OPERA

BY T. R. YBARRA

HARCOURT, BRACE AND COMPANY · NEW YORK

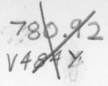

24724

TO PENNY

CONTENTS

I

DAWN

ONE

AN ASTUTE individual, this Bartolomeo Merelli, walking on a snowy afternoon along a street in Milan—astute, and with a talent for attracting both luck and ladies which had served him well in snatching for himself that golden plum, the managership of Milan's La Scala, most renowned shrine of opera in all Italy. He liked the nickname given him by the Milanese, "the Napoleon of Operatic Impresarios," deeming it a tribute to his coolness, dash and boldness in business. But just now he looked worried.

He hailed from Bergamo in Northern Italy, home town of the great Donizetti, for a few of whose earlier operas he had written the libretti; and, since his father administered the estates of a powerful and wealthy local magnate, Count Moroni, young Bartolomeo had been free to roam at will in his boyhood through the ancestral palace of the Moronis. A wild young blade, addicted to card-playing, he had hit upon the idea one day of meeting an urgent gambling debt by appropriating and selling a splendid dinner service bearing the Moroni crest. The Count discovered the theft. But, instead of getting the culprit locked up, he contented himself, in view of the elder Merelli's long and faithful service to the Moroni family, with booting Bartolomeo out of Bergamo.

After much privation the lad got a job in a theatrical agency in Milan, which brought him contacts with many theatrical folk, including a young ballerina, whom, when she left Milan, he followed in an amorous daze to Vienna, where she and he set up housekeeping together without benefit of marriage.

3

At the Vienna Opera House, where she was dancing, she so interested an old aristocrat high in the Imperial and Royal Government of Austria-Hungary that he suggested to her a similar illicit home life with himself. The lady sought counsel from young Bartolomeo Merelli as to how she should act in the face of the high official's ardent passes at her.

"Be adamant," he advised.

She was. Maddened by delay, the passionate official consulted her young adviser.

"She is so stubborn!" he wailed.

"Chastity comes high," remarked the youth, poker-faced.

"Please help me," begged the official.

"Very well."

Then Bartolomeo and the little ballerina proceeded to run the price of her virtue up to a point beyond which, they sagely reasoned, even her amorous elderly admirer would not go. Whereupon the young man informed the latter: "I have persuaded her to fall. She is yours."

Ballerina and official forthwith set up housekeeping together, the former's young lover having discreetly withdrawn from the love nest—which unbeknownst to his successor, he had shared with her—bearing in his pocket a document signed by the eminent government official appointing him Inspector General of the Imperial and Royal Austrian-Hungarian theaters. Since the job was pretty much of a sinecure young Merelli had plenty of time to resume his wooing of luck and ladies—including, among the ladies, a talented and charming young soprano singer named Giuseppina Strepponi, whom he made his mistress and the mother of a son.

Gravitating back to Milan with her, Merelli was helped by the influence of the ballerina's passionate official to add to his Vienna job that of manager of La Scala—the young lady having failed to enlighten the official as to who had preceded him in her apartment.

✦

As Bartolomeo Merelli walked along that Milan street on that snowy afternoon in 1841, a gloomy young man was also walking along it, straight toward the approaching Merelli. For one who was destined to perform a miracle, this young man, trudging gloomily through Milan's whitened streets, looked singularly unlike a miracle man. He looked much more like somebody planning to jump off a roof.

It was snowing hard in Milan. Big flakes were dropping from leaden skies, as if seeking to hide completely from view the metropolis of Lombardy, sprawling over the flat North Italian plain.

They fell on the great La Scala Theatre, most august shrine of opera in all Italy. They covered the Duomo, shrouding in a thickening garment of white its splendid façade, forcing worshipers going toward it or from it to adopt a speedier pace in their quest for shelter. They scattered and drove indoors the crowd wont to gather in fair weather on the big open space at one side of the Duomo—operatic agents, opera singers, opera conductors, musicians employed (or seeking employment) as players on some instrument or other, opera fans, hangers-on—whose custom it was to turn this open space into a sort of musical exchange.

Insistently the snow fluttered down. It cast gloom over pedestrians on the city's slushy streets. But their gloom was sunshine compared with the thoughts of that young man, as he trudged along on that snowy afternoon in 1841.

Nothing in his appearance suggested the fires of youth. As he crossly scuffed the snow aside, head bent, hands thrust limply into the pockets of his overcoat, he thought of his career, scarcely begun, as already ended.

He was a composer. Music, for him, had been a passion almost since he lay in the cradle. With melodies racing through his brain, he had journeyed to Milan, then as now Italy's musical capital, to try his luck. But the Muse had withheld

from him her favors. Two operas from his pen had been
produced by a Milanese impresario shortly before that day of
gloom and snow. To the first of them had come a small
measure of applause. It had achieved what the French call a
succès d'estime—not of sufficient substance to satisfy the
cravings of a young dreamer's soul—nor line his pocketbook—
nor fill his stomach.

His second opera had been a complete, unmitigated, resounding flop. The curtain rung down on its first performance
had been its shroud; the stage upon which those enacting
it had strutted and fretted, its grave.

Added to the bitter memory of that failure were other
memories infinitely sadder. He still winced as his thoughts
dwelt on three shattering blows struck at him by Fate in
rapid, merciless succession. Those blows had wrecked his
marriage and destroyed his home. They had left him prostrate
and crushed, shorn of happiness, bereft of hope, robbed of
the desire to go on living.

Compose another opera? He? Never! He had done with
composing and hoping.

The craving to create music, the light of his life, his dream,
his spur, the food and drink of his inner self, had vanished.
Never again would he put notes on paper! (*Within a few
years he was to turn out in quick succession three operas
which, today, more than a century later, are cornerstones of
operatic répertoires everywhere.*) Henceforth he would turn
his back on ambition! Music must vanish from his waking
hours, from the dreams coming to him in the silence of his
nights! (*Within three decades he was to compose what is
probably the most popular of all Italian grand operas.*) Let
other deluded young men thrill to imaginary acclamations
from imaginary audiences! Thus ran the thoughts of that
young man of twenty-eight. (*At 74, he was to create an opera
of sheer genius.*)

He would become a teacher! Yes, a teacher, buried under the drudgery of scales and exercises, breathing without living, with never a glance at the stars! No more would he woo the Muse! Let his pupils in their turn taste her heartlessness! (*In his 8oth year he was to stun the world with a miracle—an opera sparkling with the vitality of youth, alive with the impetuosity of youth, flaming with the fire of youth.*)

Bending his head still lower, scattering the snow under his cracked, thinning shoes with ever moodier kicks, digging his hands still deeper into the pockets of his seedy overcoat, he trudged gloomily onward. Music? Hell!

Then—all of a sudden—he ran head-on into Destiny.

Destiny, on that dark day in Milan, was impersonated by Bartolomeo Merelli, manager of Milan's La Scala Theatre. He greeted the young victim of melancholy with pleasant words; and the victim, we may be sure, countered with words which were at least polite—for he had not yet dived to such depths of despondency as to risk alienating a personage who was a monarch of "pull," a compeller of the smiles of the goddess of fortune; the man, moreover, who had put on at La Scala that youth's first two operas, the *succès d'estime* and the flop.

Ignoring the other's gloom, the impresario began to describe somewhat as follows the worries harassing him:

"Giuseppe [the young man's name was Giuseppe Verdi], I'm in a devil of a fix. I absolutely *must* produce a new opera at La Scala, and I must produce it soon. But I don't know where to find it! The other day I received a libretto from Solera—and it's a good one, full of sure-fire situations and gorgeous verses. Just the thing for Nicolai, I thought. But Nicolai, damn his pigheadedness, won't touch it—says it's anti-musical! So my plans have gone up in smoke. What am I to do, Giuseppe?"

But Giuseppe Verdi stayed as glum as ever. Not from him

would Merelli get help in his predicament. Merelli, however, falling into step by his side, craftily steered him in the direction of La Scala. There, in his office, he rummaged around until he found a fat package of pages, loosely bound together, covered with big, bold handwriting. He pushed the package into the glum young composer's hand.

"Why," inquired Giuseppe Verdi stonily, "are you giving me this?"

"Because I want you to read it. It's that libretto by Solera I mentioned to you. Grand, simply grand. On a wonderful Biblical subject. Thrills by the dozen. Take it home with you."

"I'm done with composing! Forever! I'm going to become a teacher. I'll never do another opera as long as I live!"

"Fiddlesticks!" scoffed Merelli. "Read the libretto. Set it to music." And, forcing the package of handwritten pages into the despondent youth's pocket, he pushed him masterfully to the door of the office, propelled him through it, slammed it behind him, turned the key in the lock. When Bartolomeo Merelli had a job to do as an impersonator of Destiny he did it thoroughly.

Young Verdi slunk through the snow to the bleak lodging house which was his home in Milan. He let himself into his cheerless room. He cast an unfriendly eye at the first page of the libretto which Merelli had forced upon him. On it he read:

"Nabucodonosor"
Grand Opera in Four Acts
By Temistocle Solera

With an impatient gesture of disgust he flung it across the room. As it fell to the floor it flew open to a page on which Solera had written the words of a chorus:

Va, pensiero,
Sull' ali dorate . . .

("Go, thought, on wings of gold.") Something about those lines suddenly struck a chord of sympathy in young Verdi. He picked up the libretto. He read the words of that chorus to the end. He found them beautiful—all they needed to be more beautiful still was some beautiful music.

Bah! With another moody gesture of renunciation he again flung aside the manuscript. He went to bed. Still those verses haunted him. He could not get them out of his head. He tossed, open-eyed, on creased pillow and crumpled sheets. Finally, he leaped out of bed, took up Solera's libretto yet again. And now, the Muse was at his elbow once more, smiling.

Soon he was feverishly fitting notes to "Va, pensiero." And that night, and during whole days and nights after it, he jotted down notes, notes, notes—sometimes just a few, sometimes, in a headlong rush of inspiration, hundreds and hundreds at a time.

Before long he had fashioned tunes for the entire libretto —tentative tunes of course, nothing final as yet, but still— there they were, on the table before him—solos, duets, trios, concerted pieces, everything—the full score of a full-fledged grand opera!

He dashed over to La Scala. He showed the score to Merelli. That astute individual, running his eyes over the massed notes, smiled slyly. Bright hopes of artistic triumph and pecuniary profit blossomed inside him. For all he cared, pigheaded Nicolai could go to the devil now.

He congratulated the young composer. "I'll put this on the cartellone of La Scala. (The cartellone was the list of operas planned by Italian managers for production each season at their opera houses.) And Giuseppe Verdi forgot all about his idea of becoming a teacher.

But, when the cartellone for the coming La Scala season was plastered all over Milan's billboards, there was no men-

tion of the Verdi-Solera opera. With the abruptness charac-
teristic of all theatrical managers in all epochs of history
Merelli had decided to postpone it. But he reckoned without
Giuseppe Verdi.

Conspicuous even at that early stage of his life for sudden
outbursts of fiery temper—later, in the days of his glory, they
sometimes assumed the majesty of volcanic eruptions—the
young composer wrote Merelli a letter. In it he used molten
language most inappropriate from an impecunious youth
addressing a potentate. "My opera goes on this season, or
not at all!" In after years, Verdi confessed that he had run
an awful risk that day; only by providential good luck, he
said, had he been saved from being kicked out of Merelli's
office, with his career in ruins.

But Merelli knew the artistic temperament. He apologized
to young Verdi. He smoothed down the youth's ruffled
feathers. He agreed to mention *Nabucodonosor* in a last-
minute postscript to the *cartellone* for that season.

He kept his word. Moreover, forgetting Verdi's recent unbridled vehemence, he was generous in his financial arrangements. That is, generous according to the standards of the
day. What he promised in terms of money was not much, but
it was akin to a golden shower in the eyes of a needy youth
like Giuseppe Verdi. Bartolomeo Merelli was not only fair.
He could read the future.

Lest his protégé get too puffed up by his good fortune the
impresario told him that his opera would have to do without
new scenery. It was to be put on, he said, with settings (somewhat shopworn) which had already seen service in an Oriental ballet recently presented at La Scala. Verdi, no longer a
miniature Vesuvius, nodded in acquiescence. After his un-
diplomatic outburst he was glad to find himself still on
speaking terms with La Scala's manager.

TWO

A ND NOW, for Giuseppe Verdi, came busy days and nights
working and arguing with Temistocle Solera about the
latter's libretto. *Nabucodonosor*, invariably called *Nabucco*
for short, dealt thrillingly and sonorously with a Biblical
theme centering around the captivity of the Jews in Babylon
during the reign of Nebuchadnezzar.

Librettist and composer soon became friends. A man of
great size (Verdi once called him "a species of Colossus"),
formidable strength and ferocious temper, Solera got himself
into trouble again and again with Austrian gendarmes by his
explosive objections in their hearing to Austrian rule over
Northern Italy.

But he failed to overawe Giuseppe Verdi. That reckless
youth started right in to criticize the libretto for *Nabucco*.

"Take out the aria for soprano here," he said to Solera,
"and substitute a prayer for bass."

"Like hell I will!" roared Solera. Verdi insisted, cajoled,
fumed. The gigantic librettist sizzled with rage. He glared
at his critic. One blow from his fist would have knocked
Verdi flat. But, almost always, he bowed eventually to the
young critic's wishes (often, undoubtedly, with the aid of
that most efficacious of Italian peace-makers, a table in front
of a café, with a couple of drinks on it).

Once, borrowing Merellian tactics, Verdi pushed the pro-
testing Solera into a room, locked the door, and informed
the imprisoned Colossus through the keyhole that he would
not be let out until he had altered something according to
the desires of his collaborator. An hour or so elapsed—amid
alarming mutterings from the other side of the door—and

then out came Solera, growling hideously, but with his verses changed, in conformity with the composer's wishes.

At last, one day, the tempestuous collaboration of Giuseppe Verdi and Temistocle Solera ended, without fatal results to either. But Verdi had still to argue about details with manager Merelli.

"Your chorus at La Scala isn't big enough," grumbled the young maestro.

"You'll have to get along with it as it is," said Merelli. "Not one penny more will I spend on *Nabucco*."

At this point a well-to-do Milanese opera enthusiast interposed with: "Let *me* foot the bill for the extra singers." Verdi's problem seemed solved. But, Latin-like, he was suddenly taken proud.

"I cannot possibly permit that," he said coldly, like a Spanish grandee. "I'll pay for the extra choristers myself." And he did.

At the rehearsals the singers chosen to enact the principal rôles in the new work and everybody else who heard its music being rehearsed were struck by its *newness*. Verdi's setting of Solera's words had a vigor, a nervous directness, a vibrant freshness, a rough power, distinctly different from the kind of opera that had been usual in Italy for years.

It was as if the composer, a recruit in the ranks of practitioners of the operatic art, was grappling with something inside him that he could not quite express. Not only the singers who sang the music and the musicians in La Scala's orchestra who played it but also the stage hands and carpenters busy backstage with their chores felt this new quality; dropping whatever they were doing they would cluster in the wings while *Nabucco's* arias and ensembles were being rehearsed— oblivious to everything except Verdi's notes—idle, rapt—murmuring, in their Milanese dialect: *"Che fota nova!*—What a novelty!"

On the night of March 9, 1842, *Nabucco* was produced at La Scala. According to the custom of the time the composer was allowed to sit, tucked away inconspicuously, among the musicians in the orchestra; indeed, in earlier years Italian composers of opera on first nights were supposed to make themselves useful by turning the pages of the score for one of the musicians. But young Verdi was not required to do that.

Which was just as well, for he was terribly nervous. As the opera moved along its way, sounds which to the apprehensive youth seemed alarming came from the enormous audience that filled the theater—Merelli had made such extravagant claims in his advertising for the new work that he had raised the expectations of the Milanese to fever heat and brought them out in force. There were strange noises; hoarse ejaculations that seemed to Giuseppe Verdi like angry growls, murmurs which, to his quivering mind, seemed to presage stentorian hostility, if not imminent physical violence to himself.

When the first act was approaching its close these manifestations had reached such volume as to make him fear that, as soon as the curtain came down, the audience would leap to its feet, howling for his blood.

The curtain dropped.

The hundreds of auditors broke into one tremendous roar of joy. "They did not applaud," chronicled one commentator, "they went mad." Repeatedly, the creator of the music of *Nabucco,* pushed and pulled before the curtain by his colleagues, was forced to bow, shaking with excitement, tears gushing from his eyes.

It was the same after the next act. Seldom if ever had Milan put on such a riot. The opera's brusque contrasts had life. Its tremendous ensembles set hearts to beating, blood to racing through people's veins. "This," said one of those who heard it that night, "is music for troops attacking."

Act III. The curtain rises on the members of the chorus, representing the Jews, torn from their homeland, languishing in Babylonian captivity. In their anguish they sing the words of the Lament which had so impressed young Verdi:

> Go, thought, on wings of gold,
> Alight on hilltops fair,
> Whose breezes, soft and rare,
> Our native land enfold. . . .

Solera's words. Or rather a free, very free, translation of his original Italian version of "Va, pensiero." To them, the composer had joined a melody, which, today, well over a century after it first occurred to Giuseppe Verdi, still stands as one of his loveliest (how that staunch Verdian, Arturo Toscanini, delights in it!). As the sound of it died away, the crowd of listeners across the footlights went utterly out of control. Men and women swayed in their seats. They were in delirium. They sprang up, shouting, sobbing, brushing tears aside, sending to La Scala's rafters thunders of acclamation such as that grand old temple of Italian opera had seldom if ever heard in its long life. "Bravo!" "Bravissimo!" "Ancora!" The Lament had to be repeated—and repeated again.

At the end of the fourth act, after the curtain had fallen for the last time on that memorable first-night performance, the audience broke again into madness. The young composer was compelled to come out and make uncounted bows—dazed, shaken, unbelieving.

Behind the scenes, as Verdi staggered back exhausted, from the footlights, women (also men, in exuberant Latin fashion) kissed him on both cheeks, particularly the prima donna, Giuseppina Strepponi, who had done a grand job in the leading female rôle. Wild applause, joyful shouts and compliments, came from stage carpenters, scene shifters, call boys —in fact, the rumpus behind the curtain, though smaller in volume, compared favorably in excitement with the one out in front. One can imagine the orgies of osculation staged by Merelli, the rapturous bear-hugs with which Solera the Colossus almost suffocated the composer!

In the wake of *Nabucco's* clamorous *première* manager Merelli laid before Giuseppe Verdi a blank contract. It dealt with one of La Scala's most coveted accolades to composers, the *opera d'obbligo*, leading feature of each season there—an entirely new work by one of Italy's prominent operatic composers. This accolade usually went to an established musician of high repute, a man of the stamp of Rossini or Donizetti, Mercadante or Pacini or Ricci. Now—such was the terrific impact of *Nabucco*—La Scala's manager was offering it to Verdi, practically unknown before that sensational first night of March 9, 1842.

On the contract form the terms were left for the composer to fill in. Dazed with the honor that had come to him, Verdi knocked at the door of the dressing-room of Giuseppina Strepponi. He saw riches beckoning to him, a future all happiness and gold. He needed advice. Giuseppina seemed to like him. He would get it from her.

Giuseppina Strepponi looked over the contract. Curbing young Verdi's excited babblings, she calmly reminded him that the great Bellini had received from La Scala for his masterpiece, seemingly immortal *Norma*, the sum of 8,000 Austrian lire, equivalent to about $1,350.

"You are young," she said. "You must not be too grasping. Don't ask more than Bellini got."

He took her advice. He agreed to compose a new opera for production at La Scala for the same remuneration (how pitifully small it seems nowadays!) that Bellini had received.

In addition to the payment by Merelli Verdi profited by the sale to Giovanni Ricordi, an enterprising Milan music publisher, of the publication rights of the music of *Nabucco*. For these rights Ricordi paid 3,000 Austrian lire (about $500) to be divided in equal parts between the manager of La Scala and the composer.

But Merelli refused to countenance this arrangement. His half (roughly $250) he turned over to Verdi. Merellis don't grow on every bush.

No more privations for Giuseppe Verdi! No more black anticipations of a life of soulless teaching! But, before that night of liberation at La Scala, when his thrilling triumph with *Nabucco* snatched him from poverty and obscurity, he had lived through many hard and bare years—years which had stamped their mark on him, which he never forgot.

II

STRUGGLE

THREE

I N THE autumn of the second year of the second war between Britain and the U. S., when Napoleon Bonaparte was still unbeaten and Ludwig van Beethoven still alive, neighbors said to Luigia Verdi: "Luigia, we promise that as soon as your baby is born we'll gather under your window and serenade you both." They kept their promise. So, among the very first sounds heard in this world by Luigia Verdi's little son was the sound of music. Nothing could have been more appropriate.

He was born October 10, 1813, the same year as Richard Wagner—and twenty-eight years and five months before that triumphant opening night of *Nabucco* at La Scala in Milan— in the village of Le Roncole, within the territory of what was then the Duchy of Parma, in Northern Italy. Two days later, Carlo Verdi, his father, innkeeper at Le Roncole, and his mother, Luigia Uttini Verdi, duly accompanied by a godfather and other interested parties, carried the child three miles over a rough country road to the town of Busseto, metropolis of the district. There, while the godfather held him in his arms, a priest sprinkled him with holy water, and bestowed upon him, according to local custom, a formidable string of names —*Giuseppe Fortunino Francesco Verdi*. That was the complete appellation carried away from the christening font at Busseto by that two-day-old boy—destined to become the most popular operatic composer who ever lived.

On the official document recording his birth it was given as *Joseph Fortunin François Verdi*, because Busseto and the region roundabout, as well as much of the rest of Italy, was under French rule. The soldiers of Napoleon Bonaparte, having overrun the Italian peninsula shortly before the 18th century ended, were still hanging on to a lot of it; and some time was yet to elapse before Waterloo was won and lost, Napoleon captured and exiled, and the French form of Giuseppe Verdi's name banished forever from his life except on his birth certificate.

During the long French occupation of Italy the Napoleonic yoke weighed heavily on Italians and most of them dreamed constantly of throwing it off. Giuseppe Verdi (soon nicknamed Peppino, equivalent to our Joe or Joey) was far too young to bother about it, but yarns dealing with it, heard by him in later years, may easily have done their bit in creating the smoldering dislike which he always felt for France and the French.

For one thing, during the occupation, Italians of military age were conscripted ruthlessly to help Napoleon conquer Europe. One big contingent was marched off into Russia to take part in the French invasion of that country; and, it is said, only about one in every one hundred ever got back home. Not many Italians in those years were as lucky as Gioacchino Rossini, most famous fashioner of operas in Italy, until Giuseppe Verdi helped to push him out of first place there. Having been called to service in Bonaparte's forces, Rossini, very apprehensive, presented himself before officials of the army of occupation, fully expecting to be thrown into a French uniform. But, fortunately for him, one of them was an ardent admirer of Rossinian music, and, having pulled mysterious strings to good purpose, he brought vast relief to the composer by informing him that he would not have to serve in the French army. "Which," remarked Rossini, "was a wonderful break for the French army."

At Le Roncole, Giuseppe Verdi lived through the first

years of his life in the combination hostelry and general store in which he had been born—a sort of lean-to, grimy, neglected, unpainted, behind a few forlorn trees fringing the road in front—with plaster peeling from its walls, and unglassed windows encased in ramshackle wooden shutters, opening onto a bleak stretch of dry, dusty plain—a dour dwelling in a grim region where men and women had to do cruelly hard work to make a living. He had no little brothers to play with, only a little sister who died in childhood.

He adored his mother. And if the following story about her is typical he had good reason for his adoration:

One day, when the French were being driven out of Italy by the armies of the Austrian Emperor and the Russian Czar, closing in on Bonaparte for the kill, a squad of cavalry, brutal, thieving men, galloping into poor little Le Roncole, proceeded to loot and rape and murder. Some of the villagers, in a panic, huddled, trembling and praying, inside the village church; but for the marauders that holy place had no holiness. Crowding into its aisles, drunk and profane, they continued within the walls to indulge their savage instincts.

Luigia Verdi, Giuseppe's mother, rightly guessing that the main body of the building, where fellow-villagers were shrieking and dying, was no place for her and her baby son, dashed for the entrance of the steeple, climbed the ladder inside it, gained the topmost landing, under the big bells of the church, and crouched with Giuseppe behind a pile of firewood. Neither Austrian nor Russian discovered her hiding place. And not until they had clattered away from the scene of their misdeeds did she descend the ladder, holding to it with one arm and cradling her baby with the other, and return unharmed to their home. "From her," wrote one of the many chroniclers of Giuseppe's later life, "he got his courage and indomitable will power." Today there is an inscription on

Le Roncole's church telling of how the boy's mother, by her presence of mind, "saved for art a sublime archangel."

From earliest infancy Peppino gave evidence of a passionate love for music. It was about the only thing that could snatch him from his recurrent melancholy moods. One day, in his babyhood, held in his mother's arms, he was carried into the bar of his father's inn, while a customer who loved music and had a good, true voice was tunefully singing a new song by Cherubini, a composer highly popular at that time, to the other regular patrons gathered at the surrounding tables. The babe-in-arms, kicking up his heels in glee, chuckled and gurgled and smiled contentedly.

"Ha!" cried the singer, as he finished his song. "Peppino likes my singing."

"Nonsense!" interposed another customer, who also loved music and fancied himself as a singer, but was never able to sing in tune. "What he likes is that big gold watch chain of yours."

"Well, *you* sing something."

Thus challenged, the other obliged, and, as always, promptly went off the key. The baby howled lugubriously.

While he was acting one Sunday, at the age of five, as an acolyte at the village church, little Giuseppe became so entranced with the notes of the organ accompanying the Mass that he forgot all else—the chanting priest, the kneeling congregation, everything.

"*Acqua,*" whispered the priest. (One of the acolyte's duties at this point of the Mass was to hand some holy water to the priest.) Giuseppe paid no heed.

"*Acqua!*" repeated the priest, with menace in the word. Still the little acolyte saw and heard nothing earthly. As the sounds from the organ swept over him his whole being was transported to mysterious celestial regions. Infuriated by his negligence, the priest, moving close to him, gave him such a kick that Giuseppe rolled off the platform bordering the altar, and, striking his head against the floor of the church, fainted away. When he came to he showed neither anger nor regret nor fear. He just sat up, rubbing his head, gazed toward the organ loft, drank in again the marvelous sounds coming from it—and, once more, with the world well lost, he was spirited away to his private personal heaven.

The boy's father, all honor to him, instead of disapproving of his son's absorption in music (such a dubious highway to earning a living!) bought for him a broken-down old spinet, with rusty wires, crazy wobbly legs and loose pedals. Before presenting it to little Giuseppe he had the instrument put into a passably playable condition by an expert on musical instruments residing in the neighborhood. After making the necessary repairs that worthy workman put into the cover of the spinet a note, famous in the Verdian saga, which reads: "I, Stefano Cavaletti, added new hammers and provided them with leather-covered pedals. These, together with the hammers, I give as a present in recognition of the industry displayed by the boy Giuseppe Verdi in playing on this instrument. That is reward enough for me for my trouble. Anno Domini 1821."

That moribund musical—or shall I say unmusical—contraption meant unbounded happiness to little Giuseppe. Hour after hour his fingers strummed over its yellowed keys; again and again the combinations which he made out of them brought tears of bliss to his eyes.

One day, experimenting in a haphazard manner, for as yet he had no actual musical knowledge, he happened to strike the tonic triad in C major. It delighted him. Never had he heard such a wonderful, satisfying sound.

Early next day, rushing back to the spinet, he tried to find that delicious chord again. But, try as he would, it eluded him. With more tears in his eyes, tears of anger this time,

he picked up a hammer and struck the old spinet a furious
blow with it. Had he been a little older and stronger that
blow might have ended forever the old instrument's already
precarious hold on life. Fortunately, however, it continued
functioning after a fashion, and Giuseppe, it is to be pre-
sumed, eventually rediscovered the C major chord, and assailed the instrument no more, since, long after his tantrum,
he was still eliciting magic from its battered keyboard. Today
that spinet is in Milan, where multitudes look upon it in respectful awe.

Another source of enchantment was provided for the little
boy by the performances of a ragged wandering fiddler, whose
name—Bagasset—has been preserved for us of today simply
and solely because of the part played by him in the early
years of the life of the son of Le Roncole's innkeeper.

Bagasset earned a meager living trudging from one village
to another in the Busseto region scraping his decrepit violin
at a few pennies per scrape outside peasants' homes, or in the
gustatory departments of inns like Carlo Verdi's; or, with
much more lucrative results, at weddings and other occasions
of local rejoicing. Also at funerals. Carlo Verdi used to allow
him, dusty, dirty and dropping with fatigue, to sleep in a
wretched sort of barn behind his inn, among pigs and
chickens; and, after the fiddler had entertained the inn's
habitués, he would stake the humble fellow to rough food
and raw wine.

Humble? Bagasset humble? Not to little Giuseppe! To him,
the tattered, unwashed wanderer was a messenger from a
mysterious land of ethereal song. As soon as Bagasset hove in
sight on the dusty road leading to Le Roncole Giuseppe would
rush off to listen to his unmelodious scratchings. Wherever
Bagasset went the little boy tagged at his heels.

And to the eternal credit of the seedy musician he advised
Carlo Verdi to see that his son got musical instruction with-

out any more delay. And Carlo Verdi, again all honor to him, nodding in agreement, arranged (though extra expense was emphatically not a thing to be courted in his hard life) to have the organist at Le Roncole's church, an old fellow named Baistrocchi, give his music-mad son elementary lessons in organ-playing and general musical lore.

Many years later, when Giuseppe Verdi's operas were famous all over the world, Bagasset used to come, as tattered as ever, to the composer's villa near Busseto, and play there on his fiddle as he used to do when the villa's owner was little, scraping out discordant sounds for him to whom music had brought celebrity and wealth. And Verdi, remembering those faraway yesterdays when the wandering fiddler was to him a messenger from the angels, would listen, as if memories of his boyhood were trailing clouds of glory around him. And when Bagasset was ready to shuffle away again, Giuseppe Verdi would see that his pockets were well stuffed with solids and liquids for the road, and, better still, with money.

Within a short time little Peppino succeeded Baistrocchi as organist at Le Roncole's church, after the old fellow had taught the young boy all that he was capable of teaching. Thus, Giuseppe Verdi, somewhere around his twelfth birthday, became a professional musician, a calling which, followed by him to the end of his long life, was to bring him gold and fame.

But neither of those useful commodities was exactly conspicuous when old Baistrocchi stepped down from the organ loft at the church of Le Roncole and young Peppino stepped into it. He was, as regards renown, still unknown even to the people of Busseto, three miles away. And, as for riches, he received as regular payment for his organ-playing something like ten dollars a year.

However, there was extra money to be earned by rattling

off gay tunes for church weddings and mournful dirges at
funerals. That brought in, say, another ten dollars per annum.
Twenty dollars for twelve months. A princely sum, little
Peppino doubtless thought to himself.

FOUR

SOME time after Peppino Verdi had started out on his job
as organist at the church of Le Roncole, Carlo, his
father, valiantly resisting all temptations to put the boy to
work at his general store or his inn, turned his thoughts instead to getting him decently educated. Carlo Verdi realized
that his son's native village was not capable of providing the
brand of schooling to which the far-sighted parent felt him
to be entitled. He decided that Peppino, in the interests of
the higher education, must spend his weekdays in neighboring
Busseto.

Now, Busseto, like many other similar Italian communities
of a few thousand souls, had a goodly sprinkling of persons of
culture and refinement, conversant with the arts. And these
worthy persons were particularly proud of their town's reputation of being ultra-musical. When Emperor Charles V and
Pope Paul III met there in the 16th century to discuss solemn
affairs of state, some music-minded Bussetians trooped forth
to welcome them, old chronicles aver, with "splendid concerts."

And, in subsequent centuries, Busseto had taken pains that
its reputation as a little highbrow center of the arts should
not be allowed to wither. So Giuseppe's father arranged that
his son was to get *board and lodging* in the home of a worthy
cobbler of Busseto, at the rate of eight cents daily.

Also it happened that his father in stocking his store at

Le Roncole with the staple run of articles most welcome to his customers—wine, macaroni, liquor, sugar, coffee, tobacco, oil, cheese, sausages—dealt largely with a wholesaler of Busseto, one Antonio Barezzi, with whom he was on friendly terms. So he made a deal whereby his son, when not at work in his classes or asleep in his bed, was to help at the Barezzi emporium.

This, for the little boy of Le Roncole, was an exceptional piece of good luck. For Barezzi, besides being a prosperous business man, was an enthusiastic devotee of music, a player on several musical instruments, including one with the mellifluous name of ophicleide, and, best of all, head of the Busseto Philharmonic Society, an association of amateur local music-lovers, who met regularly at the Barezzi residence to regale one another with selections from meritorious old masters of music. Soon little Giuseppe was busily copying out the various parts for the musicians participating in the concerts at Barezzi's house, acting occasionally as conductor, and even composing musical pieces out of his own head. These the Philharmonic Society, more and more impressed by the musical ability of Peppino, consented to play at some of their cultured gatherings.

Giuseppe also composed marches for the Busseto Municipal Brass Band, which, as in numerous other Italian towns, enjoyed high distinction among the townspeople, and the band played them in Busseto's principal square with much fervor and din, and their creator became more and more a little local John Philip Sousa.

For many years Giuseppe Verdi failed to outgrow this early brass band epoch; one of his principal defects, which was to give acute pain to his detractors, was the uninhibited brassiness of the orchestra in his operas. In his earlier scores the orchestration is perfunctory (how often do his critics writhe because of his "guitar orchestra!"). Verdi's early orchestration often shows a small-boyish partiality for noise. Incidentally, one of the young man's stentorian Busseto effusions was adjudged by him some years later of such merit that he stuck it bodily into his *Nabucco* score.

Besides going to school, taking music lessons, helping Barezzi in the grocery business, playing the organ every Sunday at Le Roncole (for which, once weekly, he covered the six miles from Busseto to that village and back on foot) and taking part with increasing frequency in the concerts staged by the ophicleide virtuoso and his friends, he also read eagerly at Busseto's Library, especially literature and history, seeking to "penetrate the past," as someone said.

And there was something else to keep Giuseppe busy. Barezzi had a young daughter, Margherita, with whom the youth performed piano duets. Moreover, shortly after going to live with the Barezzis (they had invited him to come over to them from the cobbler's) Giuseppe became a regular member of the Busseto Municipal Brass Band. He played the big drum.

For general knowledge and music respectively, young Verdi had two teachers, a priest named Pietro Seletti and a musican, Ferdinando Provesi. Both were competent imparters of learning; and Provesi, the organist at Busseto's principal church, had won distinction as a composer of light operas, several of which had been performed at Italian theaters. Seletti drilled the young man in the three R's and other regulation studies, including Latin. Provesi pounded into him the rudiments of musical theory and much lore, technical and historical, concerning masters of the musical art, among them, particularly, Palestrina—whom Giuseppe revered to the end of his life—and Mozart, of whom he seems to have got too much of a dose from Provesi for satisfactory digestion, since he remarked long afterward that for a time he could hardly bear to listen to Mozartian music.

In all his studies young Verdi showed such industry and intelligence that both his teachers were generous in their praise of his proficiency. Says his biographer Francis Toye: "He worked so hard and so successfully at Latin that Seletti complained of the time he was wasting on music. He worked so hard and so successfully at music that Provesi complained of the time he was wasting on Latin." * Eventually the Latin teacher was forced to admit his mistake.

But, before doing so, Seletti, intent on preparing Giuseppe for the priesthood, tried hard to steer the boy away from music by scoffing at his musical ability. Once, having learned that a certain organist would not be able to do a promised stint at one of Busseto's churches, he said sarcastically to young Verdi: "How about your substituting for him at the organ?"

That sounded good to Giuseppe. Having obtained the job as a substitute, he poured into the church a golden stream of sound. Seletti was amazed.

"Whose music was it that you played?" he asked the boy.

"My own."

"What do you mean?"

"I made it up as I went along."

The teacher was struck speechless. After some moments, putting his hand on Giuseppe's shoulder, he muttered:

"Forget Latin. Study music." Good advice. What could Latin have done for Giuseppe Verdi compared with what *Rigoletto* did?

One of young Verdi's special jobs while he was studying under Provesi was to teach a member of the Busseto Philharmonic Society, a viola player blind since birth known as Donnino Il Cieco, the viola parts in pieces played by his fellow-members. Donnino was a wonderful improviser; not

* Francis Toye, *Giuseppe Verdi, His Life & Works*. New York, Alfred A. Knopf, Inc., 1946.

being able to read notes from printed scores he much preferred to string them together out of his head. It was Verdi's
job to enable him to play his viola selections as their composers had written them.

So Verdi, with incredible patience, played those parts over
and over again to the blind man, until Donnino, a musician
by intuition, had learned them by heart. In this way his
teacher made it possible for him to join his colleagues in favorite selections of the day, such as Rossini's *Barber of Seville*
and *Cenerentola* overtures, also highbrow quartets of forbidding difficulty—and so remarkable was his drilling by Giuseppe
that he seldom missed a note. Unfortunately, Verdi's blind
pupil died young; and, more unfortunately still, his death
was due in part to heavy drinking.

One foggy night, while he was walking, dog-tired, between
Le Roncole and Busseto, Giuseppe Verdi blundered off the
road and tumbled into a deep ditch by the side of it, filled
with slimy water and thick mud. Floundering desperately,
he sank deeper and deeper—his terrified cries for help, since
he had taken his tumble in a lonely neighborhood, were in
vain. Finally, when his predicament seemed hopeless, a
woman, happening to pass by and hearing his despairing
shouts, dragged him, exhausted and covered with slime, out
of the ditch. A few moments more and the world would have
had to get along without *Trovatore* and *Traviata*, *Aïda*, *Otello*
and *Falstaff*.

Meanwhile, Antonio Barezzi had become increasingly fond
of the strange, moody boy from Le Roncole. Behind his awk-
wardness and occasional outbursts of temper the worthy
grocer perceived golden traits—integrity, iron will power, astonishing musical ability. By now he was practically a member of the Barezzi family. And his fame as a musical wonder
grew to such proportions that from neighboring villages admirers of his noisy marches and vigorous bâton-waving hired

big buses to take them to Busseto and back. And his piano duets with Margherita Barezzi grew more numerous and protracted than ever.

All through his life Giuseppe Verdi's relations with the residents of Busseto had their ups and downs. Even after he had become a great celebrity there were Bussetians more or less hostile to him. And Giuseppe repaid their hostility to the full. But, in general, he gradually had become Busseto's favorite son and preserved that distinction through rain and shine.

In the first days of his renown somebody dubbed him the Swan of Busseto, just as Rossini, when he first burst on the Italian musical horizon, did not escape being called the Swan of Pesaro. Swannishness angered Verdi, that down-to-earth, quick-tempered hater of frills and fripperies. It merely amused Rossini who, at the height of swan-dom, satirically wrote on the title page of a Mass composed by him: "By the Old Ape of Pesaro." In Verdi's old age a movement was started by admirers to have their idol elevated to the Italian nobility with the title of Marquis of Busseto. Their idol exploded with typical ferocity. And there were those who dubbed him the Bear of Busseto. That nickname he probably liked.

Naturally, young Verdi never lost sight of the fact that he must eventually choose some branch of study capable of affording him a permanent means of earning a livelihood. Since music was to be his main line of work—on that he had firmly made up his mind—it was to music that he must turn. A regular job as church organist was, it seemed, the best bet.

So he worked harder than ever in the organ loft at Le Roncole. And his fellow-villagers felt increasing liking both for his playing and for him. They called him *il maestrino* (the little maestro). And when an aspirant for his position, formidably backed by a bishop, tried to get it away from him, the villagers banded together, shouting angrily. And they saw to it that he kept his job, even though he had no bishop hovering over him.

One day the post of church organist at the neighboring village of Soragna fell vacant, and, since Soragna was rather more important than Le Roncole, Giuseppe Verdi put in a bid for it. But, to his disgust, a rival also put in an application, and, whatever his other qualifications were, he had one telling point in his favor—"pull." He got the job.

Seated on Sundays before Le Roncole's old organ, after his weekly three-mile walk from Busseto, young Verdi continued to play and improvise and dream. After all, might he not some day become organist at Busseto? If he did, his future would be assured. Who was he to aspire to something higher than the post which had suited Ferdinando Provesi for many years?

But, as a matter of fact, the next phase of his career was not to develop either at Le Roncole or Busseto. And his good angel in its development was not to be Carlo Verdi of Le Roncole but another angel, equally generous and far more able to implement his generosity—Antonio Barezzi, the musical wholesale grocer.

FIVE

IN ONE of Chekov's plays, *The Three Sisters*, of which I heard a performance in Russian, the three principal female characters, I remember, fed up with life in a provincial Russian city, grouped themselves close to the footlights and intoned in unison: "To Moscow!" Well, the same sort of thing, *mutatis mutandis*, took place in Busseto in A.D. 1832, when Giuseppe Verdi was in his 19th year.

Just as Carlo Verdi had decided some time before that Le Roncole was not good enough for the education of his son,

so now Antonio Barezzi made the same decision regarding
Busseto in relation to young Verdi. "To Milan!" he advised
the youth.

Forthwith, preparations were made for transplanting Giuseppe to the capital of Italian music, where musically ambitious young students could fit themselves to earn a living
by composing music, playing it, teaching it, or doing all three.

In the 17th century an epidemic of plague at Busseto had
moved those who had lost children in it to create the Monte
di Pietà e d'Abbondanza, a sort of Memorial Trust Fund, the
income from which had been used ever since to help finance
deserving young men wishing to qualify themselves for one
of the liberal professions. Barezzi and other influential Bussetians succeeded in having part of the proceeds of this Fund
allotted over a period of two years to Giuseppe Verdi.

That meant 600 francs—about $120 yearly—not enough to
pay Giuseppe's expenses in Milan for board, lodging, music
lessons and unavoidable etceteras. So Antonio Barezzi promised to make up the deficit. (With his first royalties Verdi later
repaid him. And, some forty years later, when he was old and
affluent and famous, he donated a fund producing the equivalent of $200 yearly, to be added to the four existing scholar-
ships provided by the Busseto institution.)

After bidding good-bye to relatives and friends, including
the Busseto Brass Band, Giuseppe Verdi set out for the famous
city where he was to begin his conquest of the world of opera.

On arrival there he went to the home of Antonio Seletti,
brother of his teacher in Busseto. There he found warm
welcome; indeed Seletti's brother invited him to share his
home, an invitation which the green, bewildered, small-town
lad, who knew nobody in the big city, was glad to accept.
More than half a century later the son of the hospitable
Signor Seletti was still keeping the room which Verdi had
occupied in his house with the furniture exactly as it was

when young Giuseppe lived in it. And, today, on the Seletti residence, there is an inscription informing passers-by that it was the home of Giuseppe Verdi when he was living in Milan "learning the rudiments of an art which made him immortal."

In Milan there was at the time of Giuseppe's arrival a well-known Conservatory of Music; and to the important musicologists running that institution (among whom the most important was named Basily) he promptly applied for admission as a paying pupil. Considering all the time that he had given to the study of music at Le Roncole and Busseto he doubtless felt no fear of rejection. But such confidence, if he had it, was misplaced. The exercise submitted by him to the Committee on Admissions failed to find favor. And the unimpressive bucolic appearance of the youth gave no hint of present ability or future eminence. The examiners found fault with the way he held his hands. And his shoulders. And his elbows. "There is nothing to be done with this lout!" "He's too old to change."

The judges refused to admit him. That refusal is famous. By issuing it, those bigwigs called to themselves the attention of posterity.

Of course, the members of the tribunal that rejected Verdi may have acted in strict accordance with their consciences. After all, in the youth before them they saw merely a black-bearded, black-whiskered individual, hardly better than a country bumpkin—and Verdi himself in later years admitted that the musical exercise submitted by him to the Conservatory authorities was very bad indeed. And the average age of students was between 9 and 18, whereas Verdi was over 18. Also, there were few beds in the institution and only one piano. Nevertheless, the members of the Committee, Basily and the rest of them, must often have wished during their subsequent years on earth that they had handed down' a different verdict.

After the sentence, one of the Rejection Committee advised young Giuseppe to find himself a private music teacher. He suggested a friend, Professor Vincenzo Lavigna. So to Lavigna the disappointed boy went, and with Lavigna he arranged to take the music lessons which now must needs be substituted for those refused him at the Conservatory.

Under his new teacher young Verdi worked hard, and, luckily for him, Lavigna became fond of the shy youth from the "sticks." Like Provesi, Lavigna was well grounded in the mathematics and mechanics and cold scientific structure of the musical art. He was a *contrapuntista fortissimo*—a fanatic on counterpoint. Also, again like Provesi, Giuseppe's new teacher was the composer of several operas which had earned for him some success. (I wonder what percentage of Italians in the early part of the 19th century grew to man's estate without composing at least one opera. 10 per cent? 15 per cent?) Lavigna proceeded to pound into his new pupil fugues and more fugues and still more fugues.

In addition to his teaching, Lavigna also officiated as *maestro al cembalo* in the orchestra at La Scala. This means that he acted as conductor seated at the piano, still referred to in this period by its original name of *cembalo*. And thereby hangs a tale: once a French journalist, relying over-much on his knowledge of the Italian language, wrote an article in which the term *maestro al cembalo* figured—and all Italians who happened to read it had a good laugh because the Frenchman had translated the phrase "teacher of cymbal-playing."

Lavigna was a friend of Basily, head of the committee at the Milan Conservatory which had rejected Verdi—and that gave the latter a grand chance for revenge. One night, when Basily was visiting Lavigna, he sounded off on the subject of the deplorable lack of musical knowledge shown at a recent examination by the applicants for the post of organist at a church in nearby Monza. All of them, fumed Basily, had failed to produce a satisfactory fugue on a subject chosen by him. Lavigna, pointing to his pupil, Verdi, quietly studying in a corner of the room, suggested to Basily that the young man be allowed to try his hand at constructing the desired fugue. So Basily's subject was handed to the youth.

In an amazingly short space of time Verdi produced the fugue. Basily saw at once that it was constructed correctly and that the young man had, just for good measure, tacked onto it what musical experts call a double canon.

"Why did you add that?" Basily asked Giuseppe.

"Because," calmly answered the young student, "I thought the subject pretty thin."

Soon Giuseppe met a group of socially prominent amateurs of music (including Count Renato Borromeo, of a positively super-noble family), who sang or played various instruments at the Filodrammatici Theatre, under the direction of a youth called Masini. The latter usually left the direction of rehearsals to three assistants, each of whom took his turn at polishing up the performers in preparation for opening nights. Following the advice of his teacher, Lavigna, Verdi attended some of the rehearsals.

One night all three of Masini's assistants played truant, to the consternation of their chief, who had so long neglected rehearsing that he did not feel up to tackling it at such short notice. Suddenly he had an idea: Why not have young Giuseppe Verdi conduct at the piano? The work being rehearsed was a formidable one, Haydn's *The Creation*. "Just play the left hand," advised Masini patronizingly.

Supremely confident—seldom in his long life was Giuseppe Verdi so near despair as on that snowy afternoon in Milan shortly before the *Nabucco première*—he seated himself at the piano. At sight of his threadbare, semi-rustic clothes and gen-

erally plebeian appearance, the delegation of singers and in-
strumentalists from the Milan Social Register sniffed contemptuously. But the bucolic youth, nonchalantly hitting the
keys with his left hand, waved the other at the aristocratic
performers with the manner and convincing authority of a
seasoned conductor. At the end of the performance everybody
concerned in the proceedings crowded around him, uttering
enthusiastic congratulations.

After that, a great light burst on Masini and his three
assistants: unanimously they dumped all their duties on
Giuseppe Verdi. From that time onward he was conductor,
driller, rehearser, accompanist—Poohbah Verdi, in fact. *The
Creation* had to be repeated again under his direction; also a
third time, by stentorian local demand, with the theater
chock-full of the élitest élite in Milan.

And there was still another performance, at the residence
of the Austrian Viceroy, who lorded it over the Milanese in
the name of the Austrian Emperor, and had provided especially for the occasion a bona fide Austrian Archduke, complete with uniform, medals and hauteur. The Archduke
undoubtedly felt that he was conferring a great honor on
the humble musician from Le Roncole. Verdi, already, like
most young Italians, strongly anti-Austrian, indubitably
thought otherwise. But what could he do? It would hardly
have been practical politics to throw his bâton at the Archduke. Or bang the Viceroy over the head with a bass viol.

One day, Verdi's good angel, Antonio Barezzi, that Mae-
cenas in the grocery business, journeyed from Busseto to Milan
to see with his own eyes how things stood with his protégé.
Appearing at Lavigna's house he asked the teacher-composer-
maestro-al-cembalo for a report on his pupil's progress.

"My friend," said Lavigna, "Peppino has all that is needed
for success. He is serious. He studies hard. He improves steadily. The day will come when you and I will be proud to have

helped him. Before long Italy will rank him among her geniuses."

Delighted, Barezzi returned to spread the good news in Busseto. And Giuseppe continued on his way to musical fame by composing for his noble friend Count Borromeo a cantata for a big wedding in the Count's super-aristocratic family. Another flattering honor for the lad from Le Roncole! So flattering indeed in itself that Count Borromeo saw no need of paying young Verdi anything for it.

In 1833, in the midst of his rising good fortune, 20-year-old Giuseppe heard that his former music teacher, Provesi, had died in Busseto. That threw wide open the question of the successorship to Provesi's post of church organist there, which had long figured in the imagination of Antonio Barezzi, his benefactor, and Carlo Verdi, his father, as the immediate —even, perhaps, as the final—goal of all the youth's musical studies.

No more Milan! At least not for the present. Possibly no more Milan at all. Giuseppe hurried back to Busseto.

SIX

BACK in Busseto it was by no means all plain sailing. Antonio Barezzi, of course, was heart and soul for having Giuseppe, his protégé, decked now with Milanese laurels, appointed to the post of church organist. Behind him, packed into a large, loyal phalanx, his friends of the Busseto Philharmonic Society, who liked, respected and admired Giuseppe, were of the same mind.

But there were others in the field with radically different ideas regarding the successorship to the late Ferdinando Provesi. Though his post as organist had depended on ecclesiastical favor, Provesi had been a man of independent tinge, who had on occasion lampooned the local clergy in various satirical articles. His victims had never forgotten it. Like teacher, like pupil, they reasoned.

So they presented somebody else for the post, one Giovanni Ferrari. And when the pro-Verdi backers looked over Ferrari's supporters they found among them *two bishops!* Twice as many as Giuseppe had been up against in Le Roncole, when he had sought the position of organist there! With not even one prelate to brandish at them what chance had young Verdi? Again he lost out. Ferrari was chosen as the organist in Busseto's church.

Tremendous was the wrath of the Busseto Philharmonic Society. With true Latin abandon they paraded through the streets of the town, burst into the organ loft at the cathedral, where Ferrari was to do his organ-playing, ferreted out the sheets of music which he would need for doing it, bundled them together with vindictive zeal, and marched away with them in triumphant vengeance. Despite their young friend's setback they elected him with enthusiasm to the directorship of the Philharmonic Society, which Antonio Barezzi had relinquished shortly before.

The pro-Ferrari faction did not take things lying down. At once they got busy trying to put the Philharmonic Society out of business. Since it was an organization for the promotion of one of the arts, it had been receiving for some time an annual grant from the municipality of Busseto to help it pay expenses. Its enemies, incensed at the high-handed doings in Ferrari's organ loft, tried to get the municipal authorities to withhold the Philharmonic's annual stipend. In this, however, they failed. The Philharmonic continued to get its subsidy.

The war went on with great fury. Quarrels were staged indoors and outdoors, on the streets and in cafés. Lawyers were summoned to change people's wills. Suits for slander were started. Engagements between lovers were broken off. Creditors abruptly demanded payment for debts of such long standing that they had become honored local landmarks.

When the Franciscan friars allowed music by young Verdi to be played in their church in Busseto large squads of pro-Verdi fans ceased going to the cathedral and went to the Franciscan church instead. And, through no efforts on his part, Verdi got valuable publicity out of the ructions.

The demand for his services at nearby villages broke all records; and when he set out for some one of them he was escorted to his destination and back, amid proud tootling of brasses and banging of drums, by the Busseto Brass Band.

One result of all this was to alienate young Verdi from the church in which he had been brought up—but not from religion in itself, it must be emphasized.

All through the Ferrari war Giuseppe had held himself aloof, and now, in defeat, he gave early evidence of a capacity for standing up with fortitude to the bludgeonings of adversity which, in later life, was to become a regular Verdian specialty.

He calmly went about his affairs, learning and teaching music. Once he returned to a pupil nine Austrian lire for a lesson he had given him, because, the young teacher said, "the lesson had not been worth the money."

After his return to Busseto from Milan he had again gone to live with the Barezzis; and, in their home, he had resumed the piano duets with Margherita Barezzi, the daughter of the house. And now it became apparent that these duets had not been devoted exclusively to music. Soon Giuseppe and Margherita were in love with each other. The young man asked Barezzi for Margherita's hand in marriage.

"*Ma sì, ma sì!*" bubbled Antonio. "Yes, indeed! I shall certainly not refuse the hand of my daughter to a young man

who, though poor, has will power and ability worth far more
than wealth." Quite the copybook father. The wedding took
place in 1835. (I do not know whether Ferrari provided music
from the organ loft.) Giuseppe had taken a step up socially.
In the eyes of Italians of his day his family at Le Roncole was
far from ranking on a par with the Barezzis of Busseto.

After a year or so of married life Giuseppe decided that, in
view of his added responsibilities as a married man (and as
a father—a son, Icilio, had been born to Margherita), he
must once more try his luck in Milan. Soon the young couple
were installed there in modest quarters near one of the city
gates.

Spurred by urgent necessity, expenses having grown alarm-
ingly, Giuseppe got busy looking up Milanese friends who
might be helpful. Lavigna, his teacher, unfortunately had
died shortly before. But he found an ardent ally in Masini,
who was still directing those aristocratic amateurs at the
Filodrammatici. Masini asked Verdi to compose an opera for
performance by them; and he handed him a libretto by one
Piazza, which had been touched up by our erratic acquaintance Temistocle Solera, the Wild Man of *Nabucco*.

Verdi gave up his Milan lodgings and went back to Busseto,
where, he knew, he would receive from his father-in-law generous aid for himself, his wife and his two children (by now
Margherita and he had a second child, a daughter, Virginia).

In a short time he returned to the metropolis of Northern
Italy with the finished score of his first opera—*Oberto, Conte
di San Bonifacio*. But—Masini was no longer director at the
Filodrammatici. Standing up manfully to this additional blow,
the young composer persuaded his noble friend Count Borromeo to put in a good word for him with Bartolomeo Merelli,
impresario at La Scala. Borromeo did. And Masini, though
no longer in authority at the Filodrammatici, continued to
work zealously on behalf of Verdi.

Also, best of all, Verdi appealed on behalf of *Oberto* to Giuseppina Strepponi, asking her to use her influence with Merelli—for, having circulated for some time in Milan's operatic circles, he knew a lot about the elective affinity tactics of some of their denizens, including Bartolomeo and Giuseppina. The lady agreed to recommend *Oberto* to the "Napoleon of Italian impresarios."

Her willingness to help was not entirely due to belief in the merit of the music—obviously she found merit also in its composer. And she proved that her influence with Napoleon, despite refrigeration since passionate old Vienna days, was still strong, for, when she informed her ex-lover that she approved of *Oberto*, he promptly scheduled it for production at La Scala. He also promised to provide it with an excellent cast.

Unluckily, the tenor chosen fell ill. The *première* had to be postponed. So discouraged was the composer, so beset by financial worries, that he thought again of retreating to Busseto and taking refuge again under Antonio Barezzi's protective wing.

But, suddenly, on a day when he was seated in deep dejection at a café table, a messenger from La Scala appeared before him.

"Are you the young man from Parma who wishes to have an opera produced?" he inquired. (Parma, it will be remembered, was the principal city in the Busseto-Le Roncole region.)

"I am," replied Giuseppe.

"Well, Signor Merelli wants to see you right away at his office."

Verdi presented himself before Merelli. The ruler of La Scala, in one of those quick, big-executive decisions wanted to produce *Oberto* immediately. He agreed to take on all the expenses of production. He and Verdi were to share fifty-fifty in the sales of the music. And that music publisher, Ricordi, made his first deal with Giuseppe Verdi by offering 2,000 Austrian lire for the exclusive publication rights of the score of *Oberto* and selections therefrom. That was in 1839. Today, the great music-publishing house of Ricordi in Milan is one of the best known in Europe, and it is fair to say that its progress, prestige and prosperity are, in a way, as much a creation of Giuseppe Verdi as the triumphal march in *Aïda*.

Oberto was performed under Merelli's management at La Scala on November 17, 1839. It did not make much of an impression (it was the *succès d'estime* on which Verdi later bestowed some of his gloomy thoughts on that snowy afternoon in Milan already described, before the triumphant opening of *Nabucco*). At least one of those who heard it felt for it no *estime* whatsoever, for he scribbled on a poster announcing that its composer was Giuseppe Verdi: "Get thee behind me, Satan!" But, to Merelli, it seemed good enough.

He told the composer that he would enter into a contract with him for three operas within two years, exclusively for La Scala and the Imperial Theatre in Vienna. For each of the three Verdi was to receive 4,000 Austrian francs (roughly, $675). The proceeds of the sale of the rights to the music were to be shared equally by Verdi and Merelli. (Giovanni Ricordi, by the way, was already waiting eagerly to snap up the publication rights—his prescience with regard to Giuseppe Verdi was simply uncanny.) To the young composer the whole set-up looked like permanent residence on Easy Street. He signed up with Merelli on the latter's terms. And the manager, before rushing away to Vienna on his variegated managerial (and sentimental) affairs, turned over to Giuseppe a libretto in the hope that he would set it to music.

But, when Merelli returned to Milan early in 1840, Verdi, having found the libretto left with him not to his liking, had not written down a note. Fortunately, the active manager now had another idea:

"I *must* have a comic opera for La Scala," he told the composer. "A funny one, a very funny one—*molto buffa.*" He handed over several libretti. Again Verdi was not especially pleased with the material provided. But, as Merrelli was impatient, he selected one entitled *Il Finto Stanislao* (The Sham Stanislaus), changed afterward to *Un Giorno di Regno* (King for a Day).

Then—catastrophe.

Verdi came down with angina. When convalescent, he owed the equivalent of $50 in rent, payable in three days. And such was his integrity that it never occurred to him that the money need not be paid on the exact date when it became due.

"My wife," he recounted afterward, "seeing me in a bad temper, stole out of our house, pawned her few jewels and brought back (how she ever managed it I have never discovered) the required sum for the landlord." Deeply moved, he promised to repay her with the very first money earned by him through future music-composing.

That was just a minor phase of the catastrophe.

In April, 1840, Verdi's little daughter Virginia was taken ill; a few days later she expired in her mother's arms. Then his son Icilio died. Finally, his young and adored wife, Margherita, struck down shortly afterward by an acute inflammation of the brain, followed her children to the grave. With three terrible blows fate had wiped out young Giuseppe's family. (The sequence of his bereavements, as given here, is taken from a conversation which Verdi had some 40 years later with Giulio Ricordi, head of the Ricordi music-publishing house in Milan. But, according to evidence that has since come to light, not two months but two years elapsed between the first and the third of the composer's tragic losses. If that later evidence, disclosed in Italy in 1935, is to be believed, Verdi either got mixed up in his talk with Ricordi as to the dates of the deaths of his two children and wife, which seems improbable, even after 40 years; or Ricordi, when he made his conversation with Verdi public, inadvertently misquoted the composer.)

In any case, all three deaths came before the production of *Il Finto Stanislao (Un Giorno di Regno)*.

Giuseppe Verdi now stood alone, broken-hearted. *And he had to deliver to Merelli a comic opera, a very funny one— "molto buffa!"*

SEVEN

BY A supreme effort of will power Verdi managed to finish the score of *Un Giorno di Regno*, his "comic" opera created in tragedy. It had its first performance at La Scala on September 5, 1840. It failed. Completely. Tragically. For its title "King for a Day" the cruel Milanese substituted "Fiasco of One Night."

The composer, still mourning his beloved wife and son and daughter, bitterly resented their cruelty. Twenty years later he wrote to a member of the Ricordi firm, lucratively selling operatic scores from his pen, successors to his ill-starred comic opera of 1840: "If only the public had received this opera in silence [instead they hissed], I would not have censured them. I bow to their severity, but only on one condition, that I am not asked to thank them for their applause. We poor gypsies, mountebanks, call us what you like, are forced to sell our labor, our thoughts, our dreams, for gold.

. . . The public buy the right to hiss or applaud us. Our
destiny is to put up with it."

Not quite fair. The Milanese public, after all, was in no way
responsible for Verdi's private, shattering tragedy. When he
grew older, he became conspicuous for the stoicism with
which he met misfortunes. But, what with the loss of his
wife and children and the fiasco of his *opera buffa*—("make
it funny!")—he was for the moment knocked out.

In despair the young composer asked Merelli to cancel
his contract, which obligated him to follow *Un Giorno di
Regno* with two other operas, Merelli proved himself a man
of heart and understanding, irrespective of his youthful dis-
regard for *meum et tuum*.

"Listen, Verdi," he said, "I can't force you to write music.
Perhaps some day you'll want to write some more. If you
do, just let me know two months before the beginning of
La Scala's season. I promise to produce any opera that you
compose."

Turning his back on dreams, on the very thought of music,
Verdi dragged out his life in Milan in a coma of grief. Writing years afterward his good friend, the French critic Camille
Bellaigue, said of this black period, "All through the autumn
of 1840 and the following winter the intelligence and soul
of Verdi were wrapped in a sleep that seemed like death."
According to a Busseto friend, he almost lost his mind.

He used to sit—dazed, mute, crushed—at a table in a small
restaurant called La Rosa Gialla (The Yellow Rose) near the
cathedral in Milan. Fellow-diners noticed how little he spent
for each meal—never more than the equivalent of 20 or 30
of our cents. One evening, after eating as always without a
word to anybody, the melancholy youth, as much out of
funds as he was out of happiness and hope, asked the proprietor to let him eat a few meals on credit. The proprietor refused.

Shortly after that came that snowy day in Milan. And then—*Nabucco!*

At its sensational first night, early in 1842, the public, as I have said, went crazy. Its composer was a made man. Never again did misfortunes come anywhere near to crushing his spirit. Never again was his purse without a pleasant stuffing of bank notes and gold pieces and silver coins. Overnight he became a top-ranking celebrity in Milan, all over Italy— eventually all over the world.

Managers waited on him. They pushed advantageous contracts under his nose. They begged for his signature. Hotel- keepers, shopkeepers, restaurant keepers were proud of his patronage. Shop windows blossomed out with hats à la Verdi, neckties à la Verdi. Special dishes and sauces were named after him.

And the proprietor of The Yellow Rose, now the butt of unnumbered taunts and jokes and sarcastic sallies from the sharp-tongued Milanese, received the reports of Verdi's triumph with *Nabucco* and of his subsequent victories as if they were dagger stabs aimed at himself. And, as he read each newspaper notice chronicling the climb of the formerly unknown and penniless young composer to glory, he would exclaim, in tardy repentance: "If only I had trusted that young fellow for a few meals!"

The road to renown now lay wide open before Giuseppe Verdi.

Before *Nabucco* shot across the horizon of Italy, a golden operatic era for Italian composers was seemingly coming to a dead stop.

Vincenzo Bellini, he of *Norma* and *Sonnambula* and *I Puritani,* had died in 1835. Gioacchino Rossini (*Barber of Seville, Cenerentola, William Tell*) was to devote the remainder of his life not to opera-composing in Italy, but, with a few cre-

ative interludes, to gaiety, gastronomy and wise-cracking in
Paris. Gaetano Donizetti (*Lucia, Elisir d'Amore, Don Pas-
quale, Daughter of the Regiment*) was drawing steadily nearer
to insanity and death.

These men and most of their contemporaries in the field
of Italian opera had been tossing off operas, when Verdi arrived on the scene, with astounding speed and frequency. In
all, Donizetti produced over 60 works, one of them in 8 days,
another in 11, an entire act of a third *in 3 hours*. Heinrich
Heine said of him: "He is surpassed only by rabbits." When
somebody, awe-struck at Rossini's speed in composition, remarked to Donizetti: "I hear that Rossini composed his
Barber of Seville in two weeks," Donizetti said: "I believe it.
He is so lazy."

Verdi never hit the mad pace of his contemporaries, not
even in his most prolific and careless era. Always he had some
conscience about his work. In spite of their amazing facility
and consciencelessness, the Italian Big Three—Rossini, Bellini, Donizetti—and a number of lesser composers long delighted Italy and the world with their operas. Theirs was
indeed a Golden Era. They composed as birds sing. And they
showed cynical indifference as to the quality of the libretti
handed to them. Once Rossini remarked: "I could set a
laundry list to music."

With Bellini dead, Donizetti soon to die and Rossini living
but silent, Giuseppe Verdi was to encounter, after his smash
hit with *Nabucco*, only opponents unable to challenge indefinitely genius such as his.

After its opening night in Milan, *Nabucco* swept irresistibly
over Italy. And, outside its composer's native land, it was
heard in one opera house after another. Indeed, London was
soon digesting two versions of it, both, on account of British
religious scruples, metamorphosed into anomalous hybrids by

transplantation from ancient Jerusalem and Babylon, with their Biblical associations.

One version was called *Nino,* and was not Biblical at all; the other, dubbed *Anato,* had as its background Sappho's island of Lesbos.

Nabucco in its two modified forms was not introduced to London until 1846. (It had been preceded there by two Verdi operas of later date, which will be discussed shortly.) *Nabucco's* sponsor in London at Her Majesty's Theatre was the well-known impresario Benjamin Lumley. Deeply impressed by the sensational rise of Verdi's star on the European continent Lumley had signed up the composer and spent a lot of money on advertising his *Nabucco* production and investing it with gorgeous Oriental pomp and pageantry. At the opening performance in London Verdi himself conducted.

Years afterward, in his *Reminiscences of the Opera,* Lumley wrote regarding *Nabucco* at this theater:

The opera was a decided success. . . . The libretto, although faulty in many respects, was dramatic. . . . Sanchioli [the leading prima donna], wild, vehement and somewhat coarse, excited by her power, spirit and fire, but she failed to charm. . . . The very qualities which had rendered her so popular in Italy acted somewhat repulsively upon English operagoers. The lack of refinement in her style was not in their eyes redeemed by the merit of energy.*

That last sentence fits exactly much of Verdi's early music.

Said another London critic in 1846 of *Nabucco:* "This opera is a most remarkable work. It is characterized by merits of the highest order. In the music the composer has shown himself possessed of all the legitimate sources of success. It bears the stamp of genius."

* Benjamin Lumley, *Reminiscences of the Opera.* London, Hurst & Blackett, 1864.

So far, so good—for Verdi. But, in London, *Nabucco,* like
the two other later Verdi operas which had been produced
there before it, came under the withering fire of the most
persistent and uncompromising of all objectors to Verdi's
music—Henry Fothergill Chorley, music critic of the London *Athenaeum* from 1833 to 1871. He was a most formidable
and vitriolic personage, who played somewhat the same rôle
in London in Giuseppe Verdi's life as was enacted in Vienna
by that most implacable of anti-Wagnerites, Eduard Hanslick,
in the life of Richard Wagner.

Chorley belabored *Nabucco* thus: "Our first hearing of
Nino has done nothing to change our judgment of the limited
nature of Signor Verdi's resources. . . . Signor Verdi is nothing if not noisy . . . and has hitherto shown no power as a
melodist. . . . How long Signor Verdi's reputation will last
seems to us questionable."

That was written over a century ago, before Verdi's best
phases. In the 1950 season of grand opera at the Metropolitan Opera House in New York there were *more performances*
of Verdi's operas than of those of any other composer. And
more of his works were performed during that same season
than those of anybody else. And that goes pretty much for
operatic seasons in general in our era.

Shortly after the invasion of Britain by Verdian music, a
British M.P. introduced into Parliament "A Bill for the
Better Regulation of Street Music in the Metropolitan Police
District." Giuseppe Verdi was largely responsible for that
Bill. His irresistible, unescapable, often maddening melodies
were rampant in the streets of scores of the world's cities.
And this was before *Rigoletto* and *Il Trovatore!* Barrel organs
ground them out by the mile not only in London but through-
out the rest of Europe and in the United States. Hurdy-
gurdy Verdi.

EIGHT

OUTSIDE Italy *Nabucco* is now little known. Some years ago, in the course of the Verdi resurgence in Germany, it was resuscitated in German opera houses with success. Its famous chorus of captives is still sung or played, especially on occasions when Arturo Toscanini has anything to do with the arrangements. And its overture is still heard at concerts, particularly in Italy. But, in its entirety, it is too antiquated, too much the child of a dead era, to maintain itself in the operatic répertoire. Nevertheless, there are two valid reasons why Giuseppe Verdi's first sensational hit deserves attention today, more than a century after its cyclonic opening night.

First, it is a microcosm, in a way, of the early Verdi. In it are the germs of much that he was yet to do, the good all jumbled up with the bad. In it, still struggling for adequate expression, but already unmistakably making its presence felt, is the ingredient in his music which makes what is worst in it pardonable, gilds what is best in it with golden radiance: *genius.*

In *Nabucco*, Verdi concentrates too much on the mere externals of dramatic situations, too little on their inner poetry, on their psychological significance. He sees life too much in terms of furious conflict; and, in depicting it primarily thus, he all too often neglects subtlety and nobility. Vigor, vitality, virility. These leap out of *Nabucco*—as they do out of every other Verdi score, even the worst, at some point. His was a new voice. It expressed the spirit of revolt surging through Italy.

Second, *Nabucco* was the first of the early Verdian operas which, together, built him up into a shining incarnation of Italy's struggle for independence and unity.

During Napoleon's occupation of the land, which began some years before Verdi's birth, the great majority of Italians hated conquering France. Yet, side by side with their craving for liberation from French rule went a consciousness that Bonaparte's troops had brought to the Italy of the beginning of the 19th century a whiff of fresh air, the scent of liberty, a hint of what the French Revolution had bestowed (at least in theory) on the French—Liberty, Equality, Fraternity.

Though Napoleon, after his invasion of Italy, had repudiated democracy by having himself crowned Emperor in Paris, the Italians could not forget that his domination of their native land had at least meant the elimination of Austrian overlordship there, the discomfiture of local despotisms. So, in the years immediately following Napoleon's final downfall —when Giuseppe Verdi was still in his infancy—Italian political hopes and dreams were still high and bright. *United Italy under a régime of freedom.* That was what Italian patriots wanted.

But bitter disappointment awaited them. They merely exchanged one set of foreign masters for another. France moved out, Austria moved in. Petty princelings again ruled more or less despotically. The Italian situation reverted largely to what it had been before the French invasion. Yet, refusing to be discouraged, most Italians continued to see visions of national liberty.

Giuseppe Verdi grew up in an atmosphere alive with such visions. In the Italy of his youth plans were formed, plots hatched, under the very noses of the Austrian officials. So detested were the Austrians that Italian patriots would not willingly speak to them. Habsburg uniforms and guns and bayonets, paraded constantly before the eyes of Italians, served to stoke the fires of resentment. Storm clouds grew blacker. In 1842, the year of *Nabucco*, a terrific explosion was imminent. A few years later it was to plunge Italy into bloodshed. And Giuseppe Verdi, whose sympathies and beliefs made him welcome the new ideas surging through the land, was to become a living, visible, tangible symbol of national aspirations, a rallying-point, a battle-cry, an unfurled banner.

"His music," said Rossini, "wore a helmet." Stirring choruses from his operas were seized upon by delirious crowds, roared out in electrifying demonstrations for liberty. The first Verdi chorus thus snatched from its context and utilized for patriotic ends was *Nabucco's* "*Va, pensiero*"—especially the lines:

> O, *mia patria, si bella e perduta,*
> O, *membranza, si cara e fatal!* . . .

> (Oh, my country, so lovely and lost,
> Oh, memories, cherished and cruel!)

When Italians in milling, marching multitudes sang that Lament in the teeth of Austria's police and soldiery seeking to club and prod them into silence they were not thinking of Jewish captives of thousands of years ago in ancient Babylon. Their thoughts were of Italy, their own Italy, their adored Italy, chained, in tragic captivity, to the chariot wheels of alien overlords. Other grandiose operatic choruses composed by Verdi after *Nabucco* were soon to drive his fellow-Italians to even more frenzied demonstrations for national deliverance. But I am rushing matters.

He was now the man of the hour. Men of prominence courted his company and the ladies who ruled over Milanese society liked to show him off at their receptions, and, through him, themselves. Beautiful damsels flattered him.

Among them, doubtless, were some perfectly willing to pass from the salon to the boudoir and beyond. But, as to that, all is guesswork. He who, for years, kept copies of many hundreds of items in a voluminous correspondence—who carried with him on his travels all the paraphernalia for copying letters according to the (to us) primitive methods of the day—left behind him no love epistles. And those who received them from him, if such there were, succeeded in keeping them unshared.

Bewitching glances, seductive smiles, undoubtedly came his way after his heady triumph with *Nabucco*. But all touching on his love life, his real love life, at this period is surmise, and the surmisers, despite diligent endeavors—and, in some cases, one may be sure, high hopes—have failed to buttress their guesses with solid evidence.

Had there indeed been serious love affairs for Giuseppe Verdi in the early 1840's they might have served to soften the hardness in him, which, in maturer days, became as much a pillar of his four-square character as integrity and independence and genius. But there was no such softening—not until his mellow and miraculous old age. If there was amorous dalliance in those exciting early days, it was of the kind that, however intense, leaves no mark. This curt note, sent by him to one of the women who, in the beginning of the 1840's, knew him and wanted to know him better, is probably typical of his attitude toward women in that period of torturing grief and dawning glory:

"Please understand that nobody dictates my decisions and that I refuse to become the slave of anybody."

Thoughts of Margherita Barezzi, lying in her grave—and of two little graves beside hers—account, I feel sure, for Giuseppe Verdi's escape from serious entanglements immediately after *Nabucco*. Otherwise, the adulation suddenly heaped upon him would assuredly have propelled him into the orbit of at least one female with arms itching for what

the Germans of the two world wars used to call *Einkreisung*—
encirclement.

His staunch fidelity to the heroine of his first romance was
the main reason, in all probability, for the postponement of
the definite beginning of his second. Judging from some of
the evidence, the heroine of the latter was ready for him
before he was ready for her.

She was Giuseppina Strepponi.

That attractive and accomplished prima donna, the beloved
of Bartolomeo Merelli, Napoleon of Italian impresarios, until
he turned his eyes to other hunting-grounds, had met Verdi,
as we have seen, in the days when the young composer was
trying to get his first opera, *Oberto*, produced—and he had
asked her to use her influence with Merelli to have it put on
at La Scala. She had promised to do so and kept her promise,
informing Merelli that she liked the *Oberto* music. What
she undoubtedly did *not* tell him was that there was something else about *Oberto* which she liked much better than
its music, viz.: its composer.

Soon after, she did excellent work in the principal female
rôle of *Nabucco*, as I have recounted; and, following that
opera's thunderous opening performance, she became more
and more attracted to the leonine head and severe countenance and deep-set eyes of Giuseppe Verdi.

But the young man was still too much submerged in sor-
row, too much concerned with imbibing a certain wine that
brings forgetfulness—the wine of success. He liked her friend-
liness. But his inner thoughts were still elsewhere. A trying
time for Giuseppina Strepponi—with her former lover,
Merelli, tiring of her, and Verdi unmoved as yet by her flattering interest in him.

She bided her time.

Giuseppina was born four years after Verdi's birth at Lodi

near Milan where, she used to aver, "the best milk and the best cheese come from." * She showed herself worthy of belonging to a musical family (the Strepponis of Lodi were emphatically that) by graduating with honors from that Conservatory of Music in Milan which shortly before had spurned Giuseppe Verdi. Her rise to operatic prominence was rapid: for some ten years she figured among Italy's leading lyrical sopranos, winning special praise in the works of Donizetti. Once that renowned composer was so deeply affected by her singing in his *Maria di Rohan* that he burst into tears of admiration and delight.

La Strepponi, we are told, was "most charming but not quite beautiful." She was small, with a well-made figure. With the years she grew plump. She had pensive eyes and an expressive mouth. Her wit was sharp and sudden. It cropped out constantly in her talk. And it made of her letters, of which she wrote a great many, a joy fully appreciated by those who received them.

Feminine through and through, she was "a good actress on the stage and a delicious woman off it." The quality of her beauty was of the kind that defies photographers and painters, since it manifested itself mainly in quick, flashing, elusive glances, in telling turns of phrase, punctuated by expressive intonations and inimitable gestures. Prominent in her make-up was a touch of impishness. According to the custom of the day she wore her hair in two long braids. Her nose was a bit too long, but "built on noble lines."

She had joined Merelli's operatic forces in exchange for a male singer, whom he had loaned for a spell to a fellow-impresario, a friendly enemy—at that time, in Italy, opera singers were traded back and forth like so many bales of cotton. When the amorous czar of La Scala made eyes at her, she—barely 20 years old—had no weapons to resist his

* Mercede Mundula, *La Moglie di Verdi*. Milan, Garzani, 1941.

designing advances. The son born of their union, sent to live with relatives in the country, died when he was fifteen. Referring to him in later years, and after years of married life without having any more children, she wrote sadly to a friend: "Perhaps God has punished me for my sins by not letting me taste genuine joy before I die."

Following the tremendous success of *Nabucco*, Verdi was kept busy in a number of Italian cities supervising local productions of that opera, which all Italians wanted to see and hear. He was also hard at work composing (or dreaming about) other operatic scores with which to follow his sensational triumph at La Scala. Giuseppina Strepponi, meanwhile, was also busy—she sang in *Nabucco*, or in operas by other composers, at a number of Italian opera houses. Thus, her chances of meeting Giuseppe, and vice versa, were good. Before the 1840's were half over she and he were more than friends.

NINE

DOMINATING all else on the afternoon of February 11, 1843, on the street outside Milan's great La Scala Theatre was not the aura of poetry and music, but the odor of sausage and garlic.

Ever since three o'clock that afternoon a big crowd, drawn from the humbler strata of Milanese opera-lovers, determined to be present at the *première* of an opera which, they confidently believed, would thrill them with the beauty of its music, the merit of its text, and, for good measure, the patriotic implications lurking behind both, had jammed every approach to the renowned theater.

Aware that hours must elapse before its doors would be

opened and allow them to scramble on the first-come-first-served system for cheap seats or standing space, they had prepared for the long wait by laying in bountiful supplies of sausage, lavishly munitioned with Italy's favorite condiment. When they finally surged through La Scala's portals and massed themselves inside, the atmosphere in the theater was of a nature calculated to seem vaguely displeasing even to the *Italianissimi*—the most Italian of Italians. It would have killed the average Anglo-Saxon.

This hungry throng had gathered for the first performance of Verdi's and Solera's latest effort. The turnout was pleasing to both men: they had been working hard for this opening night. Their tremendous success with *Nabucco* had touched off in them ardent craving for more laurels. Their friendship, nurtured and strengthened and solidified by furious quarreling, had impelled them to seek fame once more in common on the operatic stage. With his customary impetuosity, Solera had dived head-first into the fashioning of a libretto out of a wild conglomeration of passion, tragedy, religion, war, violent death and cognate ingredients.

The deeper he got into this hodge-podge the more delighted and excited he became. One day he came galloping into Verdi's rooms with the words of a trio for the new opera, which, he was sure, would be its high-water mark.

"Read that!" he shouted.

Verdi did.

"Isn't it beautiful?"

Verdi implied that it was.

"Well, now it's up to you!" exclaimed Solera. "Do your part! Make beautiful music for those beautiful lines!" And off he galloped.

Soon after, Verdi dashed into Solera's presence, brandishing some sheets of music, and, together, they sat down,

Verdi at the piano, Solera on a contiguous chair. Verdi played the music with which he had clothed Solera's words. He stopped. The two looked at each other.

Then, as if worked by a single, unseen spring, they leaped to their feet, threw their arms around each other, and burst into a fit of wild, passionate weeping. No wonder the old Italian operas are so exciting when one remembers what uncontrolled children of nature manufactured them!

The authorities in Austrian-occupied Milan, alerted by the patriotic ferment caused some months before by *Nabucco*, began to get suspicious regarding Verdi's new piece. Basing their first objections on religious grounds—they had heard that the forthcoming La Scala production included scenes in the Holy Land—they promptly scented sacrilege.

Cardinal Gaisruk, Austrian Archbishop of Milan, wrote an angry letter to Commissioner of Police Torresani, stating that he had heard that in the Verdi-Solera work there were religious processions; that a church was shown; and a baptism. He demanded that Torresani forbid the performance of it. Otherwise, he threatened darkly, he would write a personal letter to the Austrian Emperor.

Suitably impressed, Torresani summoned before him Morelli, La Scala's manager, Temistocle Solera, author of the words of La Scala's announced novelty, and Giuseppe Verdi, its composer. Verdi refused flatly to get into a discussion at police headquarters.

"I will not tolerate any changes!" he thundered. "Either the opera goes on as it is or not at all!"

So only Merelli and Solera went to see Torresani.

They put on a grand act. The manager explained that the scenery was already painted, the costumes in readiness, the public of Milan agog. The librettist paid a rapturous unsolicited testimonial to his verses. If Torresani forbade the presen-

tation of the work, they intoned in unison, he would be guilty
of suppressing a masterpiece.

Their eloquent duet "went over." Torresani consented to
let the curtain go up at La Scala as announced provided a
trifling change were made in the text, the substitution of
"*Salve, Maria*" for "*Ave, Maria.*"

"If you do that," the police chief told his visitors, "I will
take full responsibility."

"Agreed!" chanted Merelli and Solera. And manager and
librettist hustled to where Giuseppe Verdi was fuming in the
background and told him of the Torresani amendment.
Glumly he nodded his head in agreement. "To think," he
growled, "that I should have as a collaborator on an opera a
commissioner of police."

The new work was called *I Lombardi alla Prima Crociata*
(The Lombards in the First Crusade). It dealt with the doings
of Lombard warriors of old, in Lombardy—of which, it will
be remembered, Milan is the metropolis—and, later, embattled around Jerusalem. What with the brush with the
Austrian censorship and the regular run of headaches accompanying first nights everywhere, there was a jumpy atmosphere at La Scala on the evening of February 11, 1843,
before the curtain rose on the opening performance of *I Lombardi*. And naturally young Verdi was among the jumpiest
individuals on the premises.

Prowling around nervously backstage, the agitated composer dropped into the dressing room of the beautiful diva
Erminia Frezzolini, entrusted with the main female rôle in
the new opera. As soon as she spied him, she exclaimed:
"Either your *Lombardi* will be a great success tonight, or I'll
die on the stage!"—which, as a piece of encouragement for
the nervous youth, certainly had its flaws.

But there was no need for Frezzolini to perish à la Brünn-
hilde or à la Norma or à la anybody else. *I Lombardi* was a

tremendous hit. The first-nighters of La Scala, its "famous
and terrible subscribers," hailed it as a musical masterpiece
(which it wasn't) and a patriotic clarion-call (which it was).
Their wild applause went thundering over the footlights, and,
for the second time in his thirty years of life, Giuseppe Verdi
tasted the ambrosial flavor of acclamation, as he, Frezzolini,
the rest of the singers, and Solera, and Merelli, came before
the curtain after each act, dizzy with joy, to bow or curtsey to
their acclaimers.

The climax came with the chorus beginning "*O Signore,
dal tetto natio . . .*" (O Lord, from our homes . . .). As
an inciter of patriotic emotion it left far behind Nabucco's
"*Va, pensiero*" of the previous year.

Such was the frenzy into which it threw those who heard
it that it had to be repeated twice—nothing the police could
do sufficed to quell the near-riot that it loosed. Next day that
chorus was sung and yelled and played and wept over throughout Milan—and within a brief space throughout Italy.

To its strains, howling crowds, waving the Italian colors,
wearing Italian-tricolor cockades, roaring defiance of Austria,
marched tumultuously through the streets of Italian cities.
And policemen and soldiers, serving the Austrian emperor,
strove hard, with swinging sabers and stabbing bayonets—
sometimes with crackling volleys of musketry—to keep these
demonstrations from swelling into full-fledged anti-Austrian
revolt.

In relation to Italy's thirst for liberation there was something inspiring in the very name of the new Verdi work—
"The Lombards in the First Crusade." The first part of it had
a special local significance, in that "Lombards" could be
taken as symbolic of all Italians, and "first crusade" as allusive
double talk signifying Italy's increasingly vehement demand
for national freedom and unity, which was to bring on a
bloody climax in a few years.

After *I Lombardi* Verdi fed musical fuel to Italian patriotic aspirations in one opera after another. But never was he more successful as an arouser of delirious national enthusiasm than he was with *"O Signore, dal tetto natio."*

Calm judgment—there was some of it in Milanese papers even right after that mad first night—classified *I Lombardi* as inferior musically to *Nabucco*—and the consensus expressed in subsequent years has confirmed that classification. Shorn of its special quality as a kind of Italian *"Marseillaise"* in four acts the opera stands out as too coarse in musical texture, too much attuned to mere melodramatic effectiveness. In it Verdi again, as in *Nabucco*, tended too much to sacrifice cohesion to situation. But, in his defense, it must always be remembered, that he was working at fever heat in a dual role: as a composer and as a vanguard fighter in the cause of Italian independence. That sort of thing is rough on the artistic conscience.

When the opera was produced in London at Her Majesty's Theatre, under the direction of the enterprising Benjamin Lumley, the principal parts were taken by two of the most celebrated singers of the period—the prima donna Grisi and the tenor Mario. It was put on with scenery and dresses which, at the time, were considered unsurpassed. Lumley, in his *Reminiscences of the Opera*, wrote:

Whilst by the anti-Verdians *I Lombardi* was declared to be flimsy, trashy, worthless, the Verdi party and the adherents of the modern Italian school pronounced it to be full of vigor and originality. The one portion asserted that it was utterly devoid of melody—the other that it was replete with melody of the most charming kind. The one insisted that it was the worst work of the aspirant—the other that it was the young composer's *chef d'œuvre*.

Some time after the great hit at Milan and elsewhere in Italy of *I Lombardi* a French version of the work was con-

cocted for the Opéra in Paris. Two French writers, Royer and
Vaez, seeking to substitute for Solera's original book something to conform with current French taste, calmly elimi-
nated the First Crusade as a feature of the piece, as well as
the original background of Lombardy, in lieu of which they
dragged in scenes in the south of France.

Verdi went to Paris to superintend this bizarre production.
He found that the Opéra management, playing true to French
form, desired him to write some ballet music into his original
score. With somewhat surprising docility, Verdi came up with
the desired ballet tunes, also with several musical items which
had not figured in the first Milan production of *I Lombardi*.

Renamed *Jérusalem*, the opera, in its peculiar French dress,
was performed in Paris in November, 1847. The government
of King Louis-Philippe made the composer a Chevalier of the
Legion of Honor; and the King graciously had two acts of
Jérusalem performed for him at his royal palace of the
Tuileries.

Even these honors failed to kindle in the composer's bosom
any marked affection for France—indeed, on the occasion of
this early visit to Paris, he showed the first signs of an anti-
Frenchism which was to last him all his life.

Though he was a Latin, he couldn't get along with the
French—he resembled a cousin who dislikes a cousin. He objected to French methods of theatrical management. He told
a friend once that he never felt sure that Parisian impresarios
would pick competent singers for his operas. Unimpressed by
its fame and eminence, he contemptuously called the Paris
Opéra *La Grande Boutique* (The Big Shop). When his friend
the Countess Maffei (one of the ladies who had persuaded
him to come to her soirées in Milan after *Nabucco*) hinted
that it might be advantageous for him to settle in Paris he
exploded into a letter to her as follows:

"I am and always shall be a peasant of Le Roncole! Had I

wished to become a Parisian, I would have accepted the offer of 40,000 francs for an opera (maybe the offer might have risen to 50,000), plus one-quarter of the receipts from it at the Théâtre Italien. I might have done one opera for that theater, another for the Opéra, a third for the Opéra-Comique. I refused all three!"

Paris and the Parisians undoubtedly caused Giuseppe Verdi numerous headaches—but, then, what city did not? Quarrels with librettists, impresarios, journalists, agents beset him wherever he went—even in many a city of his adored Italy.

No, there was something in his anti-French bias which went deep—possibly it was partly an inheritance from a father and mother who had seen Bonaparte's invasion of their native land and endured the long garrisoning of Italy by Napoleonic troops. His anti-Frenchism persisted to the end of his life. He used to remark:

"The French are the greatest nation on earth, but I can't stand them for long."

Following the production in Paris of the Frenchified *I Lombardi* the latter met the peculiar fate of being translated *back into Italian*, and performed in its new form in Milan. One wonders how anybody—composer, librettists, impresarios, singers—could have expected success for this blatant rehash. However, *somebody* did—and the Milanese blasted his or her expectations by turning upon it the iciest of cold shoulders.

Like everything by Verdi, *I Lombardi* (the original one) has moments of impressive power. Such is its vitality that it is still given occasionally in Italy. Apart from those thrilling pages in its score which elicited from Italian audiences emotional agitation impossible to classify as musical criticism, there are snatches of beauty in its quieter sections. But, taken as a whole, it has left a general impression of brutality tinged with vulgarity, of art ruthlessly sacrificed to theatrical impact.

Rossini, it is said, used to put his hands over his ears and take refuge in the parts of his home farthest from the street, when bands went by playing noisy Verdi music of this period. But Rossini was not particularly well qualified as a stone-thrower, seeing that, in his early orchestrations, he had shown a strong liking for snare drums. Once an exasperated operagoer wrote to him: "Promise to stop writing for snare drums or I'll kill you!" With complete gravity Rossini replied: "I promise to stop writing for snare drums"—and went right on doing so.

In allusion to *I Lombardi,* the Verdi biographer Gino Monaldi says: *

Verdi, who in *Nabucco* tapped a vein of melody alike lofty and beautiful and original, and expressed himself in a form full of nobility and character, seems instead, in *I Lombardi,* gloomy, agitated, coarse, careless. A strange nervousness dominates him. Musical themes abound but no musical edifice is built up from them. The score of *I Lombardi* is like a great cascade of water among rocks and obstacles of all kinds, with the stream of water becoming visible as it bursts forth at some points, only to hide itself at others, never flowing smoothly and clearly.

But that score had something which swept those who first heard it out of their minds. Raw energy leaped from it.

It made evident a truth hit upon by Stendhal in writing about the Italy of Verdi's early days: that music was the form in which the Italians, vanquished by arms and by treaties, remained, nevertheless, victorious; that the theater was the only place in Italy still open to freedom of thought. In those days of defeat Italy continued to live intensely in the arts.

The words of *"O Signore, dal tetto natio"* were to the Ital-

* Gino Monaldi, *Verdi.* Torino, Fratelli Bocca, 1920.

ians who heard them on that night of tumult in Milan, to all the other Italians who thrilled to them all over Italy, a call to battle, a cavalry charge; and, turned into notes of fire by the genius of Giuseppe Verdi, they swept Italy into madness. With *Nabucco*, Verdi had become Italy's composer of the hour; after *I Lombardi* he stood forth as the symbol of her craving for liberty.

III

DRIFTING

TEN

WHAT did he look like, this Giuseppe Verdi? What kind of person was he inside? Halfway through the 1840's his character was already molded. The third of a century through which he had come had already shaped him physically and mentally into a man who could be only superficially changed by the half-century and more through which he was to go.

What attracted him? What repelled him? What thoughts swayed this conqueror on the march? What in him attracted her by whom he was to be conquered?

He was good-looking. From youth he cultivated thick, chestnut-hued whiskers and a big mustache and he let his hair grow down over his ears. He had a high forehead and unusually severe, deep-set gray eyes, under thick eyebrows. He affected the high collars of his period; and the big ties that he favored were tied, as his contemporaries said, *alla come mi piace*—"as-I-damned-well-please."

He was earthy, homespun. He was straightforward. He was uncomplicated. He would brush aside bids to introspective discussion with an impatient "I always was and shall be a peasant. A peasant from Le Roncole."

He was a good business man. Without being greedy he knew what he wanted in business deals—and usually got it. He was wary in his dealings with others—and woe to anybody who tried to deceive him! That individual seldom if ever got a second chance.

He was given to taciturnity. "Words," he said, "dissolve,

enervate, destroy." He liked action—in real life as well as in his operas. He made a guidepost in his life of the Italian proverb: "To trust is good, to distrust better."

Of an acquaintance he once observed: "He is rough. Like a bear. Like me." Despite his drive and self-confidence, he had, deep down, a substratum of humility. Hidden under his hard crust was much sensitivity. In him there cropped up at times an unexpected inclination to diffidence. "His whole life," wrote a well-known Italian author, "can be summed up in one word: sincerity." To the Countess Maffei, with whom he exchanged letters for many years, he wrote: "You don't believe it, but sometimes I weep."

All his life he was swept by sudden gusts of anger. He was practical. He was honest. His integrity was not merely passive. It was aggressive, militant. It was said of him: "When he puts his characteristic signature, enclosed in what looks like a hieroglyphic, at the foot of a business letter, it is as good as the seal of a monarch."

Once an unscrupulous journalist showed him two reviews which he had written after the final rehearsal of a new Verdi opera about to be produced. One was fulsomely favorable, the other devastating in its disapproval. Looking meaningly at the composer, the journalist inquired:

"Maestro, which shall I have printed?"

"Whichever you like," snapped Verdi. And he turned on his heel.

As he grew older he grew sunnier. Without losing his basic earthiness, he became more cultured. He gave freer rein to something that ripened miraculously in him over the years— his sense of humor. She who knew him better than anyone spoke of his "great laugh."

Toward women he could be charming, gentle, attractive. His brusqueness was often caused by his absorption in thoughts of music. What seemed rudeness was due often to the sudden intrusion into his mind of a melody which for the moment obliterated all else.

He scorned frills. He hated counterfeit. He loved liberty and democracy. He abhorred oppression. When it looked as if the Emperor Napoleon III would bring French troops to the aid of the cause of Italian liberation and unification, Verdi, in a joyful outburst of patriotism, exclaimed: "If he does, I shall revere him as much as I have always revered George Washington!" But Napoleon III fell far short of his hopes.

He despised pretentious highbrowism. He disliked having those around him try to pigeonhole and docket and classify music. "I belong to no school," he insisted. He used to stop hair-splitting with remarks such as: "In music there is something more than style. There is something more than method. There is music."

Someone said on meeting him for the first time: "His expression can be soft and vivacious. When he speaks, his whole face lights up. His incessant mobility of expression reflects the variety of his moods."

"He is kindly," said somebody else. "He feels pity for the unfortunate. The tears of the weak go straight to his heart."

He accepted with a shrug whatever Fate handed him. "Once my operas are finished," he told a friend, "I let them take the road that God and the impresarios mark out for them."

Giuseppe Verdi's next opera, his fifth, scheduled to be put on for the first time in Venice, brought him into collision with three individuals so hostile to his ideas that he had to fight them hard. To offset this, it also brought him into contact with a fourth individual so amenable to his every wish that he didn't have to fight him at all.

The opera was based on Victor Hugo's drama *Hernani,*

which became, in its transplantation to the Italian operatic stage, *Ernani*. When originally produced in Paris the play had caused a grand rumpus. In it the revolutionary French writer had challenged the accepted rules of French classical drama, which, in the view of France's conservative literary element, ought, having been good enough for Racine and Corneille, to be good enough for Hugo and all other dramatists *in saecula saeculorum*.

This alone sufficed to cause disquiet among Austria's censors. But, for good measure (or bad, according to the point of view) Victor Hugo, in his new play, had shown himself, from the political standpoint of Imperial Austria, a dangerous subversive. He had made his dramatis personae in *Hernani* utter politically iconoclastic sentiments and provided his drama with scenes (including a conspiracy against a monarch!) little calculated to enrapture Austrian officials busy bolstering Austrian occupation of Venice in the teeth of highly articulate Venetian disapproval. These sentiments and scenes were duplicated in the libretto for Verdi's *Ernani*.

So, like Police Commissioner Torresani of Milan in the case of *I Lombardi*, the chief of the Austrian police in Venice requested the pleasure of Giuseppe Verdi's company at an informal chat in his office concerning the projected production. This time—though he fumed prodigiously—Verdi went to police headquarters.

After some exciting wrangling, he came off victorious. A few small changes in the new opera, the censor told him, would be sufficient to make it presentable. These changes were duly made in the libretto—which had been fashioned out of Victor Hugo's drama by Francesco Maria Piave, recommended to Verdi by Count Mocenigo, the noble impresario of the Fenice Theatre.

Piave, a local writer who had escaped from the study of law, had, says Francis Toye, "a passion for everything theatri-

cal from plays to actresses." Little better than an obliging
carpenter in words he lasted longer at the difficult job of
providing the text for Verdi operas than anyone else who
tackled it. Whatever Verdi wanted was all right with Piave.

When, in later years, anybody scolded him for not standing up to his exacting boss, he would serenely remark, "*Il
maestro lo vuole così, e basta*" (The maestro wants it so, and
that's enough!).

Verdi had his second battle with Count Mocenigo, manager of La Fenice. For reasons understandable only to those
intimate with the innermost convolutions of the Italian temperament the Count objected violently to having a horn,
indispensable to the unfolding of the plot of *Ernani*, sounded
on his theater's sacrosanct stage.

"No horn can be blown on the stage at La Fenice!" he
declared, in outraged accents. "The idea! Never have I heard
a horn blown there!"

"Well, you're going to hear one now!" Verdi truculently
informed him. As usual, after attack and counter-attack, blast
and counter-blast, the composer won. When *Ernani* was produced on Count Mocenigo's hallowed stage it was produced
complete, with horn and horn blower.

Verdi's third passage at arms was with Madame Loewe, the
Teutonic diva engaged to play the leading woman's rôle in
the new work. Under the composer's severe thumb, Piave had
ended his libretto with a trio, the music whereof became celebrated afterward as one of *Ernani's* best tidbits. But Madame
Loewe, who possessed a sense of her own importance not
without counterparts among other operatic stars, thought
that it would be simply grand to have *Ernani* end with a
soprano solo, to be warbled by herself in the center of the
stage just before the final curtain, with all her fellow-singers
appropriately minimized.

She mentioned what she had in mind to Piave, and he, al-

ways friendly to the suggestions of others and as yet inade-
quately acquainted with Giuseppe Verdi's will of steel and
temper of fire, nodded in ductile acquiescence. He even
worked out a blueprint of the text of the contemplated solo,
which Loewe wished to sing as the climax of the opera. And
he even showed it airily to Verdi.

Verdi hit the ceiling. When he came down and got through
expressing his opinion of the proposed Loewe-Piave amendment, Piave was crushed, Loewe astounded, and *Ernani* un-
changed. The composer was so angry with the diva that,
when he was about to leave Venice shortly after their collision, he merely sent her a perfunctory postal card, instead
of staging the usual affectionate and compulsorily osculatory
farewell. Not until weeks later was the rift patched up.

Ernani was presented for the first time at Count Mocenigo's
Fenice in Venice on March 9, 1844—two years to the day
after Verdi's sensational triumph with *Nabucco* at Milan's
La Scala.

It was enthusiastically applauded. Again its success had
the same peculiar duality noticeable in that of its predecessors, *Nabucco* and *I Lombardi*: it was ascribable partly to the
music *as music* and partly to its *patriotism-arousing quality*.
The latter brought a hurricane of enthusiasm more violent
than the one engendered by *Nabucco*, only a bit less so than
the one loosed by "*O Signore, dal tetto natio*" in *I Lombardi*.

As for Verdi's music in *Ernani*, many contemporary critics
found much merit in it, and some of their successors of later
epochs have echoed their praise. But here as well as in preceding scores Verdi showed clearly that he had not yet shaken
himself free from some of the worst defects of his earliest
manner. These he learned to eschew more and more in subsequent operas, upon which rests the bulk of his dazzling
renown.

It must be borne in mind that such defects were by no

means attributable to the composer alone; a large portion of
blame for them must be dumped squarely on the shoulders of
his epoch and its musical fashions.

At best, the way of the composer is rough. Every inch of it
is bitterly contested by those whose creed it is to keep things
as they are—who usually (for a time, anyhow) have the
weight of public opinion on their side; and, in addition, have
under their control the money bags providing the where-
withal for composers to feed themselves. The one thing that
some critics cannot forgive in geniuses is that they have to eat.

The Verdi of 1844 committed in *Ernani* and in the years
immediately preceding and following it what we in the 1950's
consider breaches of good taste, excesses in noise and banality
and downright vulgarity. But was he alone in this? Was he
unique in not having sprung fully armed from the brows of
the gods of music? Richard Wagner eventually created the
Ring and *Tristan* and *Meistersinger* and *Parsifal*. But before
them did he not create *Rienzi?* Similarly, the Giuseppe Verdi
of *Oberto* and *Nabucco* and *Ernani* eventually created *Aïda*
and *Otello* and *Falstaff.*

Reforming an art is a cruelly complicated matter, not a
perfectly simple bandwagon progress. That truth both Verdi
and Wagner learned in the earliest phases of their composing;
and having learned it served not to hinder but to help them
when they strode, at the height of their genius, into the full
light of their glory.

As a source of patriotic enthusiasm, *Ernani* came close, in
its effectiveness, to *I Lombardi.* One grand chorus in it, starting with the words *"Si ridesti il Leon di Castiglia"* (Rise up,
Lion of Castile) was made in Venetian imaginations to mean
an apostrophe to the Lion of Saint Mark, symbol of the ancient power of the Queen of the Adriatic.

In the same way, when the opera made the rounds of theaters in other parts of Italy, that chorus was made to sym-

bolize the Italian nation suffering under alien rule. It touched
off tremendous mob scenes, to the regular accompaniment of
Austrian saber-swishing.

Another chorus in *Ernani*, "*A Carlo Quinto sia gloria e
onor*" (Glory and honor to Charles V), made an audience in
Rome (whose example was promptly followed elsewhere)
join with the singers on the stage in the melody, but substituting the words "Glory and honor to Pius IX," since there was
reason to believe that Pope Pius IX would become the head
of a movement for the unification of Italy. And that brought
more rioting and violence.

Outside Venice *Ernani* marched from one triumph to another. While it was being done in Bologna Madame Loewe,
who in Venice had tried to alter its ending for her personal
glorification, having heard that Verdi was passing through
that city, made overtures of reconciliation which brought the
touchy composer out of his huff and herself into his good
graces—so effectively indeed that, when a subsequent opera
of his was being cast, he chose her as its principal female
interpreter.

In Rome, while an audience at *Ernani* was volunteering
vociferous assistance to the singers on the stage, a gendarme
in full uniform, beside himself with patriotic-musical excitement, put one leg over the balustrade of the balcony in
which he was seated, and, lustily bellowing "Glory and honor
to Pius IX," threw his ornate headgear into the pit, sent
after it his coat and vest, and then hurled his unsheathed
sword in the general direction of the stage, where it stuck in
the woodwork behind the footlights, to the enormous dis-
satisfaction and considerable peril of adjacent singers and
musicians. Next, teetering on the balustrade, he started to
remove the remainder of his apparel and had almost succeeded in doing so when he was collared by a charging squad
of other gendarmes and bounced from the theater.

When *Ernani* was being prepared for its first production in

Vienna, Gaetano Donizetti, Verdi's celebrated contemporary in opera-making—who, at the time, was managing the Italian Opera House in the Austrian capital—wrote that he would give his special personal attention to the rehearsals there of the new work, a generous act which brought him a grateful reply from the flattered and appreciative composer. Other musical bigwigs also signified their approval, among them Von Bülow, the renowned piano virtuoso (he whose wife, Liszt's daughter, later discarded him in favor of Richard Wagner).

Ernani was presented for the first time to an audience in London on March 8, 1845. Before that, Londoners had already become acquainted with some of its leading musical numbers via the concert stage and the barrel-organ routes. This was particularly true of the song *"Ernani, involami,"* still a favorite among feminine bravura singers.

The reception of *Ernani* in the British metropolis was of a mixed nature. It was not a smashing triumph, nor, by any means, a failure. In judging its merits and demerits many of those who heard it stayed on the fence. The consensus among them was "I don't know." So much so that one London writer, summing up the general local attitude toward the latest Verdi offering, parodied current jargon by remarking: "The I-don't-knows have it."

Ernani pleased London in general enough to be given often during its first season there. Some critics found in the score a new confidence in the handling of musical material. Among *Ernani's* enemies in London the most virulent, as in the case of other Verdi operas before and after, was Critic Chorley of the *Athenaeum* who wrote in that regular vehicle of his diatribes: "For new melody we have searched in vain . . . all seems worn, hackneyed, unmeaning." But he added: "There is a certain aspiration in his [Verdi's] works which deserves recognition and may lead him to producing compositions which deserve success." This, coming from the fire-belching dragon of the *Athenaeum*, habitually vitriolic when confronted with Verdi scores, was calculated to make their composer go out and dance in the streets.

Paris liked *Ernani*. But Victor Hugo did not. That celebrated writer, author of the original drama from which the opera had sprung, declared in a rage that Piave and Verdi between them had horribly maltreated the child of his genius. As a result of his fulminations and those of his equally enraged adherents, there was apologetic talk of changing the name of the Verdi-Piave work as an atonement for the desecration allegedly perpetrated by those responsible for it—an idea worthy of a particularly deluded ostrich.

Adolphe Adam, even more famous as a composer than as a commentator on the compositions of others, wrote in connection with *Ernani's* debut in Paris in 1848: "Of all the operas of Verdi given in Paris *Ernani* is the one which has obtained the most success." And Gino Monaldi says of it: "When an opera lights a flame of affection and patriotism and leaves admiring memories in subsequent generations, it has achieved a great part of its object and acquired the right to occupy a glorious place in the history of the theatre."

Ernani was given for the first time in New York at the Park Theatre on April 15, 1847. It was also performed on November 22d of that same year as the opening attraction at the brand-new Astor Place Opera House.

ELEVEN

FOLLOWING *Ernani* Verdi composed *I Due Foscari*. It was given for the first time on November 3, 1844, eight months after the clamorous success of *Ernani* in Venice.

Gaetano Donizetti, whose most famous opera is that *Lucia*

di Lammermoor which still shows an amazing capacity for
not lying down and dying, as many think it should, liked the
new Verdi work. That Donizettian favorable view has about
it one astonishing point: it was inspired by a work which,
according to most of those who have commented on it, is one
of the worst that Verdi ever composed. Such is criticism. A
difference of opinion, as Mark Twain said, is what makes
horse races possible.

I *Due Foscari* is based on Byron's tragedy *The Two Foscari*.
For the libretto Verdi called again on Piave. The composer's
innate theatrical bent is shown by his instructions to his
librettist: "Make the cabaletta *energetic*, because we are
working for Rome." "Put a gondolier's song into Act III."
"Have some of the action take place, if possible, toward evening." "Have a sunset effect somewhere. That always makes
a fine impression."

The Romans turned thumbs down on I *Due Foscari*. A
contributing reason for their disdain was that the management of the theater where it was produced, foreseeing popular
acclaim, had raised the price of seats to heights which the
Romans considered outrageous. So they gave it the first push
toward oblivion.

Next on the Verdi roster came *Giovanna d'Arco* (Joan of
Arc). The libretto, based on Schiller's *Die Jungfrau von Or-
leans*, was not by Francesco Piave, temporarily shelved, but
by our old friend of *Nabucco* and I *Lombardi* days, the im-
petuous Temistocle Solera.

Solera, since collaborating with Verdi on the composer's first
two hits, had been roistering about Milan and other parts of
Italy, scribbling furiously (when he could kick himself into
it or get others to do so) and telling all and sundry, including,
occasionally, the Austrians themselves, what he thought of
Austria.

Stories still grew luxuriantly around him. For instance: One day, Verdi, impatiently expectant of a batch of verses from his Bohemian ally, had isolated the erratic librettist in an apartment, under imperious orders to turn out the verses at full speed. Unfortunately, the maestro had neglected to place beyond Solera's reach a number of bottles of wine that graced the apartment. When he returned, more impatient than ever, he found Solera fast asleep, beside a table on which were three or four empty bottles.

Striding to the table, fury in his eyes, Verdi laid a hand on the slumberer's shoulder, preparatory to giving the delinquent a seismic shock.

But, just as he was on the point of doing so, he read, on a sheet of paper before the sleeper, some scribbled verses which pleased him enormously. They were just what he needed. He relaxed his grip.

But it had sufficed to awaken Solera. Seeing Verdi standing over him, the librettist, rubbing his eyes in bewilderment, grunted: "Wh-what's the matter?"

"Nothing," replied Verdi. And he walked out of the apartment.

On another occasion, Solera, having procrastinated scandalously in completing the musical score of an opera (besides being a librettist he ventured at times into the realm of musical composition), remembered, just before the piece was to be produced, that it lacked an overture, considered by the impresario of the moment highly important. The composer had solemnly promised to turn it out on time—and promptly forgotten all about it.

At his wits' end, the composer-librettist, happening to prowl into Verdi's quarters while the latter was absent, spied, among a jumble of sheets of music, the draft of an overture, duly scored for orchestra, which Verdi had dashed off in one of his frequent creative fits. Pocketing it without a qualm,

Solera rushed off to the theater where his opera was to be given and handed his booty to the musicians there, who at once went into a fever of blowing and scraping and thumping in preparation for the imminent first performance.

On the opening night, Verdi, seated in the audience, was amazed and infuriated at being suddenly confronted with the sounds of his overture, which, intended by him for some opera of his own, now bobbed up as an item in the collected works of the unblushing Solera.

Incidentally, in those days, there was nothing remarkable in this casual grafting of a quite unrelated overture onto the main body of any opera. Rossini, in whose make-up presence of genius was as remarkable as absence of conscience, once wrote an overture for one of his early operas. The opera failed. So he used the overture for another opera. That also failed. Undaunted, he tacked the overture onto a third opera. That one went over with a bang. The Rossini prelude in question, twice threatened with an early death, is now a favorite all over the universe. It is the one played before the curtain goes up on Rossini's masterpiece—with which it has no musical kinship whatsoever—*The Barber of Seville*.

Giovanna d'Arco was first performed at La Scala in Milan on February 15, 1845. It had no luck.

Verdi salvaged the overture, which had won praise in the midst of the general shipwreck. He grafted it onto a couple of his later works. But in this carpentering he did not have Rossini's good fortune. The first on which he bestowed it dropped dead. So did the other.

Next came *Alzira*. It was based on Voltaire's tragedy of the same name, a fantastic hodgepodge laid in Peru after its conquest by the Spaniards. This time the maestro composed the score to a libretto by Salvatore Cammarano, an eccentric

Neapolitan of considerable repute in Italy, whose name has come right down to our time because it was he who provided Donizetti with the libretto for *Lucia di Lammermoor*.

Verdi looked upon Cammarano with more respect than he accorded Piave, whom he was wont to address around this time with playful brutality as "you crocodile"—which Piave, true to his creed of "the maestro can do no wrong," considered all in the day's work. Verdi exchanged several letters on the subject of *Alzira* with Cammarano, as a result of which the Neapolitan bard consented to write the words for it, thus interrupting his favorite sport—standing for hours on end without talking to anybody, propped against a pillar of his favorite church in Naples, waiting for inspiration from the Muse, and transferring it, when it arrived, into verse—after which he would calmly lie down on the pavement in front of the church and go to sleep.

Flauto, manager of the San Carlo Theatre in Naples, wanted Verdi to journey to that city to help put on *Alzira*. But the composer, afflicted with a bad stomach-ache, informed Flauto that he did not feel up to making the journey. To bolster his refusal he enclosed a medical certificate attesting to the genuineness of the stomach-ache. Refusing to take his illness seriously, Flauto kept on urging him to come to Naples; and he advised him to take wormwood for his troubles and assured him that they would be cured once and for all if he would only gaze fixedly for a while at Vesuvius.

The composer took exception to the tone of this letter. Unquestionably, he was not well. But there was also in him a touch of hypochondria. In old age, his vigorous health was to become legendary, to be hailed as miraculous—but to the end of his long life he used to worry not only about actual symptoms of illness but also about those imaginary ones dear to the hypochondriac.

So Flauto's airy talk of Vesuvius-cum-wormwood rubbed

him the wrong way. Who was the San Carlo manager to pre-
scribe medicine and talk about Vesuvius as if that noted vol-
cano were an M.D.? Not until he was good and ready did
Verdi turn up in Naples.

Alzira was given at the San Carlo Theatre there on August
12, 1845—Verdi operas in those days were certainly being
turned out with almost Rossinian-Donizettian speed! Five
in less than two years and a half! Verdi liked the way its first
audience received it. But subsequent audiences killed all hope
that it would tread the road to real success. It has been called
the worst of all Verdi's operas. *Requiescat in pace.*

After unlucky *Alzira* the composer drove himself to the
creation of another opera entitled *Attila.* He was helped anew
by the spirit of liberty rising up all over Italy. Francesco Piave
was picked to do the libretto. But he saved himself from
being apostrophized as a "crocodile" by turning the job over
to Temistocle Solera. *Attila* was presented for the first time
in Venice March 17, 1846. Based on a tragedy by Werner,
it included a scene between Attila and Ezio, a general of the
tottering Roman Empire, in which the latter suggested to the
Hun the partitioning between the two of them of the whole
known world in a duet containing these lines:

> *Avrai tu l'universo,*
> *Resti l'Italia a me!*

> (Take thou the universe,
> But leave Italy to me!)

To this the Venetians reacted as had other Italian audi-
ences to earlier settings by Verdi of similarly stirring words.
There was a wild scene of unloosed frenzy in the theater. Soon
"Avrai tu l'universo" became a patriotic chant all over Italy.
Whenever the portrayers of the Roman and the Hun sang it,
as Verdi's new work swept in triumph from one city to an-

other, it aroused more stentorian commotions. And again, in evaluating these commotions, it was difficult to determine where patriotism left off and musical appreciation began.

Friends of Verdi hailed *Attila* as the best thing he had done. It re-established him as Italy's most promising composer in the operatic field. But his rehabilitation, it must be admitted, was due largely to the unreflecting frenzies of patriotism into which *Attila* threw Italian audiences. And this was not to the advantage of his artistic development.

Having decided that her voice had passed its prime, Giuseppina Strepponi in 1847 gave up the operatic stage. Migrating from Italy to Paris she set up there as a teacher of Italian *bel canto*. She created around herself quite a little salon, which interested celebrities of the caliber of Chopin and Berlioz. That same year Verdi joined her. He had his mail sent to her address in the Rue des Victoires.

Later, the two took a house in Passy, then almost open country, and lived in it together. Giuseppina had means of her own and Giuseppe was making more money every season. So they were independent financially and free to do pretty much as they pleased. In Paris their unsanctified union, being an everyday matter, especially in the artistic-musical circles in which they moved, aroused neither surprise nor censure.

In 1848, after a year of his second romance, Verdi's royalties from operas already composed and from advances on contracts for new ones were streaming in so satisfactorily that he bought the country estate of Sant' Agata a few miles from Busseto. It was certainly no beauty spot externally—one of its chief assets was what someone called "a depressing but invaluable river"—but it was peculiarly alluring to him because of the freedom which its solitary situation afforded.

Its acres and dwelling house were set down squarely on the plain of Parma—which also held Busseto and Le Roncole—

hot and dusty in summer, cold and bleak in winter. Gradually
Sant' Agata completely captivated Verdi and Giuseppina also,
though at times its wintry desolation made her sigh for a spell
of city life. Once life on his own property "got" him Verdi's
delight in it never flagged.

In one of her typical letters, strongly suggesting the mischievous imp inside her, Giuseppina told a friend: "Verdi
is up at dawn, examining wheat and corn and grapes and
returning so tired that it is impossible for him to write. Our
tastes are exactly the same regarding sunrise but, whereas he
likes to be up and dressed when it comes, I prefer it from my
bed."

She subordinated her life to his. He dominated her—without overawing her. Always she loved him—and she had pretty
ways of expressing her love. "I kiss you on your heart," she
wrote him once. And, for the sake of "*il mio* Verdi" as she
usually called him (other favorite apellations were "my bear"
and "my white bear") she endured uninterrupted weeks of
cold weather at Sant' Agata. At first, anyhow. In proportion
as her influence over him became greater she managed to
spend less time in winter at Sant' Agata and more in big cities.

Sant' Agata's hold on Verdi became uncanny. All the peasant in him came out as he gazed on his domain. Once he remarked: "If this beautiful weather continues I shall have my
bed taken out of my room and put into that grove of trees
over there." Yet, at the beginning, it was Giuseppina who
turned him to love of country life.

Despite his insistence that he was always a peasant of Le
Roncole, city life, and, above all, the smell of the footlights
in city theaters, had from youth worked their sorceries on
him. But, eventually, he never knew genuine, lasting content-
ment except when he could turn his back for a while on Milan
and Venice and Rome, Paris and London, and hurry back to
the dust or snows of his Italian Eden.

For that is what Sant' Agata came to mean to him, thanks in large measure to the love, tact, charm, wit and worth of Giuseppina Strepponi.

Giuseppina's emergence as the châtelaine of Sant' Agata just as if she were Verdi's wife touched off a big buzz of gossip in nearby Busseto.

A small provincial Italian city of the 19th century was no Paris, that eternal condoner of laxness between the sexes. Busseto looked wryly at Giuseppe and Giuseppina living together on their country estate in a partnership which no priest had made official. It uttered a scandalized collective "It just isn't done!" There had always been an anti-Verdi faction among the Bussetians. And loud was the clamor raised by members of that faction—and by others now swept into its orbit.

The unhallowed romance of Giuseppe and Giuseppina impressed unfavorably even Antonio Barezzi, Giuseppe's faithful patron and friend, the father of his deceased wife, for whom the composer had long been one who could do no wrong. The worthy musical grocer was moved to write an expostulatory letter to Giuseppe on the subject. For once the rock-solid friendship of Giuseppe Verdi for Antonio Barezzi was jarred: Verdi answered Barezzi's letter in stinging language. The gist of his remarks was that Busseto was a backwoods community infested with narrow-minded slaves of intolerance, whom it behooved to mind their own business and the sooner the better.

Fortunately, once he had got that off his chest, Giuseppe continued to be as fond of Barezzi as ever and as grateful to him. And Barezzi, after a while, was not only reconciled with his adored protégé but actually installed as a practically permanent guest at Sant' Agata, looked after and petted and coddled and made much of by—Giuseppina Strepponi!

TWELVE

SHAKESPEARE fascinated Giuseppe Verdi. Yet the Italian composer neither spoke nor read English. Only through translations into Italian, one by a friend of his, Carcano, or into French, could he come to know the great Englishman. Verdi placed Shakespeare above all other writers of tragedy, including the Greeks. "The only true character in Aeschylus," he used to complain, "is Clytemnestra. One does not know whether all the rest are gods or mortals."

At first his impulse to look to Shakespeare for musical inspiration was largely theatrical, not literary. What he wanted at first was not Shakespearean poetry or Shakespearean philosophy but Shakespearean plots. What interested him particularly were the dramatic situations abounding in Shakespeare's plays, not the beauty of their language nor the depth of the motives influencing their characters as the latter moved, Fate-impelled, into and out of those situations.

For this arbitrary limitation of outlook Giuseppe Verdi made noble atonement in the two operas of his old age, his masterpieces. But until they came along and were appareled by him in music of an excellence which he had never before attained, Shakespeare, to him, was scarcely more than just another source of possible libretti, just another Victor Hugo or Schiller, on whose works he might drape effective dramatic music.

It was mostly in this spirit that he considered the great Englishman when he sought something to follow *Attila* and found it in *Macbeth.*

Piave was asked to come to austere Sant' Agata from the gay life of Venice. He received instructions from his exacting master surpassing in scope and volume everything that had gone before in their one-sided association. In fact, Verdi practically wrote out much of the actual text for the to-be-processed *Macbeth* in his own prose and ordered Piave to put it into verse. Never had he gone so far in usurping the other's functions. But Piave didn't mind. He did just as he was told. His not to reason why.

So Verdi briefed his pliable coadjutor and the "crocodile" versified Verdi's rough prose out of Shakespeare (via translation). That the composer, despite his temporarily well-nigh exclusive interest in the theatrical side of libretti, realized how unliterary a fellow Piave was is shown by his getting his good friend Count Maffei, husband of the lady who exchanged letters with him so frequently, to salt-and-pepper the Piave product with verses of his own manufacture. Maffei was a writer of elegance, known as "the poet with the honeyed tongue." And, like his wife, he was among Giuseppe Verdi's best friends.

The new opera went into rehearsal in Florence. At rehearsals Verdi proved himself as autocratic as in working with Piave. But now his methods were of undiluted benefit to all concerned.

Just before the opening, the composer told Lady Macbeth (soprano) and Macbeth (baritone) to come with him into the foyer of the empty theater and go over again one of their duets (there were no dress rehearsals on the stage in the Italy of that time).

Macbeth objected. He was in medieval costume, he pointed out, and, besides, he had already rehearsed the duet 150 times.

"Well, put on a modern coat and a modern pair of pants and rehearse it for the 151st time!" snapped Verdi. And that is just what Macbeth did. At the world *première* of the opera in Florence (March 14, 1847) that duet was one of the hits of the show. Early and late in his career Verdi was a grim

disciplinarian. He drove his singers mercilessly, but few among
them, when they assessed the results of his severity, failed to
admire him. He was Arturo Toscanini and W. S. Gilbert
rolled into one. Those whom he drilled and re-drilled grumbled and smarted under his sternness. But always they respected him and often they loved him.

In his new opera Verdi reappeared as Italy's leading maker
of patriotic operatic thrillers. One chorus (words by Maffei,
not by Piave) beginning

> *La patria tradita*
> *Piangendo c'invita;*
> *Fratelli, gli oppressi*
> *Corriamo a salvar . . .*

> (Betrayed, our country calls to us in tears,
> Brothers, let us succor the oppressed . . .),

promptly taken by the first Florentine audience at *Macbeth*
as an allusion to Italy's foreign-dominated plight, aroused
such mad outbursts of patriotism that the police had to come
surging into the house. Keeping an eye on explosive Verdi
opening nights and taking charge of them after they had exploded was in those days a regular part of an Italian police-
man's unhappy lot.

Macbeth, in its operatic form, was hailed by some as a masterpiece. In it were hints of the greater Verdi who was soon
to take over—of the still greater Verdi of his greatest period.
Some of the music had new qualities hinting at "music
drama" as we of today understand that phrase. Verdi, obviously, was reaching out, thinking, striving.

His *Macbeth* was revived with gratifying results in Germany during the recent Verdi resurgence there. Its first performance in the United States was at Niblo's Garden in New
York City in 1850.

Its composer was well pleased with it. In 1865 he thought it worthy of a drastic revamping for Paris. And he showed further his partiality for this, his first attempt to turn Shakespeare into opera, by dedicating it to a man for whom he felt boundless gratitude and deep affection—Antonio Barezzi, his father-in-law and true friend. To Barezzi he wrote:

"I dedicate to you my *Macbeth*, which I love so much. My heart offers it. I ask that your heart accept it."

He followed *Macbeth* with a work which was the first to have its *première* outside Italy. Composed to a libretto by Count Maffei (thoroughly tampered with by Verdi himself), it was based on Schiller's *Die Räuber*. Entitled *I Masnadieri* (The Robbers), it had its initial performance in London July 22, 1847.

Before it reached the footlights there those engaged to sing and act in it, who included the world-renowned Jenny Lind and the celebrated basso Lablache, went through wearying rehearsals. No effort was spared that might help the opera to success.

Jenny Lind's performance was rapturously applauded. And, to some extent, the audience at the opening night listened with favor to Verdi's score. But *I Masnadieri* failed. The first performance was marred by an outburst of untimely amusement when Lablache, a giant of a singer, supposed to be starving to death in prison, emerged from his dungeon with not an ounce of his gigantic person missing.

But Manager Lumley of Her Majesty's Theatre, firm in his belief that Giuseppe Verdi was the coming man in Italian opera (and how right he was!), suggested to him that he become the successor of the well-known conductor Costa at Her Majesty's. He offered the young maestro a tempting salary; and he agreed to put on in London a new Verdi opera every year during the three-year term of the contract. This put

Verdi at a crossroads. He half-agreed with the dictum that "when once the bâton is taken up the creative faculty disappears." Nevertheless, he was willing to take a chance.

But Lucca, an Italian music publisher, with whom he was having temporary dealings (the Ricordi firm had not as yet tied him up securely) made Verdi's decision for him by refusing to release him from an agreement to compose within the near future two new operas. The next conductor at Her Majesty's Theatre was not Giuseppe Verdi but Michael William Balfe, the Irishman who composed that sentimental favorite of our grandparents, *The Bohemian Girl*.

Verdi had mixed opinions about London. Early in his acquaintanceship with it he complained to his friend Muzio about the food—thus joining the serried multitudes of other Latins rendered unhappy by Britain's suet pudding, vegetable marrow, meat uncontaminated by condiment and kindred British gastronomic phenomena. To the Countess Maffei he wrote:

"Of London I can tell you little because yesterday was Sunday and there was not a soul to be seen. I find all this smoke and smell of coal disagreeable. It is like living on a steamboat. The climate takes away all desire to work."

But he liked London's big, impressive buildings, the cleanness of his lodgings, the air of immense wealth apparent all around him.

"If only London had the sky of Naples!" he confided to the Countess, "I think it would be unnecessary to long for Paradise. Oh, if only I could stay here a couple of years and take away with me a sack full of blessed money! But what's the use of wasting time on such ideas? Never would I be able to stand the London climate!"

Returning to Italy in a huff Verdi composed, for impresario Lucca, *Il Corsaro*, on a libretto by Piave, based on Byron. Piave's work, says Toye, was "partly incredible, partly unintel-

ligible," and he calls Verdi's music for it excepting a few
numbers "a wilderness of conventionalism."

Next, Verdi got back on his old job as a mouthpiece for
Italian patriotism.

The Revolution of 1848 had come and gone. After some
hard fighting and much high hoping Italian battlers for independence had been defeated, due largely to the military ability of their octogenarian opponent, the Austrian Marshal
Radetzky. But, just as in Verdi's earlier years, Italian yearning for liberty, to the fostering of which he had contributed
so effectively with *I Lombardi*, *Ernani*, *Attila* and *Macbeth*,
remained still very much alive. And he promptly set to work
to keep it so with his next opera, *La Battaglia di Legnano*.

Though dealing ostensibly with an Italy of centuries earlier,
the fact that it was a thinly disguised appeal based on the
contemporary Italian situation stuck out all over it. As a ringing call to Italians to rally after their recent reverses it was
worthy of the Verdi of "*O Signore, dal tetto natio*" and "*Avrai
tu l'universo.*"

The libretto, provided by the eccentric Cammarano, was
a bold exhortation to anti-Austrian sentiment in Italy. It sent
its audiences into paroxysms of patriotic fervor. One Italian
gendarme, after joining the singers on the stage in one of its
heady songs, threw himself in uncontrollable excitement over
a balcony railing, and landed, sword, pistol and all, among
the patrons of the orchestra seats, without losing his life or
seriously damaging his limbs, or theirs. (Verdi's early music
certainly had an extraordinary effect on gendarmes.) After a
while, in the occupied portions of Italy, the Austrians, tiring
of the wild demonstrations which *La Battaglia di Legnano*
kept stirring up, forbade further performances of it. It was revived some years later under the title of *L'Assedio di Haarlem*
(The Siege of Haarlem)—in deference again to the old ostrich
theory that if you changed the name of an opera you com-

pletely changed its nature and political connotations—with
the cast transformed into Dutchmen and Dutchwomen supposedly quite devoid of anti-Austrian sentiments and without
the remotest interest in the cause of Italian liberation.

Next, Cammarano was put to work on a libretto based on
Schiller's *Kabale und Liebe*. Verdi, with the score of this new
work buzzing in his head, went to Naples to complete it, and,
after its completion, to help at rehearsals. For the new opera
(its title was *Luisa Miller*) was to confront its first audience
at that most famous of Neapolitan theaters, the San Carlo.

After a short time he wished to go away from Naples. He
had become involved in a quarrel with the San Carlo management and had never liked the place anyhow. But the municipal authorities, working hand in hand with the San Carlo
crowd, dug up a law forbidding anybody to leave town without a special passport—and then blandly refused to give him
one.

Flying into one of his volcanic rages, Verdi barricaded himself in his hotel suite, and, from one of the front windows,
poured horrid epithets at the policemen grouped picturesquely
in the street below—and the policemen bellowed upward
equally horrid rejoinders—and the infuriated maestro shouted
that, if permission to leave Naples were denied him, he would
demand the right of asylum aboard a French frigate, anchored
conveniently in the harbor, right off-shore from the hotel.
After further assorted vociferation—listened to with truly
Neapolitan absorption by a big crowd growing bigger every
minute—the police shrugged their shoulders and went away.

A truce was declared between Verdi on the one side and
the Neapolitan municipal government and the San Carlo
management on the other. Verdi did not board the frigate.
And, on December 8, 1849, *Luisa Miller* was duly produced
at the San Carlo. But its composer's troubles were not yet
ended.

From the very moment of his arrival in Naples his friends had taken drastic steps to protect him from one Capecelatro, an ardent pro-Verdian, reputed far and wide to have a highly malignant evil eye. Whenever Verdi left his hotel for the theater or anywhere else, his friends surrounded him in a solid phalanx; and, when he returned, he again became the center of a vigilant hollow square—while, on its outer rim, Capecelatro yearned in vain to express his pro-Verdianism by an enthusiastic embrace.

But, on the opening night of *Luisa Miller*, while Verdi was backstage between the third and fourth acts, Capecelatro, eluding the watchful bodyguards, rushed up to the composer's side, beaming with joy, exclaimed, "At last, maestro!" with dramatic fervor, and threw his arms around Verdi with such violence that he knocked him off his feet, and at the same time dislodged a heavy piece of scenery, which narrowly missed cracking Verdi's skull. Together, the two rolled on the floor—Capecelatro's embrace was a sort of hammer-lock—until friends, dashing in from all directions, rescued the victim from his explosive admirer.

But—Capecelatro had made good his reputation as a redoubtable wielder of the evil eye. Superstitious Neapolitans sagely rationalized the incident thus: "Capecelatro embraced Verdi just before the fourth act of *Luisa Miller*, didn't he?" The fourth act is the best act of all, isn't it? Yet the San Carlo audience received it coldly, didn't they? Well . . ."

From Italy *Luisa Miller* went to London and Paris and America. Some liked it, some did not. The later faction found plenty to praise in it. Arrigo Boïto, poet and composer (of whom I shall have much to say in pages farther along in this book) told his friend Camille Bellaigue, the French music critic, with regard to one of the opera's arias ("*Quando le sere al placido* . . ."), that nobody not an Italian could realize what ecstasy that melody awakened in a truly Italian soul.

Shaking himself free of Naples with its unfriendly policemen and evil eyes Verdi next turned his attention to an opera called *Stiffelio*. It was produced at Trieste November 16, 1850.

When I was in Trieste some years ago I read on the façade of a house on the water front an inscription stating that, "on these premises, inspired by the blue skies and soft breezes of the Adriatic, Giuseppe Verdi composed *Stiffelio*." Well, all I can say is that those skies and breezes fell down badly on the job. *Stiffelio* flopped.

In *Nabucco* the young Verdi had shown the first signs of the traits that were destined to remain typical of him all through his career, in all his operas—bad, bad-good, good-bad and good: melodiousness, power and drive.

As he progressed, these basic characteristics became less and less obscured by the blemishes typical of the early Verdi —crudity, bad taste, undue neglect of the orchestra in favor of the singer, lack of refinement, ignoring or subordination of the psychological element. Finally, in his two supreme achievements, the good qualities of his music emerged in glorious completeness, strengthened and solidified to an extent only hinted at even in the best of his previous operas.

In *Nabucco's* successor, *I Lombardi*, considered qua music, he took a step backward. But he concealed this musical retrogression somewhat by emerging as a symbol of Italy's yearning for freedom.

In his next opera, *Ernani*, he added to his stature in his native land, both as a maker of music and as an arouser of patriotic sentiments, while, at the same time, definitely establishing himself on the musical horizon outside Italy as a new voice, a new musical impact, a new force to be reckoned with.

For some time after *Ernani,* Verdi's course, taken by and large, was disappointing. He composed too much. Too rapidly. Too carelessly. Impresarios clamored for his work and he stilled their clamor by sometimes conscienceless, often mechanical, production of operatic scores.

Verdi produced *Nabucco* in 1842, *I Lombardi* in 1843, *Ernani* in 1844. After that he ground out nine operas in six years—and it is a wonder that they did not bring him to disaster. None was entirely bad. But none was really good. In several there were clear signs of what he might do if he only would—hints of the extraordinary improvement in his art that lay before him. All had moments of Verdian melody, Verdian power, Verdian drive. But none, despite transient success as musical achievements or inciters to patriotic enthusiasm, or a combination of both, brought their composer solid approval from contemporary critics and even less from critics applying to opera later standards of evaluation.

If Giuseppe Verdi had stood pat after *Luisa Miller* his name would be scarcely better known today outside Italy than the names of forgotten contemporaries of his era—as Pacini, say, or Petrella or Mercadante or the Ricci brothers. And certain works of Rossini, Bellini and Donizetti would be better known today than anything of his—for, in Verdi's output during the first half of the 19th century, there was nothing comparable in durability with Rossini's *Barber of Seville,* Bellini's *Norma* or Donizetti's *Lucia di Lammermoor.*

But critics of the mid-20th century should not be overhard on the Verdi of the mid-19th. He was young. He needed money. Impresarios offered it to him. He took it. He gave them in return operatic scores in the style to which they were accustomed—sometimes mere potboilers, hastily patched together.

For this he has been too much pilloried by armchair detractors of a later era, unwilling to temper their disapproval

by a just study of the facts, by consideration of Giuseppe
Verdi as a human being, not merely as a musical abstraction.

Intolerance often makes such carpers grossly unjust. Finding in the works of a composer like Verdi glaring faults they
magnify the faults and minimize the reasons for them. They
appeal to rules established long after the death of such composers—rules which may be forgotten tomorrow. And that is
shamefully unfair. "There is a certain type of good taste,"
declares Francis Toye, "which is the hereditary enemy of
genius." That is a line for which immortality should be arranged.

IV

SUNRISE

THIRTEEN

"THIS opera has no chance whatsoever of staying in the operatic répertoire."

Thus the music critic of a French magazine. His remarks were inspired by a new work by Giuseppe Verdi, which had been seen for the first time in Venice in 1851.

Of all the multitudes of wrongheaded asseverations refuted by the passage of time that one is among the wrongheadedest and refutedest.

The generation to which our great-grandparents belonged hailed the opera in question with joyous cheers. The generation of our grandparents thought the same way about it. The generation of our parents continued to thrill at it and weep over it and clamorously applaud it—despite a rising tide of highbrow criticism. The present generation hails it as one of the masterpieces of a composer who today is riding a foaming wave of popularity.

Venice again. Again La Fenice, scene of *Ernani's* riotous first night. A new impresario now, Signor Lasina, in place of Count Mocenigo, noble hater of horn solos backstage. And, in place of *Ernani*, a brand-new opera by Giuseppe Verdi.

Discussions about it are on. Each one of them has been a battle. The casting of the new work has occasioned furious dispute. Who shall be the prima donna? All look to Verdi. He imitates the Sphinx.

"Cruvelli?" ventures somebody.

The composer nods. Apparently he is pleased. Around him eyes brighten.

"An excellent singer," mutters Verdi.

Eyes sparkle. Furrows are ironed out of foreheads.

"But she's crazy."

Eyes darken. Foreheads crease. And the discussion goes round and round again in maddening reiteration.

Rehearsals are on. At one of them the entire company— soprano, contralto, tenor, baritone, basso, full male and female chorus—are gathered on the stage around the composer. Everybody is nervous, tense. Giuseppe Verdi is objecting, as usual, to this, taking exception to that. He is badgering first this singer, then that one—striving as always for perfection— unattainable but always to be striven for.

To him, with wrinkled brow, temperament-propelled, strides the tenor.

"*Maestro, mi manca un pezzo.*" Maestro, in my part there is one song lacking. My solo in the last act . . . Unless . . ."

"Tut, tut. I know. Don't worry. There's plenty of time before the opening."

One day later. Same setting.

"*Maestro, mi manca un pezzo.*"

"Don't bother me. I'll give it to you in plenty of time. . . ."

"But . . ."

"Let's get on with the rehearsal."

Next day.

"*Maestro, mi manca . . .*"

"Come over here!" Verdi takes the tenor into a corner and hands him a sheet of music. The tenor looks at it. His eyes light up. "Bravo, maestro!" He starts singing.

With terror in his glance, Verdi grabs the tenor's sleeve with one hand, puts his other hand warningly to his lips.

"Listen!" he whispers. "I want you to make me a solemn promise. I want you to vow not to let anybody in Venice hear that tune before the opening night. Don't sing it. Don't hum it. Don't whistle it. Not on the street. Not at a café. Not in your home. Not on this stage. Promise now!"

The tenor promises.

Final rehearsal.

All music of the new opera has been gone over again and again—except that tenor solo. Now, at last, with the whole company crowding around him, Verdi tells the tenor to sing that song.

The orchestra plays the short prelude. The tenor begins to sing. A rustle of delight comes from his fellow-singers. It changes, as he finishes, to a wave of applause. Somebody starts humming.

Frowning fiercely, Verdi turns to the assembled company:

"Listen! I want you to make me a solemn promise. I want you to vow not to let anybody in Venice hear that tune before tomorrow's opening. Don't sing it. Don't hum it. Don't whistle it. Not on the street. Not at a café. Not in your homes. Not on this stage. Promise now!"

They promise.

Opening night of the new opera. Last act.

For the first time—the first time in tens of thousands of times—an audience hears from the orchestra the electrifying bars preceding that solo. The tenor begins to sing. A hush falls over his hypnotized hearers. He finishes.

A frantic storm of cheering shakes the theater. Hundreds in the audience are on their feet. They are shrieking. They are howling with delight.

"Ancora!" The song is repeated. "Bravo!" It is repeated again. "Bravissimo!"

As that audience leaves La Fenice after the final curtain, it is singing, humming and whistling that tune. Next morning it is being sung, hummed and whistled on every street and square in Venice, at every café. Ever since it has been heard

innumerable times all over Europe and the Americas and in
every part of Asia, Africa and the antipodes to which singing,
humming and whistling Europeans and Americans have penetrated. Giuseppe Verdi was perfectly well aware when that
ditty occurred to him that, unless he took the most drastic
steps, it would sweep all over Venice, until, when the curtain
went up on the first performance of the opera containing it,
it would sound like such old stuff to the first-nighters that
they would brand him a shameless plagiarist. Verdi knew his
Venetians. And all the rest of his fellow-Italians.

There is only one word for the effect which that song has
had on the human race for an entire century—maddening. It
is known as *"La donna è mobile."* It is sung, as everybody
knows, in Giuseppe Verdi's *Rigoletto*. I doubt whether a
catchier tune was ever composed.

But, before the opening night, Verdi, his librettist Piave, impresario Lasina, and all their helpers, male and female, in all
categories—the company, the orchestra, the backstage squad,
everybody in the front part of the theater, including the box
office—went through hell.

The new work was based on Victor Hugo's drama *Le Roi
s'amuse*. When Hugo's play had been given in Paris it had
occasioned such outraged displeasure that it had been
promptly withdrawn. Critics adjudged it utterly immoral.
In it, they averred with heat and horror, vice was exalted at
the expense of virtue. Also, there were political undercurrents.
Hugo himself thought that these, not immorality, were really
in the minds of the play's foes—especially the rough treatment he had meted out in it to a French king, Francis I. So,
when Verdi and Piave and Lasina were readying it, in its new
guise as an Italian grand opera, for its Venice opening night,
the Austrians (again intrenched solidly in Northern Italy after
the abortive Italian revolution of 1848) sat up and took notice.

What? An opera based on *Le Roi s'amuse?* Ha! They scented trouble. Had not Victor Hugo depicted a king sunk in profligacy—a royal roué of the most abandoned type? That was no way to depict a monarch, even though he had lived a couple of centuries ago and was all that Victor Hugo said he was!

However, according to rumor, they were going to base their objections primarily on the immorality of Hugo's theme in general. And these rumors assumed such alarming bulk that Verdi and Lasina got deeply worried. It looked to them like a case of no *Rigoletto* at La Fenice.

But librettist Piave remained unperturbed. He knew to a certainty, he told his nervous colleagues, that the production of *Rigoletto* would be permitted. Apparently, he had some mysterious private grapevine, leading (so he thought) straight into the mind of the head censor. All will be well, he told them repeatedly, with the mysterious mien of a combination Sherlock Holmes-Machiavelli. Reassured, Verdi repaired to Busseto, to get to work in earnest on the score for the new opera.

Whereupon, with deadly suddenness, the Austrian-inspired Bureau of Censorship in Venice struck.

It issued an edict forbidding the production of *Rigoletto* in Venice. And with it went a stinging rebuke to composer, librettist and impresario for daring to think of committing such a heinous outrage in a city of such a high moral character.

Verdi (back from Sant' Agata, wild-eyed) and Piave and Lasina were in despair. Rushing to the censorship offices they pleaded and stormed. Nothing doing. They had almost given up the battle when one of the censors, Martello by name, made a brilliant suggestion: why not turn Francis I into a mere Italian Duke of Mantua, a ducal profligate (there had been one such in Mantuan history), his seduced victim from French Blanche into Italian Gilda, etcetera, etcetera.

Eureka! Verdi, Piave and Lasina solemnly signed an agreement promising to make these changes and others, on which Martello and the other censors insisted. The skies cleared. The sun shone again. Verdi returned to Sant' Agata.

And Machiavellian Piave, who had been in such deep disgrace with Verdi that a present of cakes and fish had failed to placate the angry maestro, again climbed back into his boss's good graces. Having finished making the required changes in his libretto and having wheedled the final green light out of the censorship department, he jubilantly wrote to the composer: "Te Deum! Gloria! And a couple of hallelujahs!" And impresario Lasina drew a tremendous sigh of relief and a tremendously relieved Verdi returned to Venice from Sant' Agata for the opening night of *Rigoletto*—March 11, 1851—a date to be starred and double-starred and triple-starred in all chronicles of Giuseppe Verdi's sensational career.

Rigoletto was a howling success from start to finish. And that is the sort of success it has been ever since everywhere. At La Fenice it was given 21 times during the first few weeks of Lasina's season. Soon it was running riot all over Italy—and everywhere else where there were opera houses available to house it and impresarios on hand to take charge of its production. People went wild over *"La donna è mobile"* and *"Caro nome"* and the *"Bella figlia dell' amore"* quartet. Here and there the censors stopped it, shocked that a duke should be shown as liking the ladies—with the result that it had to be given in some cities under an assumed name—*Viscardello, Clara di Perth, Lionello. . . .*

Outside Italy it was soon arousing audiences to frenzies of approbation: in Austria, Hungary, Bohemia (now Czechoslovakia), Germany. In England one critic found it lacking in melody—*Rigoletto!!* His lone voice was promptly overwhelmed.

France had to wait some time to hear it, because Victor Hugo, author of the drama on which the opera was based, objected violently to what Piave and Verdi had done to his child. And he was long successful in preventing its production at the Italian Theatre in Paris. Finally, the manager of that theater sued the outraged dramatist, who lost his case and was condemned to pay costs—a trying verdict to one who loved the incense of adulation and triumph, to whom being a national idol in France was, as a friend of mine used to say of almost everything pleasant, "duck soup." Irrespective of rights and wrongs, there can be little doubt that, in Victor Hugo, vanity ran neck and neck with genius. Giuseppina Strepponi, who knew him in Paris, once remarked: "What wouldn't he give to see his own funeral!"

Previous to the Paris production of *Rigoletto* more trouble was occasioned because the Escudier brothers, Verdi's representatives there, thought that the best way to push their client's interests was to disparage rival composers. This engendered a rather hostile atmosphere toward Verdi.

Rigoletto was finally sung in Paris with the beauteous Frezzolini and Madame Alboni in the principal feminine rôles, the celebrated Mario as the wicked Duke, and the noted baritone Corsi as the Jester.

It duplicated its Venetian success. The new Verdi work was given in Paris 100 times that season, oftener the next. And it got a firm hold on French favor, which it has never lost.

Later, it was given in French at the Paris Opéra, with a bit of ballet sandwiched into it (to the authorities of the Opéra an opera without a ballet seemed indecent). There too, it was acclaimed. And even Victor Hugo, joining like a good sport in the applause, remarked, after the singing of the renowned quartet:

"If only I, like Verdi, could make four people talk at the same time in such a way as to make the public grasp both what they were saying and what they were feeling!"

The French magazine (*La Gazette Musicale*) in which had appeared the article whose author glibly consigned *Rigoletto* to oblivion in 1852, now tried to make amends. In a subsequent article in its pages (I do not know whether by the same critic), after *Rigoletto* had been parading in triumph for some time, is this:

Rigoletto marks an immense advance in Verdi's manner. . . . From now onward he will no longer mean to us a fiery composer, enamored of power and noise, sacrificing to excessive sonority both charm and grace. He has put plenty of these latter two qualities into *Rigoletto.* . . . And that is why we, who have often criticized him, have nothing but praise for him today. If we have changed our style with regard to him it is because we find that he too has changed his own style, and for that we congratulate him sincerely.

Commenting on *Rigoletto's* appearance in French translation at the Opéra, another local writer said:

"This is the first true success won by Verdi in Paris. And it was a brilliant success. Since the opening night it has never flagged."

Once, when Verdi was a guest at the home in Paris of Rossini, the latter put on in his honor a rendering of the *Rigoletto* quartet with Adelina Patti singing Gilda, Alboni as Maddalena, and Mario as the Duke. Incidentally, Rossini remarked, after attending a performance of *Rigoletto* in Paris:

"It is this opera that has made me finally recognize Verdi's genius."

But—back to Venice. In that city, where *Rigoletto* was first heard, Venetian gondoliers continued to sing "*La donna è mobile*" on the Grand Canal, and the passengers in their

gondolas continued to hum it, and Venetians of all social
gradations continued to whistle it in and out of tune on the
Merceria and the Riva degli Schiavoni and the Rialto:

> Damsels are flighty jades
> Ever of change in quest,
> Making of love a jest,
> Faithfully yours—and mine!

And Francesco Piave, author of the words to which Giuseppe Verdi had fitted the most maddening of melodies,
happening, as he strolled across the Piazza San Marco, to
spy a young ex-mistress of his whose love for him had cooled,
and hoping for renewed amorous dalliance, sidled up to her
and warbled tenderly in her ear:

> Damsels are flighty jades
> Ever of change in quest . . .

to which she instantly retorted:

> And you're the stupidest
> Of lovers asinine.

FOURTEEN

IN *Rigoletto* a new Verdi speaks. A better Verdi. A Verdi
hinting at still better Verdis to come. Crudities it has, clap-
trap, bits of childish naïveté. (The difference between the
comically vengeful pirates in *The Pirates of Penzance* and the
"*Zitti, zitti*" conspirators in *Rigoletto* is that Gilbert and Sul-
livan *intended* to make their pirates absurd and *pretended* to
make them blood-curdling, whereas Piave and Verdi *intended*
to make their conspirators blood-curdling and succeeded in
making them *absurd*.) But why waste time on the flaws in

timeless, seemingly deathless *Rigoletto?* Whose operas are
perfect? The flaws in Verdi's music for *Rigoletto* no more
affect its underlying, pervasive worth and force and beauty
than thorns hide roses or dust dims gold.

Take *"Questa o quella."* Judged purely from its surface,
what is it? Nothing but an outburst of cynical self-adulation
from the profligate Duke of Mantua, re-living old escapades,
savoring new? But, in the light of the singer's imminent
seduction of the daughter of Rigoletto, his unsuspecting
Jester, it assumes dark, cruel meaning.

Take Monterone's curse. It is dismissed by some as blatant
melodrama. But, judged by what it hints at—by its effect,
above all, on Rigoletto, hitherto heedless and as immorally
cynical as his ducal master—it instantly becomes ominous,
portentous, endowed with something of the pity and terror
of ancient Greek tragedy.

Take the scene between Rigoletto and Sparafucile. The latter, it will be recalled, stopping Rigoletto on a narrow, dark
byway of Mantua, offers his services to the Jester as a professional murderer, should anything arise in his line of business. Again bare theatricalism? Maybe. But what excellent
theatricalism!

As yet fate has not felled the Jester. Disaster is not yet at
his throat. But, the Sparafucile theme—and what a theme it
is!—hisses balefully in the orchestra, heavy with the presage
of terrible doings to come. The Jester and the murderer con-
verse in hushed recitative—and, not in their whisperings, but
in that theme, imbedded deep in the orchestra, the melody of
their grim dialogue is carried—a writhing melody, coiled and
sinister, a snake set to music.

And *"La donna è mobile."* Taken on the mere sound of it,
on its rush and impact, what is it? A maddening ditty. But
with what genius Verdi handles it in the last act of his *Rigoletto,* in that act concerning which Francis Toye blurts out,

in uncontrollable admiration: "I would not willingly change a single note of it!" (Amen to that.)

First, introduced with electrifying suddenness, that ditty pictures the Duke, lust-ridden, predatory, heartless. But, when it reappears on the Duke's lips behind the scenes, with hideous irony, revealing to Rigoletto that his plot of revenge has failed, what horror lies in it, pointed up and illuminated by its very lightness and lilt! And what a gem of psychological insight it becomes!

And the storm. What a chance for Verdian din, for resurrected memories of the Busseto Brass Band. But where now are such memories? Gone. Dead.

Instead, flashes of lightning, made practically visible by a few notes on the piccolo—thunder subtly expressed by quiet chromatics, by subdued, ruffling sounds in the orchestra—all the awful power of tempest artfully suggested, never brutally externalized.

But—in *Rigoletto* all roads lead to the quartet. In that number, at one bound, Giuseppe Verdi comes into his own. While the Duke and Maddalena on one side of the stage, Gilda and Rigoletto on the other, glide into that thing of beauty and subtlety and genius, the Verdi of 1851 reveals, in one glorious flash, the coming Verdi of 1871 and 1887 and 1893. In all the composer's career preceding the quartet in *Rigoletto* there is nothing with equally convincing touches of characterization.

The Duke—cynicism, amorous lust, depravity; Maddalena —coarse coyness; Gilda—anguished love on the brink of self-immolation; Rigoletto—gloating anticipation of a revenge doomed in the end to shattering awakening—all these leap from Verdi's setting of that great quartet, take shape inside every audience's minds, make all sit hushed—unconscious of everything else; enthralled, on the very edges of their seats— while genius reveals, note by note, the inevitability of human destiny, using as its instrument of revelation melody which, to me—and to millions of others, I am sure—is Italian operatic music in its full and glorious flowering. With that moment of musical ravishment sounding in one's ears who would care to scrutinize *Rigoletto's* shortcomings as an opera? For them, in that quartet, Giuseppe Verdi made honorable, complete amends.

This new Verdi is no longer content with manufacturing thrilling, dramatic situations. No longer is he shying at psychological problems, running away from them. No, he is facing them, grappling with them, solving them. *Rigoletto* is the first real sign of the Giuseppe Verdi destined to round out a full and rich career, at a point where most men have done their life's work and are getting ready for death and burial, with an opera that is a miracle.

Immediately after hearing the *Rigoletto* quartet performed in Venice for the first time Verdi told the baritone Varesi: "I'll never do better than that." (He was mistaken.)

By the way, in preparing *Rigoletto*, Verdi had a daring idea, but lacked the nerve to go through with it. He wanted the principal love duet to be sung by Gilda, the heroine, and the Duke, her seducer, in the latter's bedroom, supposedly immediately after the seduction. "But—think of the censors and parsons!" he remarked—and dismissed the scheme from his mind.

Rigoletto did not get to the United States until four years had elapsed after its opening night in Venice. It was presented to an American audience on February 19, 1855, at the old Academy of Music in New York City. It was given for the first time at the Metropolitan Opera House in that city on November 17, 1883, just after the start of the Met's first season. Marcella Sembrich was the Gilda. Twenty years later

Rigoletto was the opera selected for Enrico Caruso's American debut.

Rigoletto's success has been world-wide—but nowhere does it win the hearts of those who hear it as it does in its native Italy. There it is a part of people's lives—a treasure belonging jointly to everybody. Its tunes go with the air every Italian breathes, with the thoughts he thinks, the dreams he dreams. Nowhere, to my knowledge, is this truth better expressed than in the following—written not by an Italian but by a Frenchman, a friend and admirer of Verdi, Camille Bellaigue:

I remember that, toward the end of an afternoon in Rome, on the terraces of the Pincio, I was listening to a military band playing—and playing well—Beethoven's sublime *Leonore* overture. But—I hardly recognized it—or, rather, I misunderstood it. This was not my fault any more than it was Beethoven's. But—the circumstances, the time, the place—all made it seem strange to me, out of place, alien. I failed to be impressed, under the palm trees, by its severe tones; and its evocation of Beethoven's saintly but sombre heroine had, for me, no power against the golden enchantment of the approaching Roman evening.

A few hours later I was coming out of a second-rate popular theatre. There, mediocre singers had just sung *Rigoletto* for humble folk. But—how those Italians, every one of them, had understood that Italian music of theirs! How some of them had grasped, others merely felt, its rush and ardor and life! How they made me realize that this music is not the product of profound meditation, of scientific method, but the outpouring of instinctive genius, of passionate improvisation!

I walked along with slow steps under the starlight. Young voices of young lovers blended with the sound of the waters of the Trevi fountain the refrain of the Duke of Mantua's song, "*La donna è mobile.*" And I realized that a little song can be a thing of greatness, since it can contain and express all the mystery of youth and plashing waters, of spring-time and the night.*

* Camille Bellaigue, *Verdi*. Paris, Henri Laurens, 1912.

Giuseppe Verdi now stood triumphant. He knew that, in *Rigoletto,* he had found himself; and, like Montecristo in the play, he might have cried: "The world is mine!"

But into his joy came sharp grief. His mother, whom he adored, who adored him, died three months after *Rigoletto* drove the Venetians to frenzy. From her little village—and later from Sant' Agata, where, at his insistence, she had gone to live—she had marked his victories with loving attention. And each time he had returned to her from one of them she had given him the same love as on the day in his babyhood when she had saved him from threatening death in the church steeple of her village.

He buried her in a nearby cemetery. By the side of her grave, forgetting ambition and applause and glory, Milan and Venice and Paris and London, he wept broken-heartedly—transformed from the great Giuseppe Verdi of those great cities into her little Peppino of Le Roncole.

Most of the time while Verdi was attending to the details of the production of *Rigoletto* Giuseppina Strepponi was getting to feel more at home every day at Sant' Agata. From the beginning of her taking up residence there she had liked it (except in the dead of winter) and her liking not only grew but communicated itself to her companion.

At first his affection for his Sabine farm was more moderate than hers; eventually, however, it left hers behind. At Sant' Agata Verdi proved to the full the truth of what he often said of himself: "I am simply a peasant." And yet, when he was taking his ease on his estate, with her whom he loved and who loved him, famous and affluent, among his best friends, it was said that nobody was more the grand seigneur than this peasant from Le Roncole.

And the affection of Giuseppina for Giuseppe and his for her grew in proportion to the growth of their attachment to

Sant' Agata. In the *Rigoletto* days, knowing that Francesco
Piave was an assiduous rounder, she wrote to Verdi in mock
alarm, warning him against "that devil," inplying that com-
poser and librettist were roistering in the small hours about
Venice, while she led a life of bucolic innocence at Sant'
Agata.

"Tell Piave from me," she instructed Verdi, "to indulge
his erotic tastes in the company of cronies of his own stamp."
She knew well that *il mio* Verdi had no leaning toward amorous nocturnal prowlings à la Piave; and she was so sure of her
Verdi that she could pretend that she thought he liked them.

With what zest and joy he would escape from his work in
cities to Giuseppina and Sant' Agata! And, as his train steamed
in to the nearest railway station, she would be waiting there
for him. "The smoke of the locomotive," she wrote once to
one of her many friends, just before going to meet him, "will
announce to me the return of Mago [another of her nicknames for him] and that will mean the return of our good
times."

As soon as he reached his country estate he became the
country squire. Immediately, city life was forgotten as he
wandered again with his dogs over his fields, inspected his
horses and herds and flocks, discussed crops with his majordomo, and, best of all, puttered around in his garden.

His garden!

Giuseppina wrote to their particular friend, the Countess
Maffei,

At first when we started planting that garden it was *my* garden.
But now he reigns over it like a czar. At present I am reduced to
one small corner of it. I make it clear to him that he has no right
to poke his nose into that corner. But I can't say that he obeys
this rule. However, I have found a way to make him behave. I
threaten that, if he interferes with me in my part of the garden,
I shall not plant flowers there but cabbages.

And in allusion to Verdi's habit of bossing the workmen doing odd jobs on the estate:

"Ah, that's the weakness of *il signor maestro!* If I tell him that one of his operas is no good he doesn't care. But if I criticize his qualifications as a foreman then the sparks fly!" *

Part of the secret of her hold over him was that she was not afraid of him. Most of those who came into contact with him felt flutters of fear. But not Giuseppina Strepponi. The very fact that she gave him nicknames proves that. Nicknames for Giuseppe Verdi! Why, the mere idea of doing so was enough to shock most of his friends!

One of them, who for years was on the best terms with him, summed up that side of the great composer when he remarked that, if he got into animated conversation with Carducci, one of Italy's most celebrated and most respected poets, he would lay his hand now and then in the excitement of the moment on Carducci's shoulder. "But," he would add with something like a shiver, "lay my hand on Verdi's shoulder? Never!"

That, however, was not Giuseppina's way at all. She respected Giuseppe's privacy. She deferred to him constantly. She acknowledged that at Sant' Agata he was king. But she showed her respect and her deference and her submission to his sovereignty in her own special way and that was a way which, to practically everybody else who knew him, was outrageous familiarity. And he loved it.

Once she had the audacity to write:

"You have the heart of an angel, but, in some things, the bony part of your skull is so thick that if it came to the notice of the great Gall [the celebrated phrenologist] it would give him ideas for an additional section for his famous book on phrenology."

* Mundula, *op. cit.*

And once, when their friend De Amicis was talking with her in one corner of a room at Sant' Agata while Verdi, in another corner, was conversing with another friend about expeditions to the polar regions, Giuseppina, with her accustomed fearless *gaminerie*, remarked to De Amicis, pointing to Verdi:

"He's in an awful frame of mind. He always is when he's composing a new opera. You have no idea how dreadful he is when he's at work. You just don't know that man!" De Amicis roared with laughter. Verdi, across the room, inquired:

"Giuseppina, what are you talking about over there?"

"Nothing much," she replied, with a mischievous look at De Amicis. "I, too, was merely mentioning polar bears."

And soon Verdi was back in his study, composing music at high tension and Giuseppina was attending to her household duties and thinking up another piece of impishness.

Though she adored and admired Verdi she never let adoration and admiration blind her to her own importance in his life. Once, after one of his triumphant successes, Giuseppina, busy with her work in running Sant' Agata, remarked: "After all, everybody can't write *Aïda*. Somebody is needed to pack and unpack trunks and make out the laundry lists."

Nobody knew him as she did. None of those conscious of the hardness in him knew him half as well. Giuseppina was quite aware of that hardness. Often she must have suffered from it and deplored it before old age softened and mellowed him. Yet, long before that happened, out of her unrivaled knowledge of him, she wrote to him, during one of his enforced absences from Sant' Agata:

That which makes the world raise its hat to you is something to which I never, or almost never, give a thought. I swear to you, and you will not find it difficult to believe me, that often I feel a sort of surprise that you know about music.

Though it is a divine art, of which your genius is worthy, the magic qualities in you that fascinate me, that I adore, are your character, your heart, your indulgence toward the errors of others while being, at the same time, so hard on yourself—your charitableness, filled with shyness and mystery—your proud independence—your boyish simplicity—all qualities appropriate in one who has been able to preserve in himself a fierce virginity of ideas and sentiments in the midst of the sewer of humanity.

Oh, my Verdi, I am not worthy of you! Your love for me is an act of charity, a balm for a heart that is often filled with sadness when it appears to be happy. Keep on loving me, love me even after death, that I may present myself before God's Throne of Judgment rich in your love and in your prayers, oh, my redeemer! *

FIFTEEN

ONCE upon a time a young Spaniard named Antonio García Gutiérrez submitted to the management of a theater in Madrid the manuscript of a play that he had written. The management, having found it highly meritorious, accepted it for production and promptly started rehearsal, thus bringing to the young dramatist agreeable dreams of bright literary fame and rich pecuniary reward.

But, in the midst of his dreaming, the Spanish government of the period coldly informed him that he was liable for immediate service in the Spanish army, and that—unless he was lucky enough to draw from an urn provided for the occasion a number exempting him—he would have to go through for several years the regular round of peacetime marching and drilling prescribed for conscript soldiers.

Señor García Gutiérrez drew Number One. That meant shouldering a musket. Of course (according to an old Span-

* Mundula, *op. cit.*

ish custom) he could have bought a substitute to shoulder it
in his place. But he had no money. So he resigned himself to
the prospect of a weary spell as a soldier, with no time left
over for literature.

But—that play of his proved a thundering success. And the
box-office receipts were so satisfactory that he forthwith
bought himself a substitute and returned with enthusiasm
to playwriting. All of which has nothing to do with my subject except this: young Señor García Gutiérrez' play, transformed into an operatic libretto and produced in 1853 as
Giuseppe Verdi's next offering after *Rigoletto*, has been ever
since as popular an opera as mortal man ever composed.

The name of the García Gutiérrez play is *El Trovador*. The
name of the opera fashioned from it is *Il Trovatore*.

Verdi, having somewhere run across a copy of that Spanish
play, was instantly attracted by it—and, over the years, in the
midst of other matters commanding his attention, he had
never forgotten it.

Its gloom and grandeur—the somber melodrama of its setting—its lurid succession of kidnappings and murders and ex-
ecutions—its brutal contrastings of love and hate, pity and
fury—its sinister gypsies and prancing soldiery and lugubrious
monks and exalted members of the Spanish aristocracy, male
and female, all beset by the most harrowing tribulations—
were right up the Verdian street.

All over the universe opera-lovers were thirsting for Verdi's
next opera—for it must be remembered that he who, as a
ragged, penniless little peasant boy, had strummed and day-
dreamed at the broken-down old spinet in Le Roncole, was
now the most sensationally successful living composer.

And he was keen to remain just that. There must not be
another sagging away, he resolutely told himself, from high
achievement, as there had been in some of the operas which
had followed *Nabucco's* triumph. He must now create some-

thing to maintain the standard set by *Rigoletto*. The world
was at his feet. It must stay there. And the way to keep it
there, he decided, was to get that Spanish play by which he
had been so much attracted transformed into an operatic
version preserving, unweakened, its ferocious blood-and-thun-
der elements, enabling him to provide the resultant gory,
noisy hodgepodge with a thrilling, melting Verdian score.
That he was at the height of his power as a fashioner of melodrama set to music he felt—*he knew*. His next opera must
prove it to the world. Forward march!

Who was to work with him? Francesco Piave? No, not this
time. Salvatore Cammarano? Ha! The very man! Already, as
we have seen, Verdi had collaborated with Cammarano, in
Alzira and *La Battaglia di Legnano*.

So, having dispatched to that eccentric poet at Naples, a
copy of the García Gutiérrez play, the eager composer ex-
horted the Neapolitan versifier to squeeze out of it a libretto
containing every bit of the fire and passion and gore and
gloom of the original.

Cammarano got down to work. And soon Giuseppe Verdi
had in his hands a first draft of the book for *Il Trovatore*.

Not hot enough! Not gloomy enough! Verdi sputtered and
swore. Nevertheless, keeping within the bounds of parliamen-
tary language despite his disappointment—throughout their
association, as I have said already, Verdi never pushed Cammarano around as he did docile, unretaliating Piave—the composer enclosed with his next letter to the Neapolitan a
detailed sketch (indeed, it was practically a full scenario) of
what he wanted.

As usual, when he meddled with a libretto, it diverged
seriously from what the author had first jotted down. But
Cammarano, instead of exploding in the outraged manner of
Temistocle Solera in the days of *Nabucco* and *I Lombardi*,
conformed without over-much protest to the exactions of the

composer and worked into the finished product the abrupt contrasts and savage vehemences and ruthless, over-drastic compressions demanded by his driving, cocksure collaborator. Meanwhile, the latter sat down to concentrated composing.

But, before the work was finished, Cammarano was taken ill and died. The libretto was completed by another Neapolitan named Bardare, suggested to Verdi by his friend Cesare de Sanctis, also a native of Naples. It was De Sanctis who brought to Verdi's attention the fact that the widow and children of Cammarano had been left in dire poverty, whereupon the composer, with typical generosity, paid to her not only the entire amount agreed upon for the complete libretto but 100 ducats besides.

Completing the score of *Trovatore* was a hard task. Not only was Cammarano's death a shock, but Verdi's father fell ill and for a while seemed on the point of death. Fortunately, he recovered. No wonder the composer, thus beset, was in a terrible humor.

While, as he used to say, he was "martyrizing" the *Trovatore* libretto with notes, he refused crossly to do an opera requested from him by his staunch admirer Lumley of London, now in charge of the Italian Theatre in Paris. And he broke off relations with La Scala in Milan because, according to him, it had put on his *Macbeth* in such a lamentable manner that it had failed to please the Milanese. And he had a row with the Parisian impresario Roqueplan—"that filibuster." And he quarreled with his publishers, the Ricordis, (grown fat with prosperity largely through selling Verdi music) over the translation rights of *Luisa Miller*. Dark days for Giuseppe Verdi. But to what a glorious sunrise their darkness was to succumb!

In a few weeks the last verses for the new opera, by Cammarano and Bardare, had been joined to the last notes for it by Verdi. *Il Trovatore* had been born. As I write, more than

100 years later, it shows not the slightest signs of approaching death.

For the first night the Apollo Theatre in Rome had been selected. Opera-lovers in the Eternal City had been agog for weeks about the coming event—as indeed had been those of the rest of Italy and many other countries. The fact that on the night chosen for the *première* (January 19, 1853) the waters of the Tiber, brimming over their banks as a result of heavy rains, were oozing through the streets and flooding the sidewalks adjacent to the Apollo, did not suffice to keep an immense crowd away from the theater. With feet soaked to the ankles, trousers covered with mud and slime, hundreds stood waiting for the doors to be opened; and, when the curtain went up, the theater was jammed to the topmost gallery seats with shivering, dripping, dirt-caked Romans.

Il Trovatore eclipsed their brightest anticipations. It won an immense, glowing, tumultuous success. The Apollo shook to delirious joy. "It was," wrote one commentator, "a triumph such as only Giuseppe Verdi can hope to achieve." The pattern set that night was duplicated all over Italy and Europe and all other parts of the world where operagoing was cultivated.

Today it is still being duplicated everywhere by operatic managers who have the astuteness to put *Il Trovatore* on yet again, to the opulent enrichment of their purses. Within the first year of its life Verdi's new opera proved itself one of the most potent magnets in operatic history. The composer, delighted, wrote to his friend Count Arrivabene: "If you go to India or the interior of Africa you will hear something from *Il Trovatore*."

At the present time it exerts over all those who see it and hear it undiminished drawing power. Most people yield willingly to that power. Others yield reluctantly. But all *yield*.

Is there an anti-Verdian anywhere with the nerve to vow, with hand upraised, that not once during a performance of *Il Trovatore* did his heart beat faster or his eyes moisten or his feet start tapping the floor (not even during the "Anvil Chorus") to the irresistible thrill and compelling melody and overwhelming dramatic rhythm of Giuseppe Verdi's music for that most melodramatic of operas?

Azucena, the tragic gypsy-mother in *Il Trovatore*, elicited in 1853 and still elicits an immense amount of praise alike as an individual, a symbol and a vehicle for some of Verdi's most impassioned and melodious music. From the time of his first reading of the Spanish play on which the opera is based he was strongly drawn to this brooding, vengeful, half-insane character. (Indeed, his original idea was to call the opera *Azucena*.) From her first appearance on the stage she shows qualities that catch and hold the attention of the audience. Any woman portraying her must certainly be a bad singer and a worse actress if she cannot "put over" adequately *"Stride la vampa"* in the first act or *"Ai nostri monti"* in the last. The former, as a revealing blueprint of the somber personality of Azucena, of the basic somberness of the opera as a whole, is a masterpiece; the latter, though it has gone through a century of corroding, tarnishing, exasperating barrel-organ popularity, remains one of the tenderest of all Verdian songs. Both still live, after ten decades of inadequate rendering, cruel burlesque and furious denunciation without becoming hopelessly hackneyed in their essential effectiveness. Incidentally, is it not reasonable to assume that much of the tenderness instilled by the composer into *"Ai nostri monti,"* that wonderful picturing of nostalgia and mother-love, is due to the desolation caused in him by his own mother's death less than two years before?

Il Trovatore's climax is its last act. There, once and for all, overpoweringly, Giuseppe Verdi, the genius of melodramatic grand opera, made good. And there he is apparently firmly intrenched for another century. Though it is the reddest of red rags to many highbrows the public still thrills and weeps at the shattering contrasts and unerring impact of the tower scene in that act.

Despite all Verdi's defects—and many of them cry aloud to the heavens in *Il Trovatore*—the overwhelming majority of operagoers are totally unable to sit unmoved through that scene—as they listen to the monks chanting the deadly notes that herald the imminent execution of the prisoner Manrico —as Leonora, his beloved, shuddering at the horror of the coming tragedy, sings of her love and despair in agonized accents—as the prisoner bids her a last farewell in notes that seem literally to soar out of his dungeon and rise to regions of hope and peace.

Every time I hear *Il Trovatore* I am struck anew by this soaring quality in the opening of the tenor's song—those notes, which, as an Italian critic says, "are projected into a limpid realm of musical light." What a contrast to the grim *Miserere* of the monks, to the anguished lament of Leonora! The same soaring quality, for me, lies also in the tenor's entry into "*Ai nostri monti,*" after Azucena has sung its opening part.

SIXTEEN

B ROWSING through reviews of *Il Trovatore* during its century of existence I am tempted to dub it the on-the-one-hand-on-the-other-hand opera *par excellence*.

"On the one hand, the beauty of its melodies is undeniable; on the other hand, the taste of some of its scenes is execrable."

"On the one hand, parts of it are good; on the other hand, parts of it are bad."

"On the one hand, it is full of power; on the other hand, it is brutal and vulgar."

Never was criticism of an opera so cautiously balanced. Never were critics so unable to come out flat-footed one way or the other.

The libretto drew many unkind words from commentators of a century ago—and it is still drawing them today. An Italian critic declared that Cammarano's text created obscurity where everything was simple and tended to make the action illogical. Librettist and composer alike were belabored by the same writer when he said: "There is in *Trovatore* no authentic psychological exploration."

And then comes the invariable "on the other hand":

"If, of these three operas [*Rigoletto*, *Trovatore* and the next to be discussed, *Traviata*], *Trovatore* ranks lowest as an organic whole and is farthest from perfection, it is perhaps the most powerful, the most Verdian, in its triumphant melodic quality, its atrocious dramatic violence, its merciless tumult of raw passions."

"They say that this opera is too sad, that there are too many deaths in it," said Verdi, when he read some of the criticisms of *Il Trovatore*. "But—in life, is not everything death?"

And now back to the army of on-the-one-hand-on-the-other-hand critics:

Periodically, after a succession of conventional or trivial pages something emerges and hits you, as it were, between the eyes, something elemental, furious, wholly true. *Il Trovatore* has been reproached with vulgarity, and the reproach is not unfounded. But this vulgarity is the vulgarity of greatness, a by-product of the vitality and passion without which there can be no great art. . . .

Nobody has ever surpassed the magnificent collection of tunes assembled by Verdi in *Il Trovatore*—tunes throbbing with sincerity and emotion. . . . Verdi's score . . . remains a remarkable expression in music of the romantic, hot-blooded drama of chivalry. . . . All over the world . . . *Il Trovatore* captured the heart of the public if not the admiration of the learned. It has by no means lost the first even today, while its claim to the second seems greater, not less, than formerly. *Il Trovatore* . . . may be regarded as the apothesis of both the good and the bad qualities of early Verdian opera.*

Trovatore stands out in the minds of most of us as a masterpiece of fury and fire, of brute force and overwhelming violence. Some of its outbursts of elemental savagery are more like blows than songs. Manrico's terrific denunciation of Leonora for her supposed treachery has been likened, in its unbridled vehemence, to the wild cry of a wounded beast. As for *"Di quella pira"*—who anywhere can think without a thrill of that impossible, tasteless, stentorian, convincing, irresistible manifestation of Verdi's genius? It has been burlesqued and lampooned and derided; its notorious high C has ruined the tempers of critics and the throats of tenors. On the other hand . . .

When Cavour, after working indefatigably for the unification and aggrandizement of Italy, heard the news that the war against Austria for which he had sought and found allies for the Italians, the war which he had looked upon as the final step in the liberation of his country, was at last a reality, he did not burst into patriotic eloquence. He did not shed tears as an outlet for all the pent-up emotions coursing through his mind. He did not shout. He did not rant. All that would not have expressed what he felt. Instead, he hummed *"Di quella pira."*

✦

* Toye, *op. cit.*

On its triumphal march through Italy *Il Trovatore* struck a snag for a while in one Italian city, Naples—the city where Cammarano, its librettist, had resided.

Also resident there (and quite one of its most important and celebrated citizens) was the composer Mercadante, who, before Giuseppe Verdi came along, was well to the fore as an aspirant to the place in the estimation of Italy's opera-goers left vacant by Rossini, Bellini and Donizetti. Mercadante, inordinately jealous of Verdi, worked hard to put obstacles in the way of his success all over Italy; and, when these did not work, in seeing to it that the newcomer, whom he considered an interloping upstart, should make no headway in Naples.

For some time Mercadante succeeded. Such was his influence with the Neapolitans that they lent themselves to cabals and plots subtly designed to prevent Verdi from being a success in Naples. But, when *Il Trovatore* burst on the operatic horizon—when news of its tremendous success reached Naples from nearby Rome, the scene of its riotous first night—there was revolt even among the most pro-Mercadante Neapolitans.

They insisted on hearing the new Verdi hit. The great Teatro San Carlo not being available (partly, perhaps, through Mercadante's skulduggery) *Il Trovatore* was announced for performance at another local theater. There, the singers, having got hold of a copy of the *Trovatore* score, studied it feverishly, all bunched around it, memorized every word and note in an incredibly short space of time, and put it on, almost without decent rehearsal, just as soon as they possibly could. As everywhere else it brought down the house. And Mercadante, we are told, walked around town "growling like a bear with a sore head."

This must have been all the more pleasing to Verdi because Naples was notorious among singers and librettists and composers for mobilizing just about the most ultra-captious and disagreeable audiences in all Italy. Milan, they used to wail, was bad enough, and so were Rome and Florence, but—Naples! Dire tales were told of the awful things that had befallen opera folk there who had displeased Neapolitan audiences and the Neapolitan local authorities.

One prima donna, after being hissed at the San Carlo, philosophically shrugged her shoulders and turned her back on the hissers. Immediately she was hustled off the stage by the police and thrown into a dungeon cell, where she languished in solitary confinement for several days and was released only when the time came for her to do her stuff at the San Carlo, when gendarmes took her out of her cell, delivered her at the stage door, and returned her to prison after the end of the performance. A similar fate befell a tenor who, also made the target of hisses, clearly showed that he did not hold with that sort of thing: he, too, went to prison, but, not being a lady and hence entitled to special favors from the gallant city government, he was kept locked up *for an entire week.*

Eventually, Naples—imagine the disgust of Mercadante!—became a great stronghold of pro-Verdi sentiment. It was said that so great was the passion of the Neapolitans for his music that, in a day when outrageous liberties were often taken with operatic scores by conductors, nobody dared in Naples to change a note of Verdi's product. If anybody attempted to do so Neapolitan audiences rose up *en masse* and howled with rage.

Nevertheless, Verdi could not forgive Naples for the variegated troubles it had caused him. He was particularly sore with the management of the San Carlo Theatre there. In that he resembled Enrico Caruso. Though a Neapolitan devoted to the end of his life to the city of his birth the greatest of tenors conceived a grudge against the San Carlo which he resolutely refused to forget.

Caruso was engaged to sing at the famous (and dreaded) Neapolitan temple of opera in 1901, the year of his first tremendous success at La Scala—also, incidentally, of Verdi's death. On first nights two mutually hostile factions in the audience, captained by two musical noblemen of Naples, monopolized the best seats and what was one faction's meat was the other's poison.

On the night of Caruso's first appearance at the San Carlo the house was packed. Caruso sang. One of the factions signified approval. That was enough for the other faction. It immediately registered violent disapproval. The first faction leaped to its feet. Awful Neapolitan epithets were exchanged. After a while things calmed down. Ruffled tempers subsided. There were no casualties. The performance was resumed.

But Enrico Caruso had been wounded to the heart. He remained unforgiving to the end of his life. Never did he consent to appear again before a Neapolitan audience as a professional singer. His love for the city where he had been born remained unshaken. Years later he said to a friend:

"Of course I'll return to Naples! Always. But never to sing. Only to eat spaghetti!" *

Il Trovatore had its first night in Paris (in its Italian form) in December, 1854. And it was introduced to London May 11, 1855, with Mesdames Frezzolini and Viardot as the leading ladies and the renowned tenor Tamberlik as Manrico. From England Tamberlik went to St. Petersburg, where he triumphed again as the luckless hero of Trovatore.

In Paris the opera had another first night (this time in French) at the Opéra January 12, 1857. With a ballet added of course, with a new "Soldiers' Chorus," and under the title of Le Trouvère it had again immediate and enormous success.

* T. R. Ybarra, Caruso, The Man of Naples and the Voice of Gold. New York, Harcourt, Brace & Co., 1953.

In 1863 *Le Trouvère* reached its 100th performance in Paris, in 1872, its 200th.

Il Trovatore was given for the first time in the United States at the Academy of Music in New York on May 2, 1855. There were unfortunate shortcomings that impaired the quality of the New York first night: for instance, the tenor Brignoli, much applauded in his heyday, sounded, according to Richard Grant White, an able and caustic critic of the period, like a "bleating sheep"; and he looked like "one of those figures of a man made by a child by sticking two skewers into a potato." Another flaw of the evening was Signor Amodio who did the Count di Luna—the effect of his villainy was badly diminished by his resemblance to "a plum pudding on a pair of sausages." Obesity also marred the rendition of the rôle of Leonora by the prima donna, Bena Steffanone, likewise of "notable amplitude." Much of this was offset, however, by Verdi's music—and by the fact that the Azucena was "a formidably handsome woman."

For Giuseppe Verdi 1853 was a wonderful year. Not satisfied with producing *Trovatore* he was to follow it, ere that year was out, with the third of his Three Unkillables, destined like *Rigoletto* and *Trovatore*, to sensational, durable success. He was already at work on that other opera while the applause for *Trovatore* were still resounding in his ears—yes, back at work again, striding up and down at Sant' Agata, like a grumpy polar bear—while Giuseppina Strepponi, imperturbably philosophic, getting into his way as little as possible, ran the place with her usual casual efficiency.

At Sant' Agata she surrounded herself with pets. She was fond of monkeys. And parrots. Particularly parrots. Rarely was Sant' Agata without a bevy of them. Apropos of one of them called Lorito she wrote to the daughter of Verdi's Parisian agent, Escudier (who, with the rich proceeds of his commissions from Verdi operas, had built himself a villa near Paris which he named *Il Trovatore*):

"Lorito can sing *'La donna è mobile.'* Also, *he composes music.* How about asking your father whether he thinks it will pay him to acquire the publication rights to Lorito's compositions?"

She wrote her impish letters with Verdi reading by her side, or fidgeting around in his study, or digging in his (formerly her) garden, enjoying as much as she the rural life of their estate.

At Sant' Agata he forgot all about the world of etiquette and formality and bowing and kowtowing. As a matter of fact they always meant very little to him in city or country. Once, in answer to an inquiry from the young son of one of their friends, De Sanctis, regarding the maestro's many medals, she wrote to the lad's father:

"Tell him that they're at the bottom of some box or other, where nobody can find them but myself. . . . They are toys given to great men by tens and to little men by thousands. . . . Teach your son to look on them as Verdi does."

SEVENTEEN

IN 1848, a few years before the music of *Rigoletto* and *Trovatore* had flashed across the busy mind of Giuseppe Verdi, to the great advantage of his snowballing celebrity, Alexandre Dumas the Younger, son of the Alexandre Dumas who had captivated multitudes of readers with *The Three Musketeers*, *The Count of Montecristo* and other tales of superlative thrill and derring-do, diffidently showed to his father a play which he had just finished. It was entitled *La Dame aux Camélias* (*Camille*, to us). The elder Dumas read it and tears gushed from his eyes, and, with characteristic child-like exuberance, he embraced his son enthusiastically, blubbering: "My boy, you have written a masterpiece!"

The play was produced in Paris. It was a hit. Much of its success was due to the fact that it gave thousands of those who saw it—and many more thousands who heard about it—the shock of their lives.

It was furiously berated by press and pulpit. It was branded as an outrageous assault on the decencies. It was considered "most erotic." It was denounced as a glorification of wrong living. It was vehemently belabored as an unprincipled undermining of the sanctity of marriage. It was spat upon as a hymn to harlotry. And Giuseppe Verdi, having attended a performance of it during one of his sojourns in Paris between spells of composing at Sant' Agata, immediately chose it as the basis for his next opera.

To him it had none of the horrors apparent to its detractors. And the passage of time has confounded them and vindicated him.

We of the present are wont to consider the play of the younger Dumas—and the opera eventually constructed from it by Verdi's librettist (Piave again)—as no more than an old-fashioned, stodgy, stuffy presentation of the facts of life, a very much diluted and fumigated dose of what the dramatists of our own times are dishing up every day with impunity. What was instantly apparent in it to Giuseppe Verdi was contrast, that quality so dearly beloved by him as an ingredient of opera à la Verdi—contrast between sensual love and pure love—contrast of clashing personalities and clashing beliefs.

He also saw in it a shining opportunity to express new stirrings of his genius, of a type almost unknown to him up to then, to the still greater advantage of the reputation which, with typical energy, he was building up for himself in the teeth of every rising competitor, even the most formidable of all of them, Richard Wagner.

So he turned to Piave. And that faithful little yes-man

("Verdi's tame librettist," somebody called him), having listened to the maestro's commands with uncomplaining plasticity and nodding head, muttered as always: "Thy will be done." Whereupon, in the workroom of the Venetian writer, set in the midst of the beauties and gaieties of Venice, and in the study of the driving composer, hidden in the bleakness and solitude of Sant' Agata, the manufacture of the successor to *Rigoletto* and *Il Trovatore—La Traviata*—was begun.

At times, when Verdi was composing, the resemblance of his mood to that supposedly dominating grizzly bears came out strongly. He was like that in the agonies of creating *Traviata*. He sat by the hour, glowering into space, forgetting mealtime and bed-time. Giuseppina used to tiptoe to the door of his study and stand, irresolute, outside it, wondering whether to knock and let the bear growl at her, or steal away and let the dinner get cold.

On one of these occasions, while she was hesitating outside the bear-pit and somewhere in the background the chef was tearing out handfuls of his hair, she suddenly heard, played on the piano inside the room, a ravishing, tender, heart-piercing melody ("*Addio del passato*"). Leaning on the door Giuseppina stood enchanted, the tears streamed down her cheeks. As he finished she sobbed aloud.

Verdi heard her.

Leaping from the piano stool, he rushed to the door, flung it open. Striding up to Giuseppina, he caught her in his arms, crushed her to his heart.

"And now," he said, as she kissed him, still sobbing, "let's eat."

Such was the industry displayed by Verdi and such the efficacy of the remote control exercised by him on Piave, laboring in Venice, that, early in the spring of the year that had seen the first production of *Il Trovatore*, its successor was ready for the public.

Again Venice and La Fenice were chosen for the opening. From the start, the composer believed with unshakable firmness in the merit and lasting quality of his new score—and again time has borne him out and discomfited those who disagreed with him.

Unfortunately, the latter were prominently represented at rehearsals by the singers selected for the new work. They did not understand or like the novel features of the music. They missed musty, honored details which they had come to regard as essentials of Italian opera. Above all, they were disgusted at having to appear not in the costumes of some bygone century but—in garments exactly like those that they wore when they strolled on the Piazza San Marco or sipped ices at Florian's. Awful! Who ever heard of opera singers on the stage looking like everyday human beings! Outrageous! So, amid baleful mutterings, they glowered at Verdi and Piave, as the two rushed distractedly around behind the curtain of La Fenice, their thoughts on imminent tomorrow.

When that curtain went up there was frost in the air. The tenor, suddenly afflicted with a sore throat, uttered sounds less like the warblings of a lover than the cawings of a crow. The baritone, convinced that his part was secondary and, hence, beneath him, bothered little about the quality of his performance. (That part includes a song, *"Di Provenza,"* to get a chance at which baritones still scheme and dream and plot and counterplot.) Worst of all, the prima donna, destined in the part of Violetta, the heroine, to die a tragic death in the course of the evening as a victim of tuberculosis, was of a personal construction verging distinctly on the corpulent.

Their eyes alight with mischievousness, the Venetian audience watched in wicked expectation.

A ballroom scene, at the outset of the opera, was clumsily presented. The Venetians chuckled.

The tenor cawed. The baritone walked through his part. And, at each statement by the buxom soprano—lugubriously confirmed by those around her—that she was rapidly wasting away, chuckles grew louder.

The climax came in the last act, when the curtain rose showing the lady lying on a bed, which—in view of her alleged emaciation—was most inappropriately billowy.

She began to warble with much vigor (like other singers who have sung Violetta in later years—"consumptive ladies who cough pianissimo and sing fortissimo"). Seated by her side, a doctor felt her pulse. He shook his head.

"She has," he croaked, "only a few hours to live." From the bed came a sigh suggesting a melancholy hippopotamus.

The audience howled with glee. They laughed until the tears came. They rocked back and forth in their seats. As they filed out of the theater they were sure that the new opera was doomed—that never, in any theater in the whole world, would it be put on again.

In the wings Giuseppe Verdi sat in stoical silence. The baritone walked up to him to present his condolences.

"Present them to yourself," snapped the composer, "and to the other singers, your colleagues, who are too stupid to understand my music!"

That is the story of the opening night of *La Traviata*. Next day Verdi wrote to his friend Muzio: *"Traviata* last night a fiasco. Am I to blame? Or are the singers? Time will decide."

Time has decided. *La Traviata* has since become one of the most popular operas ever created.

Fortunately for Verdi an Italian impresario named Antonio Gallo, who felt about *Traviata* much as its composer did, took prompt and energetic steps to remedy matters before the new opera's cataclysmic first night should be taken as a final verdict.

After the composer had made a few changes in his score and the action had been set back a couple of centuries and the singers costumed in accordance with the period chosen, Signor Gallo, not quite daring to brave the chucklers and laughers and hissers of La Fenice, was, nevertheless, audacious enough to present *Traviata* in May, 1855, fourteen months after its failure, at another Venetian theater (the San Benedetto), where it won a tremendous triumph.

The reversal of the original verdict was sensational in its completeness. For one hundred years, *Traviata*—despite sneering here and damning there—despite changing attitudes toward opera—despite violent unheavals in public tastes and likes and dislikes—has kept its place in a category of phenomenally successful Verdi works reached up to then only by *Rigoletto* and *Trovatore*. And not for another eighteen years was another opera by Giuseppe Verdi to crash the gates of that select category and say to that hitherto unchallenged trio of Verdi perennials: "Hey! Make room for me too. Move over!"

By the side of the clapping hands which greeted the Antonio Gallo production of *La Traviata*—and other productions following it in rapid succession—were the raised hands of those who were horrified. As with Dumas, so with Verdi and Piave; librettist and composer were furiously assailed for their sympathetic portrayal of Violetta, their unshocked acceptance of her scandalous mode of living before she succumbed to true and pure passion.

New York's H. E. Krehbiel dubbed the opera, long after its first production, "an apotheosis of vice and pulmonary tuberculosis." It was adjudged "most erotic"—what a laugh that brings to us hardened theatergoers of the present.

Traviata at once became popular with lovebirds of both

sexes indulging in illicit amours. It became a symbol of revolt against conventional sex relationships. One middle-aged love-bird (female) attended performances of the shocking work repeatedly—indeed she followed it around from city to city, and, on occasion, was so overcome by what she read into it that she would suddenly get up and hurry out of the theater, with her handkerchief over her eyes and sobs shaking her frame.

Unquestionably Giuseppe Verdi had seen in the theme of *Traviata* only what he invariably saw (or thought he saw) when he picked a subject—clash and contrast, the opportunity to write exciting music for exciting situations. So the charge heard from so many sides that the Dumas subject was "erotic" must have astonished him.

Even at *La Traviata's* disastrous first night at La Fenice there were some who refused to be swayed by the prevailing thumbs-down atmosphere. More than one reviewer next day wrote of remarkable qualities in Verdi's score, sensed the newness of what the composer had done or had attempted to do. The "intimacy" of the new work struck the more perceptive members of the audience. So conspicuous was the absence of the usual Verdian fire and fury that one commentator spoke of "chamber music."

One triumphant production after another followed Antonio Gallo's bold and prescient venture; and opinions about the opera became more and more laudatory. Singled out for the highest praise was the prelude to the last act, a choice in which the judgment of the 1850's has been borne out right up to the present day. There were official critics who sided whole-heartedly with the many-headed multitude of unofficial judges in hailing "Ah, fors' è lui" and Violetta's "Drinking Song" and "Parigi, o cara" and "Addio del passato" as sheer operatic delight. Of course, there was abuse—and there still is—but, as with *Rigoletto* and *Il Trovatore*, the sneerers, irre-

spective of whether their sneers were justified, failed completely to stop the onward march of the opera from one
generation to another.

Traviata was given for the first time in the United States at
New York's Academy of Music on December 3, 1856, with
the well-known diva La Grange as Violetta. It was first presented at the Metropolitan Opera House in the same city
November 6, 1883, with Marcella Sembrich in the leading
soprano rôle.

Prima donnas delight in turning themselves into Violettas
—and, unfortunately, some among them, insufficiently endowed with good taste or good sense, sing her music with so
much attention to themselves and so little to Verdi that
they have made her famous arias notorious examples of the
worst kind of Italian vocal fireworks—thus hopelessly falsify-
ing the intentions of the composer when he wrote them with
the opera as a whole in mind, not the misguided vanity of
some of the songbirds whom it has spawned. Sung intelli-
gently and tastefully it is a joy. Some of the best sopranos
have triumphed in it on both sides of the Atlantic—Patti,
Nilsson, Melba, Nordica, Piccolomini, Lilli Lehman, Sembrich, Tetrazzini, Bellincioni, Galli-Curci, Geraldine Farrar.

The last-named lady made her American debut in it at
New York's Met. A short time before, Heinrich Conried,
then manager, said to her: "I have a birthday present for
you."

"What is it?" she inquired (with jewels or something like
that in mind).

"The rôle of Violetta in *Traviata*." And it was as Violetta
that she made her Metropolitan first appearance on her birthday in 1908.

Among the numerous renowned tenors who have sung

Alfredo in America and elsewhere are Enrico Caruso and
Alessandro Bonci. The rôle of Germont, considered an insult
to his importance by the baritone who first sang it in Venice
in 1853, is enormously popular among the baritones who have
succeeded him in the part, though its celebrated "*Di Provenza*" gets liberally excoriated by experts—notwithstanding
which the average American audience weeps and cheers as
that song goes its melting way.

Between 1883, the Met's opening season, and 1950, *Traviata* was given there 235 times (in 54 seasons), thus bettering
the record of its fellow-Unkillable *Rigoletto*, which was given
226 times in 56 seasons and *Trovatore*—170 times in 49
seasons.

After reaping the acclamations of Italian audiences *Traviata*
crossed Italy's boundaries to succeed anew in London and
Paris, St. Petersburg and Vienna and Berlin. In London, sandwiched in with the cheers, there were growls of disapproval
and snarls of disgust. Britain's ferocious and cherished "Thun-
derer," the London *Times*, spoke of the new opera's "foul
and hideous horrors." But—oh, what rich publicity! Londoners stood in long lines in front of the box office of Her
Majesty's Theatre, surged into its lobby, thirsting for a
chance to see Verdi's latest. And his old admirer Lumley,
whom ill luck had driven almost into bankruptcy, heard again
the sweet music of jingling sovereigns and crackling five- and
ten-pound notes. "Once more," he wrote nostalgically years
afterwards, "dresses were torn and hats crushed; once more
mania possessed the public."

Once more praisers and blamers ran neck and neck in
filling Mr. Lumley's theater—as their successors were to do
many years later, when a latter-day Lumley of New York
named Heinrich Conried put on at the Metropolitan Opera

House that latter-day *Traviata*, Richard Strauss's "shocking"
Salome.

And once more Mr. Lumley had good reason to thank his
stars that he had never faltered in his belief that in backing
Giuseppe Verdi he had picked a winner.

EIGHTEEN

THE "CENTRAL OPERAS"—that is what Verdi's friend, the
French critic Camille Bellaigue, called the composer's
Triple Triumph, his Indispensable Trio—*Rigoletto, Trova-
tore, Traviata.*

Bellaigue envisioned them as placed in the center of Verdi's
achievements, between the inferior operas that preceded
them and another bigger and better Big Three, of which he
was dreaming, toward which, with several false starts still
ahead of him, he was struggling.

Having in mind the great mountain climbers of the world,
I find a distinct similarity between their methods and Giuseppe
Verdi's record. That is why I like to call his Indispensable
Trio—the "Central Operas" of Bellaigue—Verdi's "Base
Camp Operas."

Would-be scalers of mountain peaks first ascend from
points at the foot of mountain ranges to some point far above
that level but far below those peaks. There they establish a
base camp—represented in Verdi's career (as I see it) by
Rigoletto, Trovatore and *Traviata.*

Then they inch upward to a far loftier camp—resembling,
in relation to Verdi's career, a certain opera by him, produced twenty years after the first of his Indispensable Trio.

Next, after a long spell of preparation, they make a still
more arduous ascent to their last camp—right under the

shining, icy, brooding pinnacle of their ambitions. That camp
corresponds, in the Verdi story, to his next to last opera.

Then—Everest!

That peak of peaks is represented in the Verdi saga by—

But again I am rushing matters. Suppose we go back to the
"Base Camp Operas."

Even the most extreme of Verdi's foes, unless they are out
of their minds with hostility, must admit that the three operas
in question, Verdi's Triple Triumph of the 1850's, are his
Three Unkillables. Certainly those foes have done their best
to kill them. But every time that *Rigoletto, Trovatore* and
Traviata have been left for dead on the operatic battlefield
they have bobbed up again serenely in the répertoires of the
world's opera houses, as cocky and full of life as ever—including the opera houses of Wagnerian Germany, which has never
lost its appetite for them.

James Huneker, one of America's most acute and most brilliant critics, whose province was the Seven Arts, but whose
first love was always music, felt their significance in the history of grand opera when he wrote in one of his books:

Rigoletto, Trovatore and *Traviata* have one cardinal merit in
addition to their miracles of mellifluousness—they prefigure the
later Verdi, the thinking Verdi, the truer musical dramatist. . . .
The neo-Verdians will have none of the middle-century Verdi—
forgetting that no man may lift himself to the stars by his own
bootstraps. Verdi offers a fine picture of crawling, creeping evolution. . . .

To *Rigoletto* in 1851 must we go in search for the roots of
the mature Verdi. In the declamatory monologues of the hunch-
back Jester are the germs of the more intellectual and subtle
monologues of Iago and Falstaff. *Il Trovatore* contains strong
dramatic situations and if the tower scene has become hackneyed,
yet how well-devised! In this much-admired, much-sung composition are to be found harmonic straws which indicate to the keen

observer the way the musical wind was bound to blow nearly a
half-century later. With *Traviata* Verdi made his first attempt at
musical psychologizing. . . . No, decidedly it will not do to over-
look the Verdi of 1850. It would be building musical history
without straw.*

And another able American critic, John Erskine, has this
to say about the Indispensable Trio:

Rigoletto is remarkable for a new kind of music that hovers
between recitative and aria; the character of the title part is a
marvelous psychological study. . . . *Il Trovatore* . . . lives by
virtue of its intense dramatic concentration. . . . To old-fashioned opera-goers *La Traviata* was no more than a display-piece
for a prima donna's voice, Paris gowns and diamonds. . . . That
period has now passed into the era of the picturesque and recent
productions have made *La Traviata* into a chamber opera of
singularly touching delicacy.†

There is a story which, I think, gives a good idea of the
evolution—or, rather, revolution—which eventually led Verdi
to his supreme achievements:

In his old age, friends around him were talking about an
opera planned by a fellow-composer, in which Napoleon was
to be one of the characters. Would not that be artistically
impossible? Turned into an operatic strutter and fretter would
not Napoleon, so clearly etched in all men's minds, become
merely ridiculous? Thus Verdi's friends questioned one another. How far they had come, in their sophisticated appreciation of the properties and limitations of grand opera, from
the mentality of the days of Rossini, Bellini, Donizetti (aye,
of the early Verdi), which saw nothing inartistic or improper
in putting into operas puppet emperors and kings, to serve as
frameworks for meaningless arias, as cogs in dragged-in-by-the-

* James Huneker, *Overtones*. New York, Charles Scribner's Sons, 1909.
† *A Musical Companion*. Edited by John Erskine. New York, Alfred A.
Knopf, Inc., 1935.

hair quartets and ensembles, rich in thrills and melody but empty of significance and appositeness!

At the height of the discussion those friends asked Verdi the septuagenarian:

"Do you think a singing Napoleon possible?"

The veteran reflected. After a moment's silence, he replied:

"It depends on what you want him to sing and how you want him to sing it."

Verdi's three huge successes of the early 1850's are striking in their dissimilarities. Resemblances they have—but differences outweigh these. Each has an individual stamp. One can scarcely imagine their composer, in accordance with the cynical old Rossini-Donizetti formula, taking something from one of the three and putting it into one of the others. Even thus early in his progress the incongruity of such a procedure begins to be apparent. In his final phase—the miraculous culmination, forty years later, of his broadening, deepening genius—such a trick would be as unimaginable as grafting a trunk on a horse or a fin on a dog.

Rigoletto gives evidence of a new subtlety in its composer. In its blend of recitative and cantabile passages it throws out hints of the "endless melody" of Wagner's ultimate style. But there is nothing resembling imitation by the Italian of the Teuton. Never were two men farther apart, less mixable, than Giuseppe Verdi and Richard Wagner.

Undoubtedly the great German affected the great Italian, but only in the sense that Wagner's forward march put Verdi on the defensive, and, in so doing, brought out what was best in him and most Italian, the very core and essence of his Italianism. The whole relationship of their respective styles, the final answer to the accusations of imitating Wagner so often aimed at Verdi, is summed up in this remark by him, in allusion to his operatic style and that of Wagner, built on symphonic lines: "An opera is an opera. A symphony is a symphony."

Had Verdi tried to imitate Wagner's symphonic framework, instead of developing to the utmost his extraordinary powers and utilizing them always as an Italian, he would in all probability have gone down fighting a losing battle. Instead, by meeting Teutonic thunder and lightning with Latin beauty and fire he still stands forth today in the fullness of his glory. *Rigoletto* foreshadows all that.

From *Rigoletto* to *Trovatore* there is, in a way, retrogression. The latter has not the subtlety of the best parts of the former. In *Trovatore* Verdi fails to employ the deft touches of characterization abounding in the somber tale of the Jester and his undoing. *Trovatore* is rough where *Rigoletto* is polished. It lacks the budding psychological insight shown by Verdi in its predecessor. It possesses nothing rivaling the adroit interweaving of emotions in the *Rigoletto* quartet. It is melodrama, raw, violent melodrama, sometimes so brutal as to be horrible.

But what a rush of melody it is! With what overpowering, overwhelming effect melody pours from it! It is as if the composer had under his hand a tap of golden sound to be turned on at will. *Trovatore's* melodiousness is sometimes poignant, melting—of a tenderness that softens and beautifies the opera's awful story, gilds its horrors, sweetens its fury. Terrible, but irresistible—that is *Trovatore*.

Compared with its two forerunners, *Traviata* presents striking points of divergence. It is more delicate than *Rigoletto*, more truly realistic. Again and again it is miniature painting—"chamber music." No presage of coming murder slinks, snake-like, through its orchestration.

It has none of the violence of angry, turgid, baleful *Trovatore*. It is more convincing. It seems far more a painting of

real life. It digs deeper into human moods and motives. In it
there is nothing quite comparable with *Rigoletto's* "*Bella
figlia dell' amore*" quartet, or *Trovatore's* "Tower Song"; on
the other hand neither of these two can show anything in their
scores in quite the same class as the prelude which Verdi
wrote for *Traviata's* last act.

So much for the describable, tangible elements in the Indispensable Trio; there remain those elements which Bis-
marck, in allusion to things which have no kinship with music,
called the Imponderables.

What makes *Rigoletto* an inescapable ingredient of countless operatic seasons? What makes *Trovatore* shake morons
and sophisticates? What is there in *Traviata* that keeps it as
alive in the 1950's as it was in the 1850's?

Is it because all three are excellent "theater"? Partly. Is it
because they provide marvelous opportunities to sopranos and
contraltos and tenors and baritones for doing marvelous singing and garnering avalanches of applause? Partly. Is it because
in them the sureness of touch of their composer never flags,
the fecundity of his inspiration never dries up? Partly. Or is
it primarily due to something that eludes explanation, defies
analysis, laughs at dissection? Certainly. That something is
genius.

In the hope that I am providing food for thought for those
who concentrate on the shortcoming of the Verdi of the
1850's to the exclusion of the good in him, I beg to submit
here something that is not about music at all but about one
of the other arts, yet, as regards that Verdi, seems to me
absolutely tailor-made—a quotation from a recent article by
Joseph Wood Krutch:

This Spring a great many people must have been reading
Huckleberry Finn at the same moments I was. How many of
them, I wonder, were reminded again how conclusively it proves

that a great work of fiction does not need to be what is called a "good novel" or, indeed, a merely "good" anything else. . . .

Much of it is so improbable as to become at times wholly unconvincing. . . . It is also episodic, clumsily plotted, and sometimes as crudely melodramatic as a dime novel. . . .

The river journey is as unforgettable as the March of the Ten Thousand or as the wanderings of Ulysses. By comparison with that fact the baldness of the plotting or the "unconvincing" aspects of the episodes is as irrelevant as the "unconvincing" aspects of the story of the Cyclops.

Once a certain degree of imaginative intensity has been reached we lose all concern with what is ordinarily called "realism." The question whether or not something is "probable" or "convincing" becomes mere fiddle-faddle. *One no longer needs to be convinced; one simply knows.* Huck floated down the river as indubitably as Hamlet saw a ghost or the Greeks hid in a wooden horse. . . .

Perhaps nothing except great energy of some sort is absolutely indispensable. Balzac once declared that "the important point is not to avoid mistakes but to have a quality that sweeps everything in front of it." *

A quality that sweeps everything in front of it. The Giuseppe Verdi of *Rigoletto, Trovatore* and *Traviata* had it.

Around 1850 Verdi's deep interest in Shakespeare, destined to be of such immense importance in the culminating epoch of his career, came back to him, particularly in relation to setting *King Lear* to music. He divulged it to Salvatore Cammarano, the eccentric Neapolitan librettist, even sent him a full scenario of what he thought a *Lear* libretto should be. Cammarano got to work on the idea. But too many other more pressing matters in opera-making were on the composer's mind. Regretfully he gave up the project for the time being.

* Joseph Wood Krutch, in *The New York Times Book Review*, May 23, 1954.

It returned to him in 1853, the year of *Trovatore* and *Traviata*, Verdi's greatest year so far. At that time he toyed with the idea not only of setting *Lear* to music but *Hamlet* as well. His friend, the poet Carcano, known in Italy as a translator of Shakespeare, had sent him a libretto based on Shakespeare's tale of the Melancholy Dane. Verdi looked it over, but drew back in fright when he considered the great difficulty of musicalizing it. "If *King Lear* is difficult," he wrote Carcano, in rejecting his libretto, "think of what *Hamlet* would be!" Incidentally, years later in Paris, Verdi went to hear the Frenchman Ambroise Thomas's opera based on *Hamlet* and disgustedly referred to it as "an insult to Shakespeare."

Later that same year, having picked out, as the possible author of a *Lear* libretto, Antonio Somma of Udine in Northern Italy, a writer of successfully produced tragedies, and, like Verdi himself, an ardent champion of Italian liberation and unification, Verdi got into correspondence with him concerning the scheme. In a vein far more respectful than the one he affected toward Piave (Somma was to Verdi no "crocodile") Verdi's letters to Somma not only throw light on the composer's growing obsession with Shakespeare but on his musical and other theories in general.

As always, he had much to tell the prospective librettist on how to run his business:

"I think monotony the besetting sin of our Italian opera. . . . Today I would refuse to treat subjects like *Nabucco, I Due Foscari*, etc. They lack variety. . . . They are played, so to speak, on a single string." And he added: "I prefer Shakespeare to every other dramatist, the Greeks not excepted." *

In October, 1853, Verdi remitted to Somma 2,000 lire in payment for the *King Lear* libretto, two acts of which had been completed by the poet-patriot of Udine. Somma duly

* Dyneley Hussey, *Verdi*. London, J. M. Dent & Sons, 1940. New York, E. P. Dutton & Sons, 1940.

finished the *Lear* libretto. But again other projects got in the way. In 1868 Verdi still had *Lear* in mind; and, even at the very end of his long career, after he had produced music for two supreme operas, both on Shakespearean themes, there were rumors that he meant to tackle *King Lear*.

These rumors were never substantiated. And, after the composer's death, he having expressly ordained in his will that all fragmentary compositions found among his effects must be burned, the music he had actually composed for *Lear*, if any, was summarily thrown into the fire. Just as well, perhaps. As *Macbeth* proved, the early Verdi was not up to doing music satisfactorily for Shakespeare. A *King Lear* of that period in all probability would have been unworthy both of the great Englishman and the great Italian.

V

TRANSITION

NINETEEN

LUCRATIVE publicity, as actors and actresses interested in self-advertising are well aware, is to be derived not alone from stage appearances but from real-life disappearances. That truth was known a full century ago to Signorina Cruvelli, engaged for the leading female rôle in the opera scheduled by Giuseppe Verdi to follow his smash hit, *Traviata*. The new work was to have its world *première* at the Paris Opéra. Just before the opening night, La Cruvelli, acting on her inside knowledge of how to get personal advertisement, suddenly disappeared. Completely. Absolutely. *Spurlos versenkt.*

Paris chuckled and worried. All over Europe people wondered and waited. Weeks passed. Still no news. In London a farce was produced entitled "Where's Cruvelli?" The management of *"La Grande Boutique"* fumed. Giuseppe Verdi stormed. As a result of the lady's disappearance and the consequent disruption of plans the management suggested to Verdi that he provide it with another opera to take the place of the one in which the fair disappearer was to have been a star. "No!" The composer threatened to pack up and get out of Paris.

Then—as suddenly as she had disappeared—Cruvelli reappeared.

With wide open, innocent eyes she confronted an incensed, expostulatory management. "But I told someone—I don't recall whom—to inform you that I was going away. You say he didn't do it—well, now really . . ."

The management tore its hair. Giuseppe Verdi exploded all

151

over the place. But there was no satisfactory substitute immediately available for Cruvelli. Swallowing their wrath, management and composer curtly instructed her to report for further rehearsals of the new Verdi work. She did—enveloped in glorious publicity.

Shortly before the first performance of Verdi's offering she sang one night at the Opéra as Valentine in Meyerbeer's *Les Huguenots*. As those acquainted with that opera will recall, Valentine, when she comes on the stage, is greeted by a fellow-member of the cast, enacting Marguerite de Valois, with the remark: "And now you will tell us about your daring journey." The audience roared with laughter. It is not on record that Giuseppe Verdi joined them.

La Cruvelli, it transpired, had been on a sort of trial honeymoon with a member of the French nobility whom she subsequently married. Most of their preview of marital felicity had been staged in Germany, for the lady's nationality was not Italian but German, her real name not Cruvelli but Krüwell. To have an Italian name, it was thought at that time, made one sing better.

Much trouble (besides the case of off-again-on-again Cruvelli) was still to precede the opening night in Paris of the impatiently awaited new Verdi production.

As early as 1848 Verdi had made tentative arrangements with the management of the Paris Opéra for a new work to follow his sensational *Rigoletto-Trovatore-Traviata* trio of thrillers and money-makers. But not until four years later did the idea assume definite shape with the signing by the composer of a contract stipulating that the score must be based on a libretto by Eugène Scribe, at that time a haughty potentate in French dramatic and operatic circles, either unassisted or with a French collaborator. It was to be delivered in six months.

But eighteen months after the signing of the contract there

was still no libretto. Verdi, in high dudgeon, told Roqueplan,
the manager of the Opéra, that, unless those in authority
there bestirred themselves quickly, he would cancel the agreement. Paris, never an agreeable place of sojourn to him,
was again getting on his nerves. He hungered for Sant' Agata.
His bad temper proved efficacious. On the last day of 1853 a
complete libretto by Scribe and Duveyrier, a collaborator, was
placed in Verdi's hands.

It turned out to be a gloomy, blood-stained affair, full of
battle, murder and sudden death, dealing with the revolt of
the Sicilians under Procida against French soldiers, who, in
harmony with the ever-recurring complications of European
history, were occupying Sicily in 1282 A.D.

The choice of subject could scarcely have been more un-
pleasant both for France and Verdi.

First, it included the massacre of the aforesaid French
troops; and, second, Procida, chief of the massacrers, was depicted by Scribe and his colleague as a species of cheap gang-
ster. In disgust, Verdi wrote to Crosnier, who had succeeded
Roqueplan as manager of the Opéra (Roqueplan had been
fired partly as a result of the Cruvelli contretemps):

"The more I think of it, the less I like it. It will displease
the French because Frenchmen are slaughtered and it will
displease Italians because Monsieur Scribe has altered the historical character of Procida, and has made of him, according
to his favorite device, a common conspirator with the inevit-
able dagger in his hand. . . . There are, God knows, in the
history of every people, good deeds and villainies. . . . But
I am before all else an Italian and will have no part in an insult to my country."

Verdi complained angrily to Scribe, and that arrogant individual merely brushed aside his protests. The composer
waxed sarcastic.

"I know," he said, "that Monsieur Scribe has a thousand

things to do which are nearer his heart than my opera. But, had I suspected in him this complete indifference, I should have stayed at home, where, to tell the truth, I was contented enough." Scribe, he declared furthermore, did not even take the trouble to appear occasionally at rehearsals of their joint work.

"I am not accustomed to such treatment!" sputtered Verdi. "And I won't stand it. Without perfect agreement success is impossible!"

One of the things that most annoyed him about the libretto was its formidable length, quite in the French tradition of the day, but repugnant to that arch-deleter and super-concentrator, Giuseppe Verdi. He declared that an opera at "*La Grande Boutique*," with its five hours of solid music, was "enough to kill a bull."

This sort of thing served to increase his already considerable dislike of *la ville lumière*. One reason for this, perhaps, was that his Parisian agents, the Escudier brothers, had again decided that the best way to make the French public appreciate Verdi's merit was to deny merit to all his competitors. They went to great lengths in doing this through inspired articles in the press and other devious methods. Soon, however, they found that they had thrown a boomerang. The tactless emphasis on Verdi's excellence at the expense of his musical colleagues caused quite an upsurge of hostility to him.

Furthermore, an undercurrent of anti-Verdianism had been started in France because Verdi, a foreigner, had been chosen to write the new opera touted assiduously as one of the main features of the Paris Exposition of 1855. Why, asked disgruntled Frenchmen, had not the honor been awarded to some native composer? Inklings of all this undoubtedly reached Verdi—and, one may be sure, lost none of their malignancy in transit.

After staying for a while in the Opéra quarter, he moved

out to one of the city's suburbs, where he again set up housekeeping with Giuseppina Strepponi, now definitely sharing
his life with him, still without benefit of clergy. But extra-
urban attractions and extra-marital bliss could not change
his prevailing unfriendliness toward the capital of France.

"Why do they all hunt in couples here?" he asked queru-
lously. "When a theatrical agent calls on me, he does not
come alone—he brings along another! When I am expecting
an interviewer—two interviewers knock on my door! When I
want to see a librettist, two librettists appear!"

The unpopularity with Giuseppe Verdi of the most popular of cities had grown. He realized what it meant to his
career. But he simply could not get to like it. There was something about Paris and France which repelled his innate Italianism. Neither passage of time nor acquisition of francs
could overcome his aversion. That it was purely a personal
prejudice he knew perfectly well. And, when some years later,
in war, the French were in dire trouble, his heart went out
to them in true sympathy, expressed with noble generosity.
But, when things were normal, France just rubbed him the
wrong way.

On one occasion, while Verdi was fretting and fuming in
France, the Countess Maffei, who had already taxed him with
injustice in his attitude toward the French, again suggested
to him the advisability of being more sympathetic to them.
It behooved him, she pointed out, to Parisianize himself at
least a little, to think, while he was in Paris, as the Parisians
did, to get accustomed to the place by more frequent and
longer sojourns. She even hinted that it might be well for him
to settle there. This brought sparks from Giuseppe Verdi,
that 100 per cent Italianissimo.

"Settle here?" he exploded. "Impossible! Why should I?
For personal glory? I can acquire none here. For money? I
can earn as much or more in Italy. Besides, I do not intend

to spend my few thousands of francs on publicity—on a
claque and all that dirty sort of thing, which seems to be
necessary here for success. The other day Dumas wrote in
his paper, in reference to Meyerbeer's new opera: 'What a
pity that Rossini is not producing his operas here today!' "
(In penning that, Verdi inferred, Dumas was alluding to the
beneficent propaganda preceding the launching of each work
by the publicity-loving Meyerbeer, the composer of the hour
in Paris.) Verdi went on: "But then Rossini had not the
German wit to set success simmering six months in advance
on the stoves of the newspapers and so prepare for the explosion of *intelligent appreciation* on the opening night!"

Finally, there was one grand devastating row at the Opéra.
Tempers were shot to pieces. Ancestries were impugned. Fur
flew in all directions. Then—the smoke cleared and all concerned recovered their reason, or part of it. By the time that
the opening night of the Verdi-Scribe-Duveyrier work arrived
composer Verdi was speaking to librettist Scribe and librettist Scribe was speaking to composer Verdi and both were
speaking to Manager Crosnier without foaming at the mouth.

Les Vêpres Siciliennes was produced for the first time at
the Opéra, June 13, 1855. That theater, meanwhile, had been
renamed the Académie Impériale de Musique, France having
become an empire again with Napoleon III in the rôle of
Emperor.

The new opera, better known by its Italian title, *I Vespri
Siciliani*, was the first opera ever composed by Verdi to a
libretto in French, also the first to have its opening night in
Paris.

It ran 50 consecutive nights—a remarkable record for that
or any other time. Cruvelli, the Disappearing Lady, won loud
applause in the big soprano part. Some critics found in the
score a decided improvement over early Verdi music.

Adolphe Adam, France's noted composer-critic, acknowledged that it had inclined him to a more favorable view of
its creator (Adam had been pretty nasty to Verdi in previous
criticisms). Another writer in a leading Parisian newspaper
praised Verdi for ridding himself of stale conventionalities
and for showing more respect than he ever had previously for
musical proprieties and dramatic truth. He added: "His writing for the orchestra shows colors and accents previously unknown in Italian music. It [*Les Vêpres Siciliennes*] is a great
and fine work."

That judgment has not been borne out. Despite its initial
warm welcome the successor to *Rigoletto-Trovatore-Traviata*
has not really caught on anywhere. Even Verdi did not like
it. He considered the libretto mechanical, its Sicilian and
French characters without reality or humanity—and, it seems,
he thought that these shortcomings had seeped into his score
and played havoc with it.

Some commentators found beautiful melodies in that
score; but others deny it even that merit. Richard Wagner,
caustically lumped it together with other melodramatic theatrical performances which he had attended and disliked in
his disagreeable allusion to "*Les Vêpres Siciliennes* and other
nights of carnage." And Camille Saint-Saëns inquired why
Verdi did not set the battle of Waterloo to music.

Produced later in Italy, under another name, with its
Sicilians and French turned into Portuguese due to censor
trouble, it failed again to please sufficiently. It just did *not*
have the sensationally dynamic qualities which its immediate
predecessors, Verdi's Indispensable Trio, had possessed in
such copious abundance as to enable them to overcome triumphantly every deficiency in words and music. Only the
overture of the new work survived the general shipwreck.
Adjudged by many the best thing of its kind ever done by its
composer it may still be heard at concerts, especially in Italy.

"Verdi tried to beat Meyerbeer at his own game," said one carper. "He failed." Scribe, too, came in for acid comment. In the opinion of one Parisian writer, the librettist's artificiality seemed "to paralyze Verdi, in whom complete, unabashed sincerity is a primary virtue."

All of which further soured the squire of Sant' Agata. The management of a new theater in Genoa asked him to be allowed to name it Teatro Verdi. "No!" (Later, he acknowledged, this refusal was due "to a whim that probably would occur to nobody but me.") He also got very cross with his publishers, the Ricordis of Milan, who claimed for themselves the royalties accruing from productions of Verdi's works in France.

"You rely too much on commas and periods," he growled. And he reminded them: "You made four times as much out of *Trovatore* as I did." One of the Ricordi partners retorted: "You can produce your operas in Pekin, if you wish, but it will be illegal."

Eventually, however, as in previous and future Verdi-Ricordi disputes, everything was ironed out satisfactorily, the bear lay down with the fox, and—many years later—the published music of the last of all the works of Giuseppe Verdi was, as usual, issued under the imprint of the Ricordi concern.

As if he had not trouble enough on his hands already, Verdi was angered by a wealthy Spaniard called Calzado, who, having taken over the Italian Theatre in Paris, was planning to put on *Rigoletto, Trovatore* and *Traviata* in unauthorized versions made in Spain by piratical publishers. (They had already deflected royalties from Verdi's pockets, in connection with garbled productions of *Luisa Miller*.) Hearing of Verdi's wrath, Calzado blandly inquired of him what it was all about.

"I am not accustomed to answer questions from gentlemen to whom I have not been introduced!" Verdi replied.

But the sun came out on this tempest also—indeed, not

long afterward, Verdi was thanking the Spaniard for favors done him in Paris. The shrewd, peasant-ancestored landlord of Sant' Agata knew well, despite his aversion for France, how valuable that country was to his musical reputation and bank balance.

Verdi now turned again to that Spanish dramatist whose *El Trovador* had been transformed into *Il Trovatore* with electrifying results. This time the García Gutiérrez product on which he cast his eye was a drama based on the story of *Simon Boccanegra*, the pirate who become Doge of Genoa, which the Spaniard had heard while serving as Spanish consul there. From Sant' Agata, to which Verdi had finally escaped from Paris, the composer instructed faithful and flexible Francesco Piave to make a libretto out of the Spanish dramatist's work about the ex-pirate; and from it Piave proceeded to concoct a hopelessly complicated and undramatic brew. How much Verdi, with his irresistible itch to undo as much as possible what his librettists did, was responsible for it I do not know —undoubtedly he made *some* changes, just to convince Piave that the world was not coming to an end. Anyhow, that libretto was enough to militate strongly against any musical score. Which was unfortunate. For Verdi, now definitely forging ahead in masterful self-confidence, gave to the new work some excellent music.

His English friend Lumley, getting wind of it, tried to tie up the new opera for London. He offered for it 500 pounds sterling. But Verdi, riding high, refused to swallow this bait —not good enough, he decided. Things were going well with him—so much so, in fact, that canny Giuseppina feared that they were going *too* well. A change for the worse, in her opinion, was bound to come—and soon. "*Midi est sonné*," she warned Verdi. (Paris had not failed to leave its mark on her vocabulary.)

Her premonition was correct. Given for the first time in

Venice March 12, 1857, *Simon Boccanegra* met a cold reception from the difficult Venetians. Its score was praised by some critics—in fact, one of them called it Verdi's most inspired work. But he could not push back the tide of disapproval.

That libretto! Most of the time when he was on the stage, the hero, who was supposed to be a man of action, persisted in providing words unmixed with deeds. Against such handicaps Verdi's score was powerless. But he never lost his belief in *Simon Boccanegra*.

Before he struck out on the road which was to lead him to the three supreme achievements of his career, Verdi essayed still another job of tinkering. As I have related, he had failed to reap success with an opera called *Stiffelio*, produced in Trieste in 1850. But, as with *Simon Boccanegra*, Verdi refused to abide by the decision of the majority of audiences and critics. He dug up *Stiffelio*, turned it upside down and inside out (in fact, he added an entirely new act to it), re-named it *Aroldo*, and bestowed it upon the management of the opera house at Rimini, in lieu of a brand-new work which they had requested of him.

Alas! In Rimini *Aroldo* flopped as hard as its parent, *Stiffelio*, had flopped in Trieste.

TWENTY

AROUND this time Verdi, having fled again from Paris to Sant' Agata, decided that there was too much parrot in his life. As usual, he found Giuseppina plentifully be-parroted. Parrots, gaudy of plumage and strident of voice, graced Sant' Agata, as she thought, or, as Verdi thought, infested it. He was fed up with the silly raucous things—especially with her principal pet parrot, named Lorito.

So, beckoning to his side his friend Giuseppe de Amicis, again a house guest and similarly anti-parrot, they arranged in secret confabulation worthy of the *Zitti-Zitti* gang in *Rigoletto* that De Amicis, alleging the necessity of a shopping tour to neighboring Busseto, should buy at a drug store there, ostensibly for use in his host's garden, a quantity of deadly poison.

On his return from Busseto, De Amicis, sidling up to Verdi, pointed to a small package in his hand.

"I got it!" he whispered hoarsely.

But he found himself talking to an entirely different person from *Zitti-Zitti* Verdi of the previous confabulation. The new Verdi, looking apprehensively about him, put his finger to his lips.

"I got it!" repeated De Amicis. And he pointed in a sinister manner first at his package and then at Giuseppina's principal pet parrot, swinging nonchalantly from its perch.

"Wahwahwah! Wheeeeee!" screamed Lorito.

Verdi took De Amicis into a corner.

"Say no more about it," he cautioned his friend. His friend was utterly mystified. Had something happened to thwart the great Anti-Parrot conspiracy?

Something had. Authorities differ as to just what. Most probably Giuseppina's secret household police, having got wind of what was brewing, had alerted her and there had been a duet between her and Giuseppe, culminating in a solo by herself.

"Aren't we going to poison the damned bird?" inquired De Amicis. Again Verdi's finger went to his lips.

"No!" he replied. "And never mention the matter again. Just tell me how much I owe you for the poison—and forget it!"

"Yahyahyah! Hawhawhaw!" screamed the parrot.

For the successor of *Les Vêpres Siciliennes* and that luckless hybrid, *Aroldo*-out-of-*Stiffelio,* Verdi again turned his eyes to the Scribe factory. Eugène Scribe may be said to have introduced into the opera-manufacturing game of his epoch something resembling modern assembly-line methods. He had one assistant, for instance, to do the framework of plays or libretti, another to put in the dialogue, a third to provide the "wisecracks"—with himself keeping one eye on general supervision and the other on the receipts.

Verdi had become interested in one of Scribe's products, which had already been set to music by a Frenchman, Auber, and an Italian, Mercadante. It dealt with the assassination in the 18th century at a masked ball in Stockholm of King Gustavus III of Sweden by unfriendly Swedish noblemen, who had drawn lots to determine which among them was to be the assassin. The possibilities of this grim plot as the basis for a tragic grand opera in typical Verdian vein seemed to be excellent to Verdi.

So he arranged with Somma, now that the plan to collaborate with the latter on *King Lear* had fallen through, to make music on a libretto to be extracted from the already existing Scribe work.

Then, thankful to get away from Paris after his variegated troubles there, the composer, with his loyal Giuseppina, journeyed via Genoa to Naples. Some time before he had signed a contract with the management of the San Carlo Theatre for the production of the projected Scribe-Somma-Verdi opera, for which he had done much of the music already. Originally called *Una Vendetta in Domino* it had become eventually *Un Ballo in Maschera* (*A Masked Ball*), by which name it is known to this day.

But if Verdi thought that leaving Paris meant ending his current worries he was grievously mistaken; the sort of farce—with him, tearing his hair, on one side, and Italian government censorship, pursing its lips, on the other—which had darkened his skies in the era of *Ernani* and *Rigoletto*—was now to be enacted with variations all over again.

Verdi had sent ahead of him for the approval of the Department of Censorship of the Kingdom of Naples a synopsis of Somma's libretto based on Scribe. Unfortunately, the censors of that particular day in that particular kingdom would look at nothing but finished products. Synopses were beneath them. The management of the San Carlo Theatre, it seems, was perfectly well aware of this rule (Verdi was not), but, reasoning that the sooner the composer arrived in Naples the better for the forthcoming production, it had neglected, with true Neapolitan Machiavellianism, to let Verdi know about it. Only after he arrived, with Giuseppina and their current pet dog Lulu (no parrot) on the Neapolitan water front (he had come by sea from Genoa hoping to get rid of a sore throat which had been bothering him for some time) was the disagreeable news imparted to him. When he had finished commenting one may reasonably guess that his throat was no better.

Eventually the complete Somma libretto was submitted to the Royal Neapolitan censors and the problem seemed on the way to satisfactory solution. But matters were plunged into confusion worse confounded by a sudden violent twist in the course of European history.

In Paris, an Italian named Orsini threw a bomb at the Emperor Napoleon III as that monarch was leaving "*La Grande Boutique*" in his imperial carriage of state. The emperor had a miraculous escape from death. Naturally, censorship departments all over Europe, including the one at Naples, were shocked into something like complete intransigence. Consider the situation: the day of the attempt on Napoleon III (in 1858) a libretto lay before the Neapolitan censors dealing not only with a conspiracy to murder a reigning monarch but showing the murder itself! Sanction such an outrageous production for Naples? Never!

Verdi promptly went into one of his tantrums. But librettist Somma, refusing to become unduly agitated, suggested that his libretto might be thrown from the 18th back into the 13th century—compared with the careers of some Italian libretti of the 19th century the life of a football seems sedentary—without injury to drama or dramatis personae. This bland suggestion added heat to the composer's rage.

"We must," he fulminated to Somma, "find a princeling, a duke, a devil, anybody who has seen something of the world, breathed the atmosphere of, say, the court of Louis XIV. My music is not for the 13th century."

After more squabbling it was decided, as a sop to the censor, to transform King Gustavus of Sweden into a mere Duke of Pomerania and make a few additional minor changes in the unhappy libretto.

But the censors, with Orsini's bomb still very much on their minds, refused to be so easily placated. Instead, they popped up with suggestions of their own, which infuriated Verdi anew.

His opera, they said, should be called *Adelia degli Alinari*. ("Which means nothing!" he sputtered.) It must be laid in the 14th century. In Florence. Its characters must be actuated by Guelph and Ghibelline sympathies and prejudices. ("About which nothing would be known in the milieu which I have tried to depict in my music!") In addition, one of the characters in *A Masked Ball*, a page called Oscar, on whom the composer had lavished particular attention, was to be changed from a foppish, humorous fledgling courtier into a martial young cavalier. ("Either Oscar goes into the piece as he is or not at all!") Finally, in the censored version, there was no murder at the masked ball, no drawing of lots there, no masked ball whatsoever! ("!!!!") Deadlock.

When he recovered the power of speech, Verdi waxed sarcastic. He pointed out that, out of 884 verses in the original libretto by Somma, 297, or about one out of three, had been tampered with—not counting other changes and deletions.

"What remains?" he asked. And he answered his own question thus:

"The title? No."

"The poet? No." (In the censored version Somma's name had been omitted.)

"The period? No."

"The place? No."

"The characters? No."

"The situations? No."

"The drawing of lots? No."

"The masked ball? No."

Suave local Machiavellis hinted that subtle influences might be brought to bear by the Duke of Ventignano, Grand Panjandrum of the royal theaters of Naples, on the Duke of Syracuse, brother of the local king, which might possibly lead—if sufficiently subtle—to the granting of a private audience by the monarch to the angry composer, at which everything might be smoothed out. But Verdi, all his life a hater of such behind-the-scenes skulduggery, refused to sanction this stratagem.

Already he had been in communication with Signor Jacovacci, manager of the Apollo Theatre in Rome, who, having got wind of the trouble in Naples, was astutely trying to get the projected opening of Verdi's new opera transferred from the San Carlo in Naples to his own theater in the Eternal City. So Verdi stood pat. Angry in its turn, the San Carlo management declared that the creator of *Un Ballo in Maschera* must abide by his contract with them. Verdi snapped his fingers. They sued him for damages to the tune of 200,000 French francs. He snapped his fingers again.

Thousands of Neapolitans rushed gleefully into the fracas. Being adherents of democracy like Giuseppe Verdi and inimical to Napoleon III, whose near-assassination had precipitated the whole row, they showed what they thought of their government's anti-democratic, pro-Napoleonic, anti-Verdian attitude by siding heart and soul with embattled Giuseppe. (Napoleon III, previously friendly to the cause of Italian liberation, was supposed to have betrayed it.)

In vociferous disorder they paraded through the streets of Naples, yelling at the top of their lungs *"EVVIVA VERDI!"* On the face of it, their yells sounded like exuberant musical appreciation, and so the Royal Neapolitan police diagnosed them—at first. But, in reality, the frenzies accompanying this outburst of popular vociferation were caused by the coincidence, discovered by some clever rioter, that the letters forming the composer's name, V-E-R-D-I, might be made to stand, in the minds of the vociferators, for Vittorio Emmanuele Re D'Italia, thus becoming thunderous acclamations of King Victor Emmanuel II of Piedmont-Sardinia, the idol of those enlisted in the cause of Italian liberation. So, once more, as in the days of *I Lombardi* and *Ernani, Attila* and *La Battaglia di Legnano,* Giuseppe Verdi found himself a symbol of Italian independence and unity.

From seething Naples he ran off in disgust to Sant' Agata, whence he wrote to the Countess Maffei:

It is impossible to find an uglier spot than this, but, on the other hand, it would be impossible to find a place where I can live with greater freedom. And this silence that leaves one time to think! And this absence of uniforms of every color! How good both are! . . . Since *Nabucco* I may say that I have not had one hour of rest. Sixteen years at hard labor!

Sant' Agata. Solitude. Tranquillity. Rest. The whistling of the wind over the bleak plain of Parma. The sound of peasant

voices. Fields. Cows. Horses. Dogs. Sant' Agata above all else
in the world was what Giuseppe Verdi wanted just now. For
a while, anyway.

TWENTY-ONE

AFTER cooling off at Sant' Agata a bit Verdi returned to
the fray in Naples. He argued in his own behalf at the
trial of the suit brought against him by the management of
the San Carlo Theatre there, which eventually petered out.
And, *sub rosa*, he continued negotiations with Jacovacci, who
urged him to take *Un Ballo in Maschera* bag and baggage to
Rome.

"But haven't you censors there also?" inquired the composer.

"Pooh" scoffed Jacovacci. "Leave them to me. I'll take care
of the Roman censors." His tone implied that they were just
a lot of marionettes jumping obediently to strings pulled by
himself. "If necessary," he added, "I shall appeal to the
Cardinal-Governor of Rome—even to the Holy Father in
person!"

But he over-estimated his influence in the Holy City—just
as Francesco Piave, on another occasion, had over-estimated
his hypnotic effect on the censors of Venice. The Roman
watchdogs were not to be hoodwinked by the demotion of a
Swedish King to a Pomeranian Duke. There must be additional drastic changes, they decreed. And this time, for once,
Verdi raised no scathing objections. His spirit was broken—
that is, for the time being. He was weary of bickering.

"Transfer the damned action to any old place!" he said
in effect. "To the Caucasus, if you will! Or to 18th century
Puritan Boston under the rule of the British!"

Withering Verdian sarcasm? Well, maybe that part about the Caucasus was. But, incredible though it may appear, the part about Boston was not.

To pacify the Censorship Department of the Papal Government of Rome the Scribe-Somma framework of *Un Ballo in Maschera,* bereft of its original Swedish background, was indeed violently transferred to *Puritan Massachusetts!*

King Gustavus of Sweden became a British colonial governor there, under the appellation Riccardo, Duca di Warwick. Another noble Scandinavian, one of the assassins in the original Scribe play, became Riccardo's "Creole Secretary"! Another character, a sort of Azucena straight out of *Trovatore,* turned up in Boston as a swarthy practitioner of black magic (so typically Bostonian). Another became a light-hearted page, easily imaginable in the Royal Palace at Stockholm, but about as appropriate to a Boston setting at any stage of that city's history as he would have been in the Caucasus. The glittering, brilliant masked ball of the original was retained as a feature of the new hodgepodge. (So Puritan.) And the opera still had as its climax the murder of Il Duca di Warwick, batting for Scribe's King of Sweden. (So suggestive of baked beans and brown bread.)

In the original drama the leading conspirators were Swedish noblemen, but in the Bostonized version they became a pair of desperadoes with the blood-curdling names of Samuel and Tom.

But there is much to be said for Verdi. First, such violence to a libretto was nothing new in his day. Second, he was so exhausted after weeks of wrangling with censors and kindred pests that he probably would not have objected to having the action of the much-buffeted piece transferred to the bottom of the sea. Third, bizarre though the transportation of the action from Scandinavia via Pomerania to Massachusetts undoubtedly was, the dramatic sequence of the opera, as

Verdi had visualized it, and the basic traits of its characters, were preserved. And, fourthly, *Verdi's score remained intact.* Nowhere in it was he obliged to insert a hymn by Cotton Mather. He sent a message to a friend in Rome (Luccardi): "Please rent an apartment for me, with cook and piano." And, journeying from Naples to Rome, he again threw himself into the operatic battle.

The new work was produced at Jacovacci's Apollo Theatre in Rome February 17, 1859. It won a resounding success.

But the composer was still in a disgruntled mood. He had been through too much. He was dissatisfied with the female members of the cast assembled by the Roman impresario, one of whom had sung the part of Oscar, Verdi's pet page in the show. Gloomily he wrote to Jacovacci: "The company provided by you was unworthy of me. Listen to the voice of conscience and confess that I showed rare restraint in not taking the score away from you and going in search of dogs that would have howled less disagreeably than those you supplied."

But this blast failed to bother Jacovacci, riding high in the wake of *Un Ballo in Maschera's* triumph. "Next season," he told Verdi, "we'll have better female singers and the public will like the piece even better and I'll make a lot of money."

Jacovacci was a celebrity in Roman theatrical circles. He was adept at pushing his own interests. And since the success of his theater was sometimes dependent on the favor of the Pope—who in his capacity of temporal overlord ruled the Eternal City—the astute impresario used to take steps to assure himself if possible of papal good will by stationing noisy claques, composed of chorus men and women, stage hands, danseuses, musicians and other persons in his employ, at strategic points along the Pope's route when the pontiff drove from the Vatican to one of the Roman churches, who would burst into wild shouts of acclamation as soon as the papal carriage came into sight. These shouts, thanks to the wily Jacovacci's sedulous preliminary coaching, bore a remarkable resemblance to spontaneity.

Incidentally, Giuseppina Strepponi, when she had sung in Rome some years before her association with Verdi, had officiated as godmother for Jacovacci's baby daughter, on whom the name Giuseppina had been bestowed in the godmother's honor.

After the opening night in Rome there was much favorable comment from critics on Verdi's music for *Un Ballo in Maschera*. Said one of them: "A huge step forward in a new manner. . . . Taking its inspiration from the moods of the characters and the movement of the action, the music in this case exercises such complete domination that in comparison with it the poetry [*i.e.*, the libretto] becomes less than an accessory. Verdi, in *Un Ballo in Maschera*, has achieved the great ideal of harmonizing dramatic truth . . . with the fluency and clarity of the popular appeal of the melodies."

Later critics have thought the same way. The opera has gained steadily in stature. "It marks an enormous advance on its predecessors," says Dyneley Hussey, "both in its grandeur as a whole and in the subtle light and shade of its characterizations. . . . Greater range is everywhere apparent. . . . '*Eri tu*' [the opera's famous baritone aria] remains unsurpassed even in Verdi's later operas as an expression of tragic suffering." *

There is marked improvement also in Verdi's conspirators in *Ballo in Maschera* compared with those in earlier Verdi operas, notably the *Zitti-Zitti* gang in *Rigoletto*. The latter take themselves so seriously that they make the audience laugh. Those in *Ballo in Maschera*, with their sinister laughter, make the audience take them seriously.

* Hussey, *op. cit.*

In *Un Ballo in Maschera* Verdi's progress in orchestration is particularly noteworthy. Gone are his simple "guitar" accompaniments, those mere subservient appendages to the vocal doings on the stage. Like Giuseppina Strepponi in relation to Verdi, the singers still dominate the orchestra, but the orchestra refuses to be overawed by them.

Particularly felicitous is the delineation of that prime favorite of Verdi, Oscar the page. Somma, the librettist, politely but firmly steered by Verdi, had finally molded that character to his exacting steersman's wishes. And the composer, under the spell of a new and surprising lightness combined with depth, fashioned Oscar's music in a vein never really worked by him before.

Oscar hints at something entirely unsuspected up to that time in Giuseppe Verdi. In the sole comic opera of his output which had preceded it, *Un Giorno di Regno,* produced when he was 26 years old, he had revealed himself as scarcely anything more than a despairing young widower, struggling in vain to put out of his thoughts a tragic triple bereavement. With the light-spirited page of *Un Ballo* he suddenly ventured, at the age of 45, into regions of music hitherto unexplored by him—regions which he was never to enter again until, after more than three decades had elapsed, he proved suddenly (aged 80!), to a stunned and enchanted world, that he had acquired a miraculous second youth.

Oscar, the page, Samuel and Tom, the laughing conspirators—with those three Giuseppe Verdi helped materially to offset the Sweden-and-Italy-in-Boston absurdity of *Un Ballo in Maschera.*

I first saw *Un Ballo in Maschera* when I was ten years old. It was one of my earliest tastes of opera. I saw it from a stage box at the Teatro Municipal in Caracas, Venezuela.

That box impinged on the stage so far that I, leaning excitedly over the railing, could peer down into the wings, and see Oscar—enacted that night by a young lady in tights who was green at the operatic game—preparing to go out before the footlights. She was suffering from such nervousness that her father, a retired singer standing beside her in the wings, was encouraging her with paternal pats on the shoulder and pecks on the cheek.

Out she went—and gathering confidence as the show progressed, she sang with much spirit a gay little song which stuck in my mind as I went home that night and has stuck there ever since. The same is true, I learned later, of many other persons exposed for the first time to *Un Ballo in Maschera.* And critics are constantly acclaiming that ditty.

When I came to realize this, I felt pleased with myself. And, many years later, when another Oscar stepped on the stage from the wings at the Met in New York, I looked upon him (or, rather, her) as the reincarnation of an old friend. And when she sang that gay little song I clapped and yelled with a vigor and sonority worthy of a trained claqueur.

After writing the above I was put on the carpet by my New England conscience: "Aren't you thinking," it inquired severely, "of Donizetti's *Lucrezia Borgia?* That also contains a young lady in tights enacting the part of a man and she also sang a gay and famous little ditty, one night, while you gazed upon her from that stage box. How about it?"

"It doesn't matter," said I. "I heard that same young lady sing both ditties on different nights in my early boyhood and both have stuck in my mind ever since. Donizetti's opera is almost forgotten. Verdi's is alive and kicking. I have decided that the ditty I remember best is the one from *Un Ballo in Maschera. Evviva Verdi!*" My New England conscience subsided.

Un Ballo in Maschera enhanced Verdi's reputation in London, despite the fact that his leading non-admirer there, Critic

Chorley of the *Athenaeum,* was against it. In allusion to the
opera composed on the same subject by Auber (un-Bos-
tonized in his case), the assassination of Gustavus III of
Sweden, Chorley remarked: "Until I heard Verdi's setting I
failed really to appreciate the worth of Auber."

Nevertheless, other London critics and the London operatic
public in general liked Verdi's new opera—and so did critics
and public elsewhere, as it won victory after victory on many
stages.

TWENTY-TWO

TEN WEEKS after the opening night of *Un Ballo in Maschera*
in Rome Giuseppe Verdi married Giuseppina Strepponi.
The date of their marriage was April 29, 1859.

The wedding took place quietly at the little village of Col-
lange (or Collanges) in Savoy, then a part of the Kingdom of
Piedmont, but later incorporated into France. It seems that
Giuseppe and Giuseppina stole away secretly from Turin to
the Savoyard village in order to have their long unconjugal
union ended by legal matrimony. As soon as the ceremony
was over they returned to Sant' Agata.

Why didn't he marry her sooner?

They had met and liked each other some twenty years before their wedding. They had become genuinely attracted to
each other (she to him before he to her) about five years later.
They had been living together for something like a dozen
years. From almost the beginning of their acquaintanceship
it had become obvious that he was the only man for her.
And, with the passage of time, it became equally obvious
that she was the only woman who really meant anything to

him. Why then did he delay so long in regularizing their relationship?

That question has often been asked but never, to my
knowledge, answered with finality. Unions such as theirs were
common in the artistic circles in which they moved—especially in Paris, where they made long stays and probably ab-
sorbed Parisian do-as-you-please morality. But there must
have been more to it than that.

I think that Giuseppe Verdi postponed marrying Giuseppina for one of the two following reasons—or for a combination of the two:

First, he delayed because he was influenced by his fiery
spirit of independence, which made him resent all meddling
by others in his personal affairs, especially from the direction
of Busseto. It may be contended that, since Antonio Barezzi,
his beloved father-in-law, was one of the principal meddlers
from that direction, it would have been logical for Giuseppe
to defer to the other's objections and get married to Giuseppina without further postponement. But, given the composer's nature, is it not more probable that the father-in-law's
action may well have increased rather than lessened his son-
in-law's obstinate stand? All his life Giuseppe Verdi was
pretty much of a lone wolf in making his decisions.

Second, the delay may have been caused by Giuseppe
Verdi's bitter recollection of the early and tragic death of his
young wife, Barezzi's daughter, and the deaths of their two
little children. This recollection, unhealed by the lapse of
time, may have made the widower feel that to Margherita
Barezzi alone belonged the right to be his wife—even after
he had lost her forever.

Again it may be contended that, if such was the case,
Barezzi's interference in Giuseppe's liaison with Giuseppina
Strepponi would have moved his son-in-law to push forward
rather than put off his second marriage, since his first wife's

father was in favor of it. But, on the other hand, the composer's character, without complications in most ways, but
veiled and darkened in others, may have been the cause of his
reacting as he did to Barezzi's meddling. The latter's assump-
tion of the rôle of spokesman for local Bussetian moral prejudices may well have been the straw that broke the Verdian
camel's back and fortified the composer in his antimatri-
monial attitude.

On the very day of the marriage of Giuseppe and Giuseppina
—April 29, 1859—the ferment in Italian politics which had
existed right through Giuseppe's 46 years of life came to a
head in the most serious explosion since the anti-Austrian
revolt of 1848.

Count Camillo Cavour, steersman of the political destinies
of the kingdom of Piedmont-Sardinia, over which reigned the
liberal, patriotic and popular King Victor Emmanuel II,
having made an alliance with France, had set out to persuade
the French Emperor Napoleon III that it behooved him to
do something concrete for the Italian cause against Austria.
After craftily predisposing the French monarch to direct action (Napoleon the Little, as Victor Hugo discourteously
called him, was keen to emulate his uncle, the great Napoleon,
by winning battles somewhere, somehow) Cavour worked
behind the scenes to bring on an Austrian attack against Victor Emmanuel, since the alliance between the latter and
France was a defensive one, obligating the French to enter
into hostilities only if the other side was the aggressor.

Austria fell into the trap. Or else she felt herself so strong
in relation to Piedmont-Sardinia that she was not afraid of
taking the initiative. A few days before Giuseppe and Giuseppina Strepponi got married in that little village on the French-
Piedmontese border Austrian troops invaded Piedmont. And

on the very day of the marriage King Victor Emmanuel called on all Italians to take up arms against Austria.

The wily Cavour's Machiavellian maneuvers had come to the culmination that he had dreamed about for years. When he heard the report of the Austrian invasion of Italian soil he believed that his beloved Italy was at last on the eve of liberation from alien overlordship. And then it was that he quietly hummed to himself the stirring notes of *"Di quella pira"* from Giuseppe Verdi's *Trovatore*.

Like practically all Italians Verdi was in a state of wild excitement. The French-Piedmontese victories that followed Austria's irruption into Italy filled him with patriotic elation. He headed with a generous donation a subscription list got up in Busseto for the French and Piedmontese soldiers wounded at Magenta and Solferino. Breaking the rule of a lifetime, he told the mayor of Milan that he would like to compose a cantata in honor of the French Emperor, to be performed in that city. He called France's ruler "the only Frenchman who ever loved Italy." And, as I have already mentioned, he remarked that if Napoleon III came up to his expectations as a liberator of Italy he would revere him as he had always revered George Washington—"and even more."

But all his hopes crashed to earth.

Napoleon III, losing interest in the war, suddenly signed with the Austrians the Peace of Villafranca, which left the dream of a free and united Italy, so dear to Verdi and millions of other Italians, pretty much where it was before. Venice and Venetia remained in the hands of the Austrians.

Verdi was bitterly disillusioned. He composed no cantata in honor of Napoleon III. George Washington's position in his private Hall of Fame was no longer menaced by the French Emperor.

Cavour was utterly crushed. In disgust he resigned his post

as Victor Emmanuel's Prime Minister and retired to his country estate.

Pursuant to the treaty, the Parma region, of which Verdi was a native and resident, held a plebiscite to decide whether it would join Piedmont-Sardinia. The vote was overwhelmingly in favor of doing so. And Verdi was one of a delegation appointed to carry the official news of the result of the plebiscite to King Victor Emmanuel, now, as Piedmont's ruler, sovereign lord over Parma and Busseto, Le Roncole and Sant' Agata. Before returning home, Verdi met Cavour. Despite the statesman's eclipse, which to some looked total and permanent, the composer still kept him enshrined as his pet political demigod.

Having heard rumors that there was a movement afoot to get the Parma district back into pro-Austrian hands, Verdi, aided by his friend Angelo Mariani, considered by this time one of the best, if not *the* best orchestra conductor in the land, plotted to supply at his own expense a supply of rifles for the Busseto National Guard, which up to then had possessed scarcely any weapon for resisting possible invasion except patriotism. But the trouble blew over. Verdi did not have to buy any rifles. "What brave, incredible times!" exclaims Francis Toye. "Mariani and Verdi gun-running. . . . Garibaldi [who had been active in the recent fighting] . . . reviving the exploits of a medieval *condottiere!* Without catching a glimpse, at least, of that spirit it is impossible to appreciate . . . the music of the period."

Emerging from retirement in 1860 Cavour was soon active again politically. His efforts culminated in the convening of Italy's first National Parliament. He asked Verdi to accept nomination as a delegate to it from his native district. At first the composer refused. That sort of honor held no lure for him. But when his demigod insisted, impressing upon him that the proper place for a man of his eminence and patriotism was in that historic Parliament, Verdi swallowed his objections and entered the race for election to it.

As a matter of fact, he had always taken pride in hailing from the Parma region and no amount of residence elsewhere had dimmed his partiality for it. He was especially proud of the high reputation of Parma and the territory roundabout as a center of musical taste.

Once, when a double-bass player in La Scala's orchestra in Milan declared that a certain passage for that instrument in a Verdi score was unplayable, Verdi wired to Parma requesting a local musician named Pinetti to call on him in Milan. On Pinetti's arrival Verdi took him to La Scala, where the members of the orchestra, amused at the appearance of Verdi's companion, who had "country bumpkin" written all over his features and gait and speech, whispered together in derision.

But not for long. Verdi asked Pinetti to play the supposedly "unplayable" passage. The "bumpkin" played it— with perfect ease. Verdi was overjoyed. *"That,* gentlemen," he jubilantly informed the abashed Milanese musicians, "is how we play in Parma!"

Presenting himself as a candidate, he won his campaign (during which he did not raise a finger to help himself or hurt his opponent) and was duly installed as a Member of Parliament for Parma.

As such, he was first and last a Cavour man. For him, Cavour could do no wrong. During his term Verdi discussed earnestly with his demigod the sort of general musical education which, as he saw it, should be made available to pupils in Italian schools. When Cavour died in 1861 Verdi was so affected that, at the funeral services for the great statesman held at Busseto, he broke down completely.

Through four more years he remained in Parliament. Then

he resigned; and nothing could move him to enter political life again.

He most certainly disliked politics. And he felt downright contempt for the general run of politicians. Apparently, he never found among them anybody remotely resembling his idol, Cavour, as seen through Verdi's eyes.

"Politicians," he remarked scornfully to a friend, "are like somebody who wishes to light one candle to Christ and another to the devil."

One day, at his desk in Parliament, instead of paying attention to the weighty matters of national policy buzzing around him, he got into conversation with a fellow-M.P. on the best way to compose music. The main thing, he maintained (so far as his personal method of composition was concerned) was to get one's ideas on paper, transmuted into visual notes, before they evaporated completely from one's mind and never returned to it. And once, during a session of the Italian Parliament, he was caught trying to set to music a debate in the manner of the *Rigoletto* quartet!

Giuseppe Verdi, again at his beloved hide-out, Sant' Agata, received one day in his mail from the outside world a communication that must have made him sit up and rub his eyes.

After his venture into politics he had been comparatively idle. Occasionally he had paid visits to Genoa, a city that stood high in his heart. He had gone hunting with Mariani; and, after the chase, he had sat at roadside *osterias*, eating rough countryside food, drinking rough rural wine, thoroughly enjoying both, like the sturdy peasant that he was and always would be.

Despite Sant' Agata and Genoa, however, he had fallen into one of those fits of bearishness that occasionally beset him all his life. He scolded his majordomo for real or imagined derelictions. And Giuseppina, who understood him if anybody

did, was unable to pry him loose from his grumpy mood.
Nothing really seemed to please him except his garden.

Some chroniclers of Verdi's career make much of these
bearish moods of his. And they are inspired to read him moral
lectures and shake admonitory fingers at him as he lies in his
grave. I prefer to dismiss these recurrent fits as stings inflicted
on him by that merciless gadfly, the artistic temperament.
That, I think, is the true reason behind them. I refuse to set
up a list of humdrum Don'ts for genius.

Into his grouch came that electrifying letter.

It was from—Russia! In those days that faraway land
seemed to persons like Giuseppe Verdi mysterious and forbidding. And now, from its depths, came a request from the
Grand Opera Department of the Government of His Imperial Majesty the Czar of all the Russias that he compose a
new opera, to be performed for the first time at the Imperial
Opera House in St. Petersburg. The Grand Opera Department of the Imperial Russian Government offered him generous payment. He was left free to choose his own subject.
But, unofficially, it was conveyed to him (his liberal leanings
were obviously well-known even to the Czar's go-betweens)
that he must not include in the new piece a scene showing
the Czar proclaiming a Russian republic.

That letter was just the tonic needed. Soon Verdi was out
of his huff. And once more there was melody in his thoughts.

Before he could really get his teeth into the new work for
Russia, however, he had to complete a task to which he had
obligated himself at the behest of London. Those in charge
of preparing the Exhibition of 1862 there had asked Verdi
to represent Italy in the fashioning of a sort of musical rainbow, to which prominent composers of other countries were
also to contribute—Auber, as the representative of France,
Meyerbeer of Germany (by the way, most people had long
ago forgotten that Meyerbeer, so long identified with Paris,

had been born in Frankfurt-am-Main); and Sterndale Bennett of England.

Verdi's contribution was a musical mosaic entitled *Inno delle Nazioni* (Hymn of the Nations) culminating in a contrapuntal dovetailing of "God Save the Queen," "*La Marseillaise*" and Novaro's setting of the "*Inno di Mameli*," which last came as near as anything at that time of Italy's disunion to being an Italian national anthem.

The contributions of Auber, Meyerbeer and Sterndale Bennett were performed according to schedule. But Verdi's was postponed. Various guesses have been advanced for the postponement, including one to the effect that the British government objected to the mixing of "*La Marseillaise*," with its connotations of a decapitated king and similarly roughly treated members of the French nobility, with "God Save the Queen."

Finally, however, it was performed at Her Majesty's Theatre, his old stamping-ground in London, where it was cheered and encored; and the composer, summoned before the curtain, bowed courteously to loud applause with no trace of bearishness.

Ever since, his "*Inno delle Nazioni*" has been allowed to slumber almost without interruption. Arturo Toscanini conducted it in New York during World War II. Its main claim to the world's attention is that the words for it were written by a man destined to be most prominent as a literary collaborator of Verdi in the latter's miraculous old age—Arrigo Boïto.

Having returned to Sant' Agata and drawn renewed strength from contact with Mother Earth, Verdi again summoned Piave from Venice on behalf of the opera which he had agreed to write for Russia. The composer had selected as a basis for it a Spanish play, *Don Alvaro, o La Fuerza del Sino* (Don Alvaro, or the Power of Destiny) which, though not by García

Gutiérrez of *Il Trovatore* days, could hardly have been gloom-
ier if it had been.

It was by a noble Spaniard, the Duke of Rivas, and it had
in full measure the grimness and somberness, violent thrills
and passion-ridden melodrama which still attracted the Verdi
of the 1860's—though now he saw them more and more as
elements to be served up seasoned with reality and psychological truth, not thrown raw over the footlights. Verdi found
the Spanish drama *"potente, singolare e vastissimo"*—powerful, original and of enormous scope. It gave him again a
lot of tense, gripping situations, crying aloud for tense, gripping music.

So Piave set to work on a libretto ground out of the Duke
of Rivas's play. And, in spite of Verdi's constant suggestions,
corrections and condensations (or, maybe, partly because of
them) he produced a mess of tangled situations further complicated by a mess of words intended to untangle them.
Verdi proceeded feverishly to provide a score.

Toward the middle of July, 1862, he set out from Italy
for Russia. The journey was a momentous and rather fright-
ening adventure (though it involved no travel over salt water).

To Russia! What manner of folk were the Russians? Were
they civilized? Were they dangerous? What sort of food did
they serve to visiting music-men? The last of these questions
worried Giuseppe Verdi so much that, sandwiched in among
the contents of his luggage—among tail coats and patent
leather shoes and a high hat and the completed score of *La
Forza del Destino* (the name selected for the new opera)—
was a liberal supply of spaghetti. Far from objecting to this
item, Giuseppina Strepponi, who accompanied him on the
great Slavic adventure, was in favor of it, for, as she remarked,
"Tagliatelli [a form of spaghetti] and macaroni will be needed
to keep him in good humor in the midst of all that ice and
fur."

TWENTY-THREE

VERDI, probably to his surprise, liked Russia. He liked the courtesy of the Russians, which he contrasted with the "impertinent politeness of the French."

His new work had its first performance November 10, 1862 —unfortunately with the Czar not looking on, because he was ill. But the monarch attended the fourth performance, clapped, called out Verdi's name, and, having summoned the composer to his presence, invested him with the Cross of the Order of St. Stanislas. In a letter home, Giuseppina, seeking to bring this solemn Slavic ceremony down to earth, explained that the Cross of the Imperial Order of St. Stanislas was "something for Verdi to hang around his neck."

She also told those at home how much she pitied the unfortunate coachmen of the aristocracy of St. Petersburg, who had to shiver hour after hour on the boxes of their carriages in freezing winter weather, waiting for their masters and mistresses comfortably enjoying *La Forza del Destino* inside the well-heated theater.

La Forza del Destino was neither a hit nor a failure in St. Petersburg. One critic found it "mechanical." Another wrote: "Never has Verdi produced so conscientious a score nor paid so much attention to the form in which his ideas are molded. The originality and beauty of the choruses is undeniable, that of the monks at the end of the second act and that following the 'Rataplan' being quite irresistible. . . . The orchestration shows very striking progress."

The beauty of the melodies was acknowledged on all sides. Singled out in St. Petersburg for especially honorable mention—as it has been elsewhere ever since—was the duet be-

tween tenor and baritone ("*Solenne in quest' ora*") which has
won fame quite apart from the opera in which it occurs
through the record made of it years later by Enrico Caruso
and Antonio Scotti. "This is not merely one of the best numbers in the opera," avers one critic, "but one of the best numbers ever penned by the composer. . . ."

"*La Forza del Destino*," says Dyneley Hussey, "is an opera
unequal in merit . . . a collection of numbers rather than
a dramatic unity."

A *collection of numbers*. They all come back to the dominant melodiousness of the opera. On the eve of Verdi's
definite emergence as a master of melody-plus-reality-plus-psy-
chology-plus-unity, he seems in this opera of his transition
period to be saying a reluctant farewell to his exclusively
melodious self with such a burst of old-time Verdian melody
as to belie alike his age and the point of general development
at which he had arrived.

Naturally, the libretto hurt the score, in Russia as well as
everywhere else. Its gloom froze those who heard it. Verdi
himself, fearing just that, had tried to inject some light into
the darkness by his musical delineation of the comic Fra
Melitone, the best thing of its kind he had done so far, more
rounded than Oscar the Page, destined to be surpassed—and
how!—only by his supreme *Falstaff*. Also, he sought to
instill a bit of gaiety via Preziosilla the gypsy and her lively
numbers. But gloom remained predominant.

And, speaking of the libretto of *La Forza del Destino*, its
author, Francesco Piave, after years of master-and-servant co-
operation with Verdi, was never to work again with him or
anybody else. While the great composer was going through
the frustrations and self-torturings of his post-*Traviata*, pre-
Aïda period of transition, Piave had been treading primrose
paths as inconspicuous for prudent wayfaring as were his
writings for literary merit. The author of the words of "*La*

donna è mobile" had not relied for his knowledge of women on hearsay.

He fell desperately ill. And, when he recovered partially it was only to lie helpless for years, robbed of the power to speak or move, with his mind, untouched, concentrated to the exclusion of all else on Giuseppe Verdi, his adored maestro, and on an illegitimate daughter, acquired along some primrose path, the thought of whose fate after his death caused him cruel anguish.

This anguish proved unnecessary. To Piave, as he lay dying, came Giuseppe Verdi—and the last agonies of his faithful collaborator's death-in-life were sweetened by a promise from the great man, great in art and great in heart, that Piave's daughter would never know want. That promise was kept. Like all Giuseppe Verdi's promises. There is truth in this tribute to him by a fellow-Italian: "He was a man who was scrupulous in the observance of his duty, whose honesty was not bounded by conditions and circumstances, whose benefactions were known only to their recipients. Had Verdi not been a composer he might have forfeited his claim to remembrance, but he would have still been a great man."

La Forza del Destino was first sung in the United States at the Academy of Music in New York on February 24, 1865. Later, its composer, fully alive to its defects, subjected his score to revision; and—more important—asked a gifted literary colleague, Antonio Ghislanzoni (destined to go down to posterity as the librettist of *Aïda*) to tinker with poor Piave's unsatisfactory product. This new version was presented to New York operagoers on February 20, 1869, with a cast including Marie Louise Swift, Anna Louise Cary, Italo Campanini and Giuseppe del Puente.

In 1918 it was given at New York's Metropolitan Opera House with Enrico Caruso, Rosa Ponselle, Alice Gentle, Giuseppe de Luca, Thomas Chalmers and José Mardones.

Since then it has been revived a number of times, usually with a more appreciative reception from its audiences. It is one of those operas which improves with the years, like certain wines.

Its steady progress is well summed up in a notice by Winthrop Sargeant on the occasion of the opera's revival in New York at the Met during the season of 1953-54, which includes this:

La Forza del Destino is not a perfect opera, but it was enjoyable for other reasons. One of these was the lusty enthusiasm with which a superb group of singers sang its fine old melodies; another was the inimitable vigor and spontaneity of the melodies themselves. There was not an Italian in the cast, but several of the Metropolitan's best Italian-style artists, including Richard Tucker, Zinka Milanov and Jerome Hines, gave it as authentic and heart-felt a reading as one would be likely to hear anywhere. . . . And, beyond and above all this, there was *the wonderful, inexhaustible musical fecundity* of Giuseppe Verdi, a composer who seems to me to grow in stature every time I hear him. . . . Part of Verdi's vitality undoubtedly lies in the more or less imponderable factor known as genius, but a big part also lies in his unaffected and eminently civilized attitude toward the aesthetics of music. . . . He seems to have understood . . . that music is the language of passion—and he seems never to have been led away from this basic definition into trying to make music something that it is not. His subject matter consists of love, hate, and kindred emotions, and he never distracts your attention from these by means of elaborate technique or by otherwise obtruding his ego into the picture. His technique is, in fact, so simple and so artfully subordinated to his subject that you almost feel you might have thought up his melodies yourself—until you try. Everywhere his music bespeaks a deep love and respect for his materials—the voices of those who sing his operas. And, finally, he is one of the most truly original of all composers, not because he makes use of self-conscious mannerisms or artificial tricks but because every tune and chord reflects the thinking of a profound and unique musical mind. *La Forza del Destino* is not his greatest work; but it is great music and great opera.*

Yet, despite its steadily greater appeal to the operagoing public in this country and abroad, it has never quite become a success—never vied with three of its predecessors and with the three great Verdi operas that followed it.

"The truth is," as Herbert F. Peyser says with acute discernment in his *Opera Lover's Companion*, "that the jostling weaknesses of *La Forza del Destino* have substantially the same origin as those which beset every Verdi opera after *Traviata* and before *Aïda*. All of them are transitional works."

Which, substituting for technical musical terminology the pithy jargon of American housewives in describing home cookery simply amounts to saying:

"They just don't jell."

TWENTY-FOUR

AFTER returning from Russia and before settling down at Sant' Agata, Verdi made a flying trip to Spain, where the compatriots of the Duke of Rivas, from whose drama *La Forza del Destino* had been drawn, were naturally keen to see what an Italian librettist and an Italian composer had done with it. It was favorably received by Spanish audiences. And Verdi took time off from supervising rehearsals and such-like by seeing a bit of Spain. At Jerez, the home of sherry, he bought a large quantity of that noble wine and had it shipped to Sant' Agata.

* Winthrop Sargeant in *The New Yorker*, December 5, 1953.

The Escorial repelled him. To his good friend Count Arrivabene he wrote from Madrid:

I don't like the Escorial (if I may be forgiven such blasphemy). It is a mass of marble, it contains extremely valuable things, and, inside it, there are some very beautiful ones, among them a fresco of Luca Giordano [note how he picks out something by an Italian] which has marvelous beauty. But, taken as a whole, it lacks good taste. It is severe and terrible like the ferocious monarch who built it.

At Sant' Agata he returned to the bucolic life, well-cushioned and with the rough edges smoothed and rounded and polished, but bucolic life just the same. Many friends visited him and Giuseppina. And, when those friends went elsewhere, there was active exchange of letters between them and the Verdis.

"See whether you can find me a good cook," the composer wrote once to a friend. "I don't mean somebody who can cook well or badly three or four sample dishes of home cookery. I must have somebody who is really a cook. Offer whatever pay you please in my name but on one condition: *he must be a cook.*" Verdi considered a good meal, like a good opera, a work of art.

And he demanded punctuality at meal-time. "Remember," he told one of his many friends in inviting him to stay at Sant' Agata, "in this house feet go under the table at six o'clock—sharp." That, however, applied only to summer. In cold weather more latitude was allowed guests' feet. Bed-time, as a rule, was nine o'clock.

Not long afterward he was back on the subject of the incumbent for the time being, of the post of Queen of the Sant' Agata Kitchen. After an unrecorded financial conference with her, he asked his friend Arrivabene to purchase some Italian Government bonds for "That Illustrious Lady, My Cook."

"She wishes to be a capitalist," he explained.

And, in a note inviting somebody to Sant' Agata who had never stayed there before, he warned the prospective guest in his own peculiar handwriting which strangely resembled printed musical notes:

"Music is never talked about here. And you run the risk of finding a piano not only out of tune but with its wires missing!"

Even at Sant' Agata, however, he kept in touch with the world outside. Having read that there was a plan afoot to publish Bellini's letters, he complained to his friend Arrivabene:

"Why dig up the letters of a musician? Isn't it enough for him to be known through his notes? No, sir! There must be letters also. Oh, what a bore being celebrated is! We poor little-big celebrities pay a high price for popularity. For such there is no peace in life or death."

Once, when he was irritated by some statement of a music critic, he described critics in general as "those who pass judgment on the works of others, but are unable to dig into the guts of a musical composition."

He was delighted when his friend the painter Domenico Morelli told him that he would soon receive a painting which the composer had commissioned from him. And he wrote to the man who had painted it:

"Art and poetry are very beautiful things, but you, though you are a great artist and a great poet, must eat and sleep under a roof. I know how you dislike talking business. Very well. Talk it with Cesarino [Cesare de Sanctis, another friend and frequent visitor at Sant' Agata], to whom I am writing today."

That started a protracted discussion which presented a financial paradox: Morelli was not interested in being paid for the painting, whereas Verdi was impatient to pay for it. Finally, the composer issued an ultimatum: he would pay exactly as much as Morelli was accustomed to receive for his paintings from Goupil, the well-known dealer through whom he marketed his work. Not one penny less. There must be no question of his getting the painting cheaply just because he and the painter were friends. "I don't believe in mixing friendship with business!"

And that perfectly fair price was what Morelli duly received. Of Morelli it was said that he was as "indifferent to money as Garibaldi." And Giuseppe Verdi had no intention of profiting from that indifference.

Far from work and its concomitant headaches, Verdi at Sant' Agata became mellow, almost jolly. "Come to see us," he wrote to someone, "but, remember—we want to laugh!"

Hovering always over "*il mio* Verdi," with her mischievous air and sunny philosophy, was Giuseppina, who adored being a hostess, who loved waiting on her famous husband, yet never let him get the upper hand of her. Of her "white bear," conspicuous for overawing impresarios and singers and librettists, she would remark patronizingly: "He's just a big boy."

She complimented her friend, the well-known singer Maria Waldmann (a Teuton) on her excellent Italian. "If I could write one one-hundredth as well in German as you can in Italian," she informed her, "my pride would make me puff out more smoke than sixty locomotives."

Her purchases sometimes presented startling contrasts—as, for instance, when she wrote to Arrivabene: "Please get me some silk ribbon and a copy of Darwin's *Origin of Species*."

And Verdi, watching with sardonic amusement her career of disbursement, would tell Arrivabene and others whom she asked to buy things for her account not to worry as to repayment "because next month she receives her allowance."

During a year when royalties from Verdi operas were particularly copious and Giuseppina's financial situation cor-

respondingly satisfactory, she decided that she would devote
some of her funds to the purchase for her husband of the
house in which he had been born at Le Roncole. But there
were insurmountable obstacles, so she gave up her generous
plan.

But, many years later, it came to realization—though too
late for her to rejoice. After the great composer's death the
Italian government, having acquired the house, turned it into
what is called in Italy a *monumento nazionale,* with its original appearance preserved as much as possible. So, today, that
ramshackle roadside inn bears a proud inscription and attracts
visitors alike from neighboring towns and from far afield,
who gaze in respectful awe at its narrow steep staircase and
its rough paved flooring and at the little room where Giuseppe
Verdi first saw the light of day, with its "little windows like
pigeonholes and glass panes no bigger than handkerchiefs."

After a sojourn with his friend, the musical director Faccio,
at Montecatini, a watering-place that was a prime favorite
with him, Verdi, back at Sant' Agata, wrote to Faccio, who
was still taking the waters:

"Please give five francs from me to the bus driver at the
hotel who drove me to the station. It was not his fault that I
lost the train. Now that I have calmed down I'm sorry that I
gave him no tip."

And, after a disgusted look at the gambling rooms in the
Casino at Monte Carlo, he commented:

"Heaven and hell side by side! Hell in the splendid rooms
peopled by so many poor damned souls. Outside—Paradise!"

Giuseppina often asked friends, who had been invited to
Sant' Agata, to make purchases for her in the cities where
they lived. And Verdi saw to it that she did not throw money
around too recklessly. When their friend Cesarino de Sanctis,
requested to buy something for her, paid a rather high price

for it, she admonished him: "You know, I am obliged to pay my expenses out of the money that I carry in my little purse, my *borsellino*—I am not supposed to knock on the door of Verdi's safe." (Incidentally, her nickname for De Sanctis, a corpulent individual, was "The Respectable Mr. Guts.") Once, when he asked her for a photograph of herself, she refused with the remark: "I am a Venus who gains by crawling into her shell."

One day, when he was passing through Paris, Verdi was requested to conduct, as a special favor to the manager of the Opéra, an extra rehearsal of one of his works that was being revived there. He consented. But the members of the orchestra, who had a high sense of their own importance, were outraged at having to work over-time. So they did little or nothing to merit Verdi's approval. At one point he told them:

"You played that part too slowly. Let's do it over again—*just a little faster.*"

They played it at a gallop. The composer turned to a representative of the manager.

"You saw? You heard?"

"*Mais, parbleu,* they want to get away, *monsieur.* They want to attend to their affairs."

"Indeed? So their private affairs are more important than the orders of the manager of the Opéra? Very well. Gentlemen, I bid you all good day." And, clapping his hat on his head, he marched out of "*La Grande Boutique.*" And he didn't come back.

Verdi's next task was the revision of his *Macbeth* for the Paris Opéra. Composed back in the 1840's, it had always been a pet with him. And this has significance: it reveals again the composer's unswerving interest in Shakespeare, which, long afterward, was to lead to two masterpieces, both based on Shakespearean themes.

He considered his revised *Macbeth* much better than the original version—which is scarcely to be wondered at, since the Verdi of the 1860's was a far superior composer to the Verdi of the 1840's.

Of course, it was pointed out to him by the master-minds of *"La Grande Boutique"* that, since the revised *Macbeth* was to be tried out on an Opéra audience, it simply *must* have a ballet—the roués of the Jockey Club, those stalwarts of the stage door, being absolutely unable to visualize an operatic work without young, shapely and morally unfettered young females pirouetting in it at some point. Before he agreed to this, however, Verdi went through some preliminary writhings in objection to such time-wasting, as he considered it.

One of the dances desired by the Opéra management was a *tarantella*. (In Shakespeare's *Macbeth!* In Scotland!) At first the peppery composer would have none of it. Possibly he thought that, if he did not show fight, he would wind up acquiescing in having Shakespeare's "secret, black and midnight hags" do a Highland fling. To his way of thinking nobody available in Paris was capable of dancing a *tarantella*. "A street urchin from Sorrento or Capri would be best for it," he remarked.

Eventually, he left the whole matter to the Opéra people. And, just before leaving Paris for Italy on one of his shuttle trips, he thus admonished the Escudier brothers, his Parisian agents, whose penchant for extravagant puffery he knew well: "For the love of God, write as little nonsense as possible about *Macbeth!*"

It was produced in Paris in April, 1865. To its composer's bitter disappointment it again failed to achieve genuine popular success. He took the slings and arrows with his usual stoicism.

And there were other things to think about.

The year 1866 was fateful for Italians. Emulating Cavour
in his ceaseless quest for allies to enable disunited Italy to
face the arch-foe, Austria-Hungary—whose troops still occupied parts of Italian soil, notably Venetia—King Victor Emmanuel II had concluded a secret alliance with Prussia, now
so strong that she was girding herself to challenge Austria-
Hungary as the dominant power in Central Europe. And
Napoleon III, he hoped, still pathetically in search of *la
gloire* which had come so easily to his renowned uncle, might
also range himself again with Italy.

So, when Prussia and Austria-Hungary went to war, Victor
Emmanuel arrayed his forces on the Prussian side. They were
beaten at Custozza, but a few days later, early in July, 1866,
the Prussians crushed the Austrians at the battle of Sadowa
(or Königgrätz, as Germans call it), thus making the skies, despite Custozza, look bright for Italy. And the irrepressible
Garibaldi, who had marched his Red Shirts into Austrian-
held territory in Northern Italy, felt, as had Cavour seven
years before, that at last Austrian rule over Italians was to be
ended.

But again these hopes were doomed to a sad awakening.
When Austria-Hungary and Prussia made peace, the Italians
found themselves practically a defeated nation. To be sure,
Austria relinquished control over Venice and Venetia, but,
instead of ceding them directly to Victor Emmanuel, she made
them over to Napoleon III, who, in turn, obligingly passed
them on to the Piedmontese monarch.

This was taken by the great majority of Italians, including
Giuseppe Verdi, as a bitter humiliation. Indeed, he resented
the affront to his country so deeply that he was reluctant to
go to Paris and even considered the cancellation of a tentative agreement to compose an opera for *"La Grande
Boutique."*

Verdi was dissatisfied with the situation at Italian theaters, including La Scala. At the latter, he grumbled, "they no longer know how to do operas." He advised the management there to employ Mariani, for that conductor, his good friend, at least for the time being, was becoming a bright star of the bâton.

He was also incensed at the ways of Paris, where "everything is sacrificed to stage effects." A particular *bête noire* to him was Madame Meyerbeer, wife of the fashionable composer, who tried to get her husband into the good graces of the musical critics by sending them costly presents just before the opening nights of Meyerbeer operas.

"What a business!" fumed Verdi to one of the Escudier brothers. "Even art becomes a matter of banking and to succeed one must be a millionaire!"

Genoa put him into a better humor, with "its climate that restores the blood and opens the lungs." And, after another short stay in Paris, he was much cheered up by relaxing at Sant' Agata again.

He kept busy breaking in a new horse (somebody once remarked that Giuseppe Verdi probably knew more about horses than any composer who ever lived). He strolled around his garden. He enjoyed the companionship of his dog Black, successor to Lulu, deceased.

The ground was now cleared for his next opera, which had been on his mind for some time.

TWENTY-FIVE

THAT new opera, based on a tragedy by Schiller, is often called by the same name as the tragedy—*Don Carlos*. But soon after Rudolf Bing became general manager of the Metropolitan Opera House in New York he received a num-

ber of representatives of New York newspapers at a press conference. Just before, he had announced in his prospectus for
the coming season at the Met that one of the season's features
would be a revival of Verdi's *Don Carlo*—not, please observe,
Don Carlos.

At the conference somebody asked: "Why do you call it
Don Carlo?"

"Because," answered General Manager Bing, "that's what
Verdi called it."

So, ever since, it has been *Don Carlo* for me.

The libretto did not come off the assembly line of the
Scribe factory. It was the joint work of two independent
French writers, Méry and Du Locle. And it conformed to the
accepted formula of operatic works destined for the Paris
Grand Opera House, particularly in length.

As carpentered by Messieurs Méry and Du Locle out of
the original Schiller it was long, very long. Had Piave handed
to Verdi anything of similar length how the Verdian cuss-
words would have crashed around his Venetian head and
how the maestro's blue pencil and scissors would have gorged
themselves on his text! But—Verdi in Paris trying to get along
with French collaborators was another matter.

So once more he swallowed his dislike for French ways
and individuals, a dislike as sincere as his expression of it
was sulphurous. Forgetting his passion for brevity, his thirst
for concision, compression and concentration, he allowed
Méry and Du Locle to go their way. After all, was it not
reasonable to assume that they knew better what was wanted
on the Place de l'Opéra than the Squire of Sant' Agata?

Eventually, *Don Carlo* was born—a French libretto
equipped with an Italian score on the basis of a Spanish story
by a German dramatist.

Verdi was back in Paris in the summer of 1866, somewhat
under the weather with a throat ailment that bothered him

so much that he interrupted work on the *Don Carlo* rehearsals by taking a course of treatment at the French health resort of Les Cauterets. There had been hope of producing *Don Carlo* at the Opéra toward the end of the year, but—to quote Arthur Pougin: "Nobody is unaware of what sort of place the Paris Opéra is and of the difficulty in starting the functioning of that ponderous machine when the preparations for the production of a new work are under way—one postponement after another, delay after delay, indisposition after indisposition, until finally the year is ended and another has begun."

Halfway through January, 1867, Verdi heard of the sudden death of his father at Sant' Agata. Again there was postponement—the composer of *Don Carlo* was utterly incapacitated by his grief.

The father had richly deserved the son's love. From the very start of Giuseppe's life Carlo Verdi had divined his genius, given him sympathy and encouragement, done his utmost to fit him for a musician's career—ever understanding, ever selfless, ever delighted with Giuseppe's growing fame. The latter had brought Carlo to live with him at Sant' Agata and from Sant' Agata Carlo's body was taken by his son for burial in a nearby village cemetery.

What a stream of recollections the funeral must have brought—of the old spinet which Carlo could ill afford but, nevertheless, had purchased for his little son; of Carlo's kindness to Bagasset, the wandering fiddler; of his generosity in paying for his son's first music lessons with Baistrocchi, the organist, at Le Roncole, and with Provesi at Busseto—such memories must have surged through Giuseppe Verdi's thoughts as he stood, weeping, beside Carlo Verdi's grave, close to that of Luigia Verdi, who had also known the days of the old spinet and the wandering fiddler and earlier still the day when she had hidden Giuseppe, her baby, from murderous soldiery in the steeple of Le Roncole's church, long before there was any *Nabucco* or *Rigoletto* or *Don Carlo*.

Pulling himself together with his usual will power, Carlo Verdi's son returned to Paris to resume the task of licking the new opera into shape for production. Formidable enough at best, the task now presented a new complication—French growlings had arisen against the forthcoming work, as they had against *Les Vêpres Siciliennes*—because Verdi, a foreigner, had again been selected to do the featured work at the Opéra in 1867, like the year of *Les Vêpres* an Exposition year in the City of Light.

But all obstacles were again overcome. On the evening of March 11, 1867, with Verdi circulating nervously behind the scenes, *Don Carlo* was given for the first time before a brilliant audience, including the Emperor Napoleon III, the Empress Eugénie and the *crême de la crême* of official, musical, literary and social Paris. Eugénie, who took being Empress very seriously indeed, signified her disapproval of the strongly democratic tendencies of the composer of the new opera by ostentatiously turning her back on the stage during much of the performance.

There was praise for the remarkable progress shown in Verdi's *Don Carlo* music. But the libretto was adjudged too heavy. As in *La Forza del Destino*, critics found in it lack of cohesion; and they were disagreeably affected by its almost unrelieved lugubriousness. Also there was a feeling that it might have benefited, despite the traditions of the Opéra, from some expert cutting.

Camille Bellaigue, in his book on Verdi, writes of the *Don Carlo* score:

"It has . . . at least the *affirmation* of something definite —of a tendency to aspire . . . of a truly noble striving to create a realistic, a more homogeneous, better-balanced work,

with a close inter-relation of each part to all the other parts—
a work that should be less an unequal rhapsody than a har-
monious organism."

"The interest arises from a conflict of characters observed
and presented with a subtlety not to be found in any of his
earlier operas," says Dyneley Hussey. "In *Don Carlo* . . . our
interest is deeply engaged by six important characters caught
in a complicated web of public and private antagonisms. . . .
Don Carlo is the first of his [Verdi's] works that may be correctly described as, in its best scenes, a true music drama."

While *Don Carlo* was running in Paris, a bust of Verdi by
the French sculptor Dantan was placed in the lobby of the
Opéra. And Méry, one of *Don Carlo's* librettists, wrote a
poem about that bust.

"In Verdi," he said, "Italian music has found its Dante."
So replete are the poet's lines with Gallic pomp and circum-
stance that I do not dare to try to translate them into English verse. Demoted to my prose, they say in part:

Yes, it is he! He, the son of the severe Muse! He, whom among
so many masterpieces composed *Le Trouvère* [*Il Trovatore*]. He,
the eagle of Alpine peaks, the eagle of lofty summits, in whose
features are blended strength and grace such as adorn the faces
of men of genius, is here brought to life, thanks to you, Dantan,
and lives for us eternally indestructible.

One can imagine what earthy Giuseppe thought of that.

Before doing his bust of Verdi, Dantan, who could wield
a pencil as well as a chisel, had made an amusing drawing of
the visiting Italian composer. It showed him seated at a piano,
his brow wrinkled in a creative frenzy, with a long lion's
mane falling over his shoulders, and his hands transformed
into a lion's claws, with one of which he was pounding the
piano's keys, while, with the other, he was feverishly writing

on a sheet of paper the notes of another operatic score. It is
on record that Verdi much preferred this outrageous libel
by Dantan the draftsman to the pensive bust by Dantan
the sculptor.

In the midst of the generally admiring comments on his
Don Carlo score Verdi now encountered for the first time an
accusation that was destined to anger him for the rest of his
life: that his music was showing the influence of the ubiqui-
tous and all-pervasive Richard Wagner.

Verdi, though he admired Wagner, always insisted that
Italian music was one thing and Teutonic music another;
that the symphonic treatment of opera was one thing and
opera in the Italian tradition something quite different. He
felt himself sufficiently endowed not only to perpetuate the
best in Italian opera of the past but to develop it in accordance with musical progress—all without wearing the mantle
of Wagner, or of any composer dead or alive.

In view of this, the accusation of kowtowing to Wagnerism
infuriated him; and his first real taste of it after *Don Carlo*
brought from him the vigorous reaction that was to be expected.

"The germs of my so-called Wagnerism," he wrote indig-
nantly to Escudier, "are to be found in the trio of *Ernani* and
in the sleep-walking scene in *Macbeth* and in many other
places." He also remarked at this time: "The point is not in
what system *Don Carlo* belongs, but whether its music is
good or bad."

Soon after the *première* of *Don Carlo* Verdi made some
changes in it, for he realized that there was something wrong
with the opera as a whole.

After 43 performances it was taken off at *"La Grande
Boutique."* In London, presented with a splendid cast, it won
a considerable degree of favor. But it did best of all at Bologna,
where, under the superlative conducting of the composer's

friend Mariani, it aroused a degree of enthusiasm unequaled elsewhere.

Don Carlo did not reach the United States until April 12, 1877, when it had its opening American performance at the New York Academy of Music. On December 23, 1920, it was given at the Metropolitan Opera House in New York with a fine cast including Rosa Ponselle, Margarete Matzenauer, Martinelli, De Luca, Didur. During the season of 1922-23 Met audiences were treated to Chaliapin's "incomparable impersonation" of King Philip, with Léon Rothier as the Grand Inquisitor. It was also included in the epoch-making revival in Germany of a number of Verdi's less famous works. And it has been back in recent years at New York's Metropolitan Opera House.

After *Don Carlo*, Verdi spent much time in Genoa, now fast becoming his favorite big city. He rented an apartment at its Palazzo Sauli, one of the many magnificent palaces which so vividly recall the grand old days of the Genoese Doges, including Simon Boccanegra. The Palazzo Sauli, perched on one of the heights encircling Genoa, afforded a fine view of the main part of the city and its splendid harbor, which helped Verdi to forget recent squabbles in Paris. The sojourns of Giuseppe and Giuseppina in Genoa grew progressively longer—to the great satisfaction of the latter, who considered Sant' Agata in cold weather unfit for human habitation.

But enjoyment of the happy combination of his country and city residences was decisively halted by the death at Sant' Agata, where he had long made his home, of Antonio Barezzi, Giuseppe's father-in-law and benefactor, one of the brightest human stars in the composer's personal firmament. The mutual affection of the two men had never flagged. Even the strongly expressed objections of Antonio to the pre-marital union of Giuseppe and Giuseppina, though bitterly resented by Verdi, had failed to shake the foundations of their friendship.

Verdi was broken-hearted. Forty years before his death Barezzi had taken him to live in his own house at Busseto, made him a member of his own family, gladly and proudly given the unknown and impecunious young musician the hand of his daughter in marriage. He had made possible Giuseppe's studies in Milan. He had never failed him. Always he had respected and admired and loved him.

"I have known many men," wrote Verdi, from the depths of his grief, to the Countess Maffei, "but never a better one. He loved me as one of his own children and I loved him as a father."

Among all his son-in-law's compositions Antonio Barezzi liked best the chorus of captives in *Nabucco*, which had first established Verdi's renown. In the last minutes of the old man's life, Verdi, who had been seated, weeping, by Barezzi's bedside, moved silently to a piano in the death chamber and quietly played that poignantly beautiful melody. Barezzi turned on him a last look of gratitude and love. The notes of that favorite song were the last sounds heard by him on earth.

VI

BREAK-THROUGH

TWENTY-SIX

In the operas of his period of transition Giuseppe Verdi was still shackled to his limitations. He was struggling against them, steadily escaping from them. But they were putting up an obstinate battle. The old Verdi died hard. Cannot we hear that tough-fibered old warrior whispering to the new Verdi: "After all, I created *Rigoletto,* didn't I? And *Trovatore?* And *Traviata?* I made the name Verdi synonymous with supremacy in Italian opera, didn't I? What more do you want? You are past fifty. You have given your best. Anything you do from now on will be anti-climax. You're on top of the world. Sit back. Relax. Enjoy yourself."

Many a composer, courted and fêted and acclaimed as Verdi had been for years, ever since the emergence of his Three Unkillables, might have heeded such whisperings. Many a composer might have gone down fighting, in self-satisfied, arrogant blindness, against younger men fully aware that nothing stands still in this world, that methods and ideals unquestioned yesterday waver today and lie prostrate tomorrow.

But not Giuseppe Verdi.

Completely conscious of the flaws in his work which had denied him the topmost triumphs he closed his ears to siren suggestions of "thus far and no further." He emulated the Spaniards, who, when they discovered the New World, changed the motto *Ne Plus Ultra* to *Plus Ultra.*

There *is* something beyond for me, Giuseppe Verdi told himself. He was famous, rich, flattered, revered. But for him

there could be no halt. Excelsior! Now, at last, he was heark-
ening to voices, which, low and fitful at first, were to become,
in his miraculously youthful old age, clear and ringing and
compelling.

In 1870 Verdi informed friends that he had been asked to
write an opera for a distant country. He did not explain. And
at first he distinctly implied that he would not do it. The
truth of the matter was that the Khedive of Egypt, glorying
in the recent completion of the Suez Canal, wished to cele-
brate that highly important event by the production in his
capital city of Cairo of an opera of imposing grandeur by a
suitably prominent composer. Naturally, among the composers considered, was Giuseppe Verdi. His price, the Khedive
knew, would be high—Verdian works commanded much gold
in the operatic market. But, with the Egyptian ruler, money
was no object. He wanted to do the thing right.

So Verdi, on one of his trips to Paris, was approached again
—this time by Du Locle, one of the librettists of *Don Carlo*.
Speaking for the Khedive's government, Du Locle made him
a generous offer. Verdi shook his head. He was in one of those
moods when the making of music for the delectation of the
universe was less alluring to him than the making of plans for
the improvement of Sant' Agata.

Du Locle, however, was not to be put off. He mailed to
Sant' Agata a short scenario of the plot of a projected opera
which he had received from Cairo. The crafty Frenchman
knew his Giuseppe Verdi. The composer read the scenario
(he thought, it seems, that it was by the Khedive himself)
and, recognizing instantly its immense dramatic possibilities,
he was all fire and flame to get down to work on music for it.
The scenario was by one Mariette Bey, a French Egyptologist
of repute, in the service of the Egyptian government, which
had granted him the Oriental title of Bey.

Negotiations started promptly. On the Khedive's side they

were conducted by Mariette Bey and Du Locle, on Verdi's by his friend Muzio, now working at the Italian Theatre in Paris. The composer asked (and got) a down payment of 150,000 francs ($30,000). He reserved full rights for all countries except Egypt. He agreed to pay out of his pocket for the libretto and to send to Egypt at his own expense a representative for supervising rehearsals there. At no point did it occur to him to go to Egypt himself. As always, he dreaded the sea, even an inland sea like the Mediterranean.

Du Locle repaired to Sant' Agata to amplify Mariette Bey's sketch under the composer's eagle eye. And, somewhere along the line, a name was selected for the new work—a name which has become rather well-known—in fact, as well-known as any name ever given to any opera anywhere—*Aïda*.

Soon Du Locle's amplified version of Mariette Bey's scenario was completed, but, like that sketch, it was in French. The next step was to shape it into a definitive libretto in Italian. Having consulted the head of the Ricordi firm Verdi eventually chose as his librettist a writer (who had begun his career as a baritone singer in opera) named Antonio Ghislanzoni.

Ghislanzoni was an individual of Bohemian leanings like Temistocle Solera, librettist of *Nabucco*. Fantastic stories grew up about him as they had around Solera.

While he was singing the part of Ezio, the Roman general, in Verdi's *Attila* in a small Italian city he suddenly felt an overpowering urge to dash off instantly to Milan. This he proceeded to do, not bothering to change from his ancient Roman accouterments. After a train ride surrounded by goggle-eyed fellow-passengers, he strode (not unnoticed) through several of Milan's principal streets, and, presenting himself at a hotel in that city's principal square, in plumed helmet and with the short sword of the Roman legionaries clanking at his side, he peremptorily shouted to the petrified clerk: "Give me a room!"

But, like Solera, Ghislanzoni, despite eccentricities, knew his business. Soon he was closeted with Verdi at Sant' Agata fashioning the libretto which has brought his name down to us—though, as with the great majority of other men who have written the words for operas, only a very few of the millions who have heard Aïda ever heard of Ghislanzoni. In the history of grand opera there have been many Verdis, but only one Boïto (the librettist of Verdi's last two operas)—just as, in the history of light opera, there have been many Sullivans but only one Gilbert. It was Ghislanzoni, by the way, who, as a guest at Sant' Agata, discovered inside the cover of Verdi's old spinet, lovingly preserved there by the composer, the note left there by the man who had repaired it half a century before.

Verdi took a hand in the Aïda libretto with a vengeance. He made suggestions. He demanded changes. He wrote snatches of dialogue. He sketched out entire scenes. "He took command from the outset," says Toye. "Ghislanzoni was only a lieutenant." But, unlike Piave, Ghislanzoni was no bending reed. He stood his ground when he felt that to be necessary. And he did some effective suggesting himself. But most of the time Verdi's ideas prevailed—as usual.

It was he who originated one of the most famous scenes in the opera, the one showing an Egyptian temple at two levels, with the lovers, Aïda and Radames, buried alive on the lower level, and Amneris, Aïda's rival in love, praying, on the upper level, to ancient Egypt's gods, quite unaware that Aïda is with Radames. Nobody else concerned in manufacturing Aïda, not Ghislanzoni, not Mariette Bey, not Du Locle, succeeded in thinking up that one.

Even Verdi, despite his self-confidence, obviously had his doubts about it, for he gave particular instructions to a friend whom he sent to Cairo for the first performance, to tell him truthfully, with no yielding to flattery, exactly how that scene struck the opera's first audience. He need not have worried.

To Verdi also occurred the idea of the scene in which the priests try Radames for treason and pronounce sentence of death on him, to a muffled, positively blood-freezing roll of drums backstage.

After Ghislanzoni left Sant' Agata with the rough draft of the Aïda libretto duly packed away in his luggage, Verdi continued to correspond with him about the opera. And, both while they were together and after they had parted, he was busy composing the music for the work destined to be the greatest popular success of his career as a composer. He was keen to meet the dead-line, which had been set for January, 1871. He kept saying: "There is little time."

But, in the summer of 1870, all plans were turned upside down by the outbreak of the Franco-German War. One catastrophe after another overwhelmed France's armies. By the beginning of the next year their foes were laying siege to Paris; and, cooped up in that beleaguered city, was Mariette Bey, who had come there on behalf of Aïda, together with all the scenery and costumes for the Cairo production, designed by French experts, which Mariette had expected to take back with him to the Khedive's capital in time for the opening.

Verdi, incidentally, forgetting all about anti-French prejudice, became whole-heartedly pro-French as the war developed. To him, it was Latinism against Teutonism, something akin to the irruptions of Alaric and Attila from bleak regions beyond the Alps into his own sunny southland. In full sympathy with the tribulations of France he devoted part of the advance for his new opera to the aid of wounded French soldiers.

After the disastrous French defeat at Sedan and the capture

of the Emperor Napoleon III by the Germans, Verdi wrote
to the Countess Maffei:

This disaster to France has sown desolation in my heart. Of
course, despite their tribulations, the French, with their *blague*
and impertinence and presumptuousness, were and are unbear-
able, but, after all, they gave to the modern world liberty and
civilization. If France falls we must not delude ourselves by believing that all our liberties and civilization will not fall with her.
Despite this, our *littérateurs* and politicians will go on extolling
(may God forgive them for it!) the knowledge and scientific and
artistic achievements of this victorious nation—but if they looked
a little more closely into the matter they would realize that in
German veins runs the some old Gothic blood and that the Germans are a nation of unlimited arrogance, hard, intolerant, de-
spisers of everything that is not Germanic, rapacious beyond all
bounds. They are a people with heads but no hearts, a race that
is strong but uncivilized.

And that king of theirs, always talking about God and Provi-
dence with whose help he is destroying the best part of Europe!
He thinks himself predestined to reform the customs and punish
the vices of the modern world. A fine sort of missionary! *

And he made this gloomy prophecy:

"We shall not escape a European war and we shall be de-
voured by it. It is not coming tomorrow, but it will surely
come. Things look very black to me."

In further allusion to the Germans, Verdi laughed in these
words at the prolixity common in some of their writings:

"They get hold of a flea or a fly and write a volume 300
pages long about each one of its legs!"

For some time communication was cut off between
Mariette Bey and his co-workers on *Aïda* outside Paris. There
was, to be sure, balloon service—Gambetta had entrusted him-

* *I Copialettere di Giuseppe Verdi*, Milan, 1913.

self to it when he escaped from the besieged city to continue French resistance against the invaders in other parts of France. But Verdi and his associates did not avail themselves of it.

In Egypt there was worry lest the composer, who had stipulated in his contract that he was to be free to put on early production of Aïda in Milan, might "jump the gun" and let La Scala have the *première* instead of Cairo. So, in default of Mariette Bey, another Egyptian government envoy, Draneht Bey, was dispatched to Italy to protect Egyptian rights.

But there was no need of any such step. True to his unvarying integrity, Verdi, even before he heard of Draneht's trip had suspended all negotiations with La Scala in connection with the production there of the new opera. He had given his promise to the Khedive. And no contract, no matter how liberally bedizened with signatures and seals, was ever better than the pledged word of Giuseppe Verdi.

Paris surrendered in January, 1871. It was now too late to transport costumes and scenery to Egypt in time for the gala season there. So Aïda's opening performance had to be postponed. Draneht Bey appeared in Italy, hoping to sign up Teresa Stolz, of the Sant' Agata inner circle, for the title rôle in the Cairo production (he couldn't get her). And Verdi, who had envisioned Muzio as his representative in Cairo on the great night, now entrusted that assignment to another friend, Giovanni Bottesini. Himself cross the Mediterranean? Never!

"If I went there," he remarked, "I might never come back —except as a mummy."

Meanwhile Aïda engendered such an orgy of publicity that Verdi, always a hater of ballyhoo, now confronted with it in as extravagant a form as the 1870's were capable of cooking up. What would he have done in the 1950's? Beside himself with disgust and irritation, he wrote to the Milanese critic

Filippo Filippi, who had rushed off to Cairo in readiness for
the *première*:

To me it seems that art, practised in this way, is no longer art
but trade. . . . I always remember with pleasure my early days,
when, almost without friends, without any personal puffery, without preparation, without any kind of influence, I came before
the public with my operas, expecting to be sniped at, perfectly
satisfied if I made some sort of a favorable impression.

But now! . . . Journalists, singers, players, members of the
chorus, directors, etc., etc., all have to contribute their stone to
the edifice of publicity, thus making a cornice of nonsensical
trifles that add nothing to the merit of an opera and may quite
possibly detract from its real value. It is deplorable, deplorable! *

Meanwhile, in Cairo, the air was electric with rumors—
some circulated by early species of press agents, some resembling Topsy. Europe had sent some of her foremost music
critics to pass judgment on Verdi's latest.

The dress rehearsal lasted from seven in the evening until
half past three the next morning. The Khedive attended it,
with a glittering entourage. And he stuck it out to the end.

TWENTY-SEVEN

THE FIRST production of the most popular of all grand
operas took place in Cairo on Christmas Eve, 1871.

The theater was filled to the roof, to the last seat, to the
last square inches of standing space. That immense audience
combined with the glitter and social pageantry and general
gorgeousness of the same sort of assemblage in Occidental
countries a special veneer of Oriental color and glamour well

* *Copialettere, op. cit.*

suited to the exotic atmosphere and background in Giuseppe
Verdi's new creation.

Rumors had swept through Cairo for weeks. Never before
had Verdi caused such a quiver of excitement and expectancy.
Never before had a Verdi first night whipped up such extravagant hopes. Never in previous years had a multitude of
Verdi-conscious operagoers been so titillated and tantalized
by preliminary publicity, that necessary evil of musical fame
which so irritated the man unwillingly responsible for it.

The Khedive of Egypt, a modern ruler who contrived to
surround himself with a species of Arabian Nights exoticism,
was present in all his glory. Flanking him sat or stood officers
in their best uniforms, prominent civilians in their best tail
coats and highest collars, many with decorative insignia in
their buttonholes. Ladies were scattered among them, bright
human stars, Occidental and Oriental, resplendently gar-
mented, artistically coiffed, bathed in the light of rare jewels.
From the boxes, foreign diplomats, accredited to the Court
of the Khedive, with their wives and daughters, attired in
raiment reflecting the latest fashions of the day, scanned the
packed house with the proper degree of languid hauteur.

Europe's most eagerly read and looked-up-to critics of music
gazed from the orchestra floor, or (if they had been lucky
enough to get invitations from boxholders) from the boxes,
at the Khedive and his entourage, at self-important diplomats and lovely ladies of Egypt and Europe.

Filippo Filippi was there, that well-known critic from
Milan, ready to tell his exacting Milanese fellow-citizens and
the rest of Italy, via the prominent newspaper for which he
wrote, what he thought of Giuseppe Verdi's latest. All the
way from Paris had come Ernest Reyer, not only a judge of
the musical compositions of others but a composer in his
own right, with much more of a leaning to Teutonic Wagner
than to Latin Verdi. On the verdicts of those two, and on a

score of other solemn verdicts from other eminent critics in
the audience, depended to a considerable degree the chances
of success of the new opera, awaited through many months
with a veritable fever of anticipation.

The first notes of the prelude send a thrill through the
house. The world *première* of AÏDA, *Opera in Four Acts,
Libretto by Antonio Ghislanzoni, Music by Giuseppe Verdi*—
I would hate to be set to figure out how many times those
words have appeared decade after decade on the world's
posters and programs and illuminated electric signs—is at last
under way.

That prelude brings mysterious suggestions of the peculiar,
indefinable atmosphere that is *Aïda*. Its first notes tell what
sort of an evening this one is to be. From exotic prelude to
heartbreaking death-duet *Aïda*, at its Egyptian opening, is a
superb success. Every act—every scene—brings tremendous applause. Here there is no question of compliment to a Khedive,
to a singer. The cheers and handclappings are forced right out
of those in the audience by something stronger than themselves, something that forbids them to sit still and keep silent.
Genius is at work on them—and from them genius exacts
what it was to exact through *Aïda*, right up to our day: approbation without stint, willingly given, rapturously expressed.

Each time the curtain falls it falls on a tumult. Triumph,
complete triumph, lasting triumph, triumph stretching out
into tomorrow and tomorrow and tomorrow, is implicit in
every note from the stage, every bravo from the spectators.
And so it has been at thousands of subsequent performances
of *Aïda* in every country in the world where grand opera is
produced.

Reyer, the Wagnerian from Paris, joined in the chorus of
joy. He who had viewed with disfavor Verdi's steady forward
march wrote to the Paris paper through which he helped to
shape French musical opinion: "If Verdi persists in this new

orientation he may lose some adherents, but he will make many converts and find followers in circles in which he has never before been received." A grudging tribute—yet more significant, in its way, than surfeits of cheering from friends.

Next morning Cairo rang with encomiums of the new work. And at once it began its triumphal march—a sort of world-wide continuation off the stage of its celebrated triumphal march on the stage—through the world's opera houses—large, medium-sized and small. At this moment, *Aïda* is being produced or readied for production somewhere, equipped with a cast and orchestra, good, bad, fair or awful—with Verdi's music, thrilling and gentle, resonant and melting, stentorian and whispering, triumphant over even the awfulest of singers and musicians and managements.

In *Aïda* Giuseppe Verdi added to his Three Unkillables of the 1850's a Fourth Unkillable of the 1870's (and 1880's and 1900's and 1950's and so ad infinitum) which, in every way, outpointed, outdistanced and outclassed the other three. To that first audience in Cairo, to other audiences in *Aïda's* first years of life, it seemed self-evident that, with this triumph of triumphs, Giuseppe Verdi had reached the uttermost limit of his powers, the topmost pinnacle of his glory.

Of course, the most tumultuous, the most riotous acclamation greeted the dropping of the curtain in Cairo after the finale of the second act.

That curtain had risen on the gateways and palaces and temples of ancient Egyptian Thebes—on ancient Egypt's nobles and priests and warriors and plebeians gathered to welcome Radames fresh from winning a great battle against the Ethiopians—on that scene, in short, as familiar as any in opera to the operagoers of the world. Here the "damn-the-expense" attitude of the Khedive of modern Egypt toward his celebration of the opening of the Suez Canal reached its climax.

The notes of the triumphal march from the long trumpets of trumpeters in bizarre apparel ring out for the first time— is it not difficult to imagine that there was a time not so very long ago when that march was unknown to everybody? The fantastic success of *Aïda*, foreshadowed already in the reception accorded to *"Celeste Aïda"* and *"Su! del Nilo . . ."* and *"Numi, pietà!"* emerges in all its fullness. When the second-act curtain falls in Cairo for the first time on Aïda and Radames, Amneris and Amonasro—on Egypt's king, surrounded by his soldiers, his huddled miserable prisoners of war, his shining trophies of victory, his hundreds of splendidly accoutered elephants—it falls on the absolute certainty of immense, unlimited, universal success. Ever since, through more than fourscore years, that air of certain triumph has been breathed again, as it was on that brilliant first night in Cairo, from the rise of the first to the fall of the last curtain, by countless other audiences in other cities, swayed by countless diversities of likes and dislikes, sympathies and prejudices, whims and emotions and tastes and temperaments, but forced into temporary enthusiastic kinship by the wizardry of Giuseppe Verdi.

Six weeks after Cairo *Aïda* took Milan by storm. In its original cast at La Scala were two good friends of Giuseppe and Giuseppina Verdi, Teresa Stolz, enacting the title rôle, and Maria Waldmann, in the part of Amneris.

Verdi, aware of the great importance of the verdict of the Milanese, had bestowed on rehearsals rather more than his usual meticulous, pugnacious attention. And he had soon got things moving as he wanted them to move, despite a boneheaded tenor, who, firmly believing that all a tenor needs to do is open his mouth and let words, decently clothed in mel-

ody, shoot out of it, met the composer's endeavors to persuade
him that he was supposed to be a human being with a peevish:
"How can you expect me to sing well and at the same time
put meaning into what I sing?" Verdi's face when he said
that must have been worth going miles to see.

Hysteria ran rampant over Milan's first *Aïda's* audience—
the opera's first European audience. It was Cairo all over
again—Cairo plus. There were thirty-two curtain calls at the
end of the performance. Finally, the audience clamored to
have Verdi come out alone from the wings and get an ovation
all to himself. But he shook his head.

"Ghislanzoni must come out with me," he insisted. And
that last call, with the riot that went with it, was shared by
composer and librettist.

Next morning the noted Italian critic Fortis wrote:

Spectators sat almost four hours, before a grandeur of creative
power, a grandeur of externalization, a grandeur not only of
vastness but of inspiration, not only of proportions but of ideas.
Everything about yesterday evening's performance was grandiose
—the audience and the spectacle, the view on the stage and the
view presented by the crowded theatre—all that one saw and heard
and felt within one's self. The impression made on the public,
the impression made by the public, the emotion of the spectators,
of the singers, of the composer—all in Aïda's triumph was grandeur. And, in the upsurge of our Italian national pride, in the
artistic vision which had brought all this into being, there was
also grandeur—as there was likewise in the work of the artists on
the stage, in the reception given them by the immense audience. . . .

Thinking of many performances witnessed by me, particularly at the Metropolitan Opera House in New York, I can
echo those words. Justly has *Aïda* been called the grandest of
grand operas.

One Italian commentator, completely bowled over by that second-act finale, remarked: "It is a painting! Yes, a painting! A painting by Michelangelo!"

Impresario after impresario hurried to produce Aïda; and the operatic public everywhere flocked to it. And still it does so; it cannot get enough of it; it clamors for more. Aïda is superb box-office. All a manager with a wobbly season on his hands needs to do is announce Aïda, sit back at his desk, put his feet up on it and watch the money roll in.

Aïda is a torrent of golden sound. It is drama neat, melodrama in excelsis. Its characters are convincing—you understand them, you sympathize with them or the reverse—though you never saw anything like them in non-operatic life. It is a constant stream of clashing contrasts. One moment it thrills, the next it chills.

The impact of that scene of triumph at the end of Act II, with its animals, spears and plumes, its beautiful color and ugly gods, its stunning outbursts of disciplined din, is almost unique in its effect. It is pure Verdi. Quintessential Verdi. It is Verdi with as much power and melody as ever—with more, as a matter of fact—but a Verdi overlaying everything with proofs of progress in his art such as he had never shown before in his life. It is the climax of Verdian power. One's ears ring and throb with the crash of it.

Then—suddenly . . .

Act III. The banks of the Nile. The opposite, the exact opposite, of the massive scene of pageantry and power that has preceded it. Its prelude—that eerie prelude, that unbelievably diaphanous and ethereal and mysterious prelude—is immeasurably removed from the splendor and pageantry of Act II.

It is not "Oriental." All through Aïda Verdi scorns typical stage "Orientalism." More than one commentator on it has been reminded of Debussy! Debussy suggested by Verdi? Impossible! Debussy, the master of hint, the king of nuance, the arch-conveyor of under-statement, of musical double-talk. And here there is no question of plagiarism. When Verdi wrote *Aïda* Debussy was seven years old.

Without having anything really Egyptian or "Oriental" about it, that prelude, and much of the rest of the music of the Nile scene—notably the unforgettable introduction to "*O patria mia*"—is the most Oriental thing imaginable. It conforms completely to the directions given by the composer to Ghislanzoni when they were preparing the opera together. "In the Nile scene," said the maestro, "*the audience must smell Egypt.*" Well, the audience does. But—and here is a paradox that well-nigh defeats elucidation—they smell an Egypt *that never existed,* under its ancient kings or at any time since—an Egypt of the senses, an Egypt of the imagination, without "reality," shorn of stage clichés—yet an Egypt completely convincing, the child of the brain of a genius, who has infused reality and Orientalism into his music without recourse to knowledge of the East or to any of the artificial aids, which the average (and more than average) composer often deems indispensable in evoking such an exotic milieu. The same impression flows from the chant of the priestesses in the temple, from the introduction to the heroine's song to Radames when she is tempting him to abandon and betray his native country. All this is an evocation of Never-Never Land. No wonder Verdi, fully conscious that he had within him the power for such evocation, once remarked: "To imitate reality is good, *but to invent it is better.*"

Of the scene on the banks of the Nile Francis Toye writes:

Has any other composer written quite in this way for the wood wind, achieved quite this expressive smoothness in his handling of the instruments? . . . The opening passage for strings, with those harmonies on the 'cellos that are the product of sheer inspiration; the soft trumpets associated with Radames's description of the imminent war; the fiery turbulence of brass and strings in Amonasro's denunciation of his daughter—all are models of what may be called psychological orchestration. The musical material itself is of the first order—first, the promises, then the fury, of Amonasro, culminating in . . . a veritable epitome of primitive passions. . . . These show a certainty of touch, a power of imagination never hitherto attained by the composer.

"Psychological orchestration!" From Giuseppe Verdi! What a long road the composer to whom that sort of orchestration could be ascribed by a competent critic had traveled since the days of the brass band in the main square of Busseto, since *I Lombardi* and *Attila*, since *Il Trovatore!*

In *Aïda*, Verdi, his genius strengthened and deepened by the supreme Verdi already developing inside him, spoke for the last time in a Niagara of melody—so violent that everything else seems to be tumbled about in a surging melodic tide. Verdi was hampered in his transitional operas by a curious faltering in his handling of these works *in their entirety*. But so tremendous, so elemental, is the brimming tide that sweeps through *Aïda* that all is carried forward with it— brutal contrast, melting song, glancing nuance, subtlety, psychology—everything!

And now—the last scene . . .

An Italian commentator, having sat through *Aïda* on its first night in Milan, was left gasping by the sheer beauty and glory of it. So much so that when the final scene rose before his eyes, with its divided temple levels, echoing to celestial melodies as lovely as anything that ever stole into Giuseppe Verdi's mind—with its chanting priests and praying princess and dying lovers—all he could blurt out was: "Before the marvelous light of genius suffusing this scene criticism must be silent!"

I sympathize with that Italian.

Every time that I have walked out of a theater, with the *Aïda* death-duet still sounding in my ears and dominating my thoughts, words have failed me. They fail me now.

Verdi at this time went to Naples in connection with an important production there of *Aïda*; but a succession of exasperating delays in his negotiations with the management of the San Carlo Theatre (he certainly had no luck with that outfit) caused him reluctantly to postpone his departure for home and created a considerable stretch of unwelcome spare time. This he utilized by trying his hand at composing something not at all in his regular line—a String Quartet.

It was performed privately before a few Neapolitan acquaintances. The composer thought so little of it that for a long time he refused to do anything about getting it published or performed in public.

In later years, after he had withdrawn his ban, it won a fair measure of success. It shows no slavish conformity with accepted rules governing such compositions—so much so that somebody remarked of it: "No German would have composed it that way." And one section has considerable affinity with music included twenty years later in the last of his operas, the crowning miracle of his old age.

After *Aïda*, Giuseppe and Giuseppina continued to oscillate between Sant' Agata and Genoa.

On the floor below the Verdis at the Palazzo Sauli in Genoa another apartment was occupied by Angelo Mariani, considered by Verdi and other experts the best orchestra conductor in Italy, and Teresa Stolz, who had been living for some time with Mariani in a union as informal and unsanctified as that of Giuseppe and Giuseppina had been for a decade or so before their marriage.

The two couples had been the best of friends for years.

But gradually a coolness sprang up between Verdi and
Mariani. Several reasons have been adduced to explain it. One
is that Mariani, given to tampering with the tempi and even
the notes of scores conducted by him, had dared apply this
treatment to Verdi's works, to the intense irritation of their
sensitive creator. Another explanation is that the rift was due
to a debt owed by Mariani to Teresa Stolz, the non-repayment
of which angered Verdi, always ultra-scrupulous in such matters. Still another, the most frequently heard, is that Verdi
and Teresa had a love affair.

A man well acquainted with Mariana and Verdi put into
print a story to the effect that once, in Bologna, where Mariani,
Teresa and Verdi were sojourning on professional business,
Teresa was so incensed at Mariani's conduct in a quarrel with
another musician that, when the conductor returned to the
lodgings which he and she had been sharing, he found that
she had left him. Later, Mariani stated that he had lost his
sweetheart "and also the friend for whom she has forsaken
me." Some incline to the belief that the "friend" he meant
was none other than Giuseppe Verdi.

Whatever the true reason for the trouble between Verdi
and Mariani, it led to the definite termination of their long
friendship. Mariani's bitterness was so deep as to lead some
commentators to believe it to have been the real motive for
his abandoning the pro-Verdianism which had characterized
him for years in favor of a pro-Wagnerism so vigorous as to
place him in the front rank of the famous Teutonic composer's champions in Italy. Applying his great musical talents
to this new orientation Mariani conducted the first performances in Italy of *Lohengrin* with such brilliancy that he earned
the delighted approval of Richard Wagner, who sent him an
autographed portrait of himself inscribed "Evviva Mariani!"

Though no longer a friend of Mariani, Verdi continued
to admire him as a conductor. Soon after their rift, in 1873,

Mariani died. Like Francesco Piave, he had, in his earlier years, loved too well. After his death both Giuseppe and Giuseppina kept up their friendship with Teresa Stolz. If there was anything between Giuseppina's husband and Angelo Mariani's ex-mistress, Giuseppina Verdi's conduct after Mariani's death contributed materially toward keeping the true details from the knowledge of the world.

After *Aïda*, Verdi was again accused—more pointedly than ever before—of having imitated Wagner. The accusation both hurt and angered him. Into his music for *Aïda*, he insisted, he, one hundred per cent an Italian, had poured the best of his Italianism. Yet carpers and sneerers saw in it imitation of the least Italian of musical geniuses! That was just too much!

Verdi admired Wagner. But between admiration and imitation lies a long road—and on that road the great Italian refused to travel. Nor, with his thoroughly Italian musical genius, could he see the slightest necessity for such traveling.

His first impressions of Wagnerian music were not favorable: he found the *Tannhäuser* overture "crazy," the mythological characters of the *Ring*, particularly Siegfried, "uncouth." With a copy of the full vocal score of *Lohengrin* under his arm, he attended in Bologna one of the first performances in Italy of that opera. On the margin of that score (it is still preserved) he penciled: "Beautiful music, when there is thought in it. Action slow—like the words. Sometimes one is bored. Beautiful instrumental effects." He did not like Lohengrin's musical remarks to the Swan. And he found the "Bridal Chorus" "unexpectedly ineffective." At some points, to express his disapproval, he crossed out with his pencil as much as whole pages of the *Lohengrin* score.

As Verdi grew older, his appreciation of Wagner increased. Toward the end of his life he said of the famous German:

"He has a right to be regarded as one of the greatest. His music, though—with the exception of *Lohengrin*—alien to our [*i.e.*, Italian] feelings, has life, blood, nerves. Therefore, it is entitled to survive."

Wagner, says Franz Werfel—alike a Teuton and an ardent pro-Verdian—was the creator of a new musical language, to which many of Verdi's contemporaries, including Gounod, Massenet, Boïto, to say nothing of the Germans, succumbed. But Verdi remained absolutely untouched by it.

Once more it must be said with the strongest possible emphasis [continues Werfel] that Verdi took nothing from Wagner. What difference does it make if fanatical Wagnerians point to some harmony here, an instrumental coloring or sequence there? That sort of thing is inherent in the atmosphere of an epoch and has no significance whatsoever. . . .

From *Nabucco* to *Falstaff* Verdi's language remains the same— and nothing is more alien to it than Wagner's idiom. The last Verdian works, *Otello* and *Falstaff*, reproached with Wagnerism even to this day, are the strongest proof of that assertion. They show no trace of symphonic treatment—instead, we find in them the entire essence of the old operatic treatment, shortened, condensed and inspired anew by genius. . . .

In them the voice remains triumphant. And the orchestra, despite its enrichment, never takes the lead, but lives and throbs only in relation to the human characters on the stage and their fate.*

How could the essentially Latin genius of the composer of *Otello* and *Falstaff*, that master of compression, condensation and concentration, ever feel at home speaking the musical language of Wagner, as conspicuous for prolixity as it is for genius? Verdi never disliked Wagner. He simply felt in him

* *Giuseppe Verdis Briefe*. Herausgegeben und eingeleitet von Franz Werfel. Übersetzt von Paul Stefan. Berlin-Wien-Leipzig. Paul Zsolnay Verlag, 1926.

alienism. Is it not inconceivable that he could have stifled this feeling so drastically as to become a Wagner-imitator? Once, in his beloved Italy, he said to his friend Gino Monaldi: "In this sunshine, under this sky, could I possibly compose *Tristan* and the *Ring*? Never! We are Italians, by God! In everything—including music!"

That, it seems to me, is the whole Verdi-Wagner case in a nutshell.

TWENTY-EIGHT

Among the great geniuses of the past, outside the domain of music, Giuseppe Verdi revered, along with Shakespeare, Dante and Michelangelo; also, as he disclosed in a passing allusion already quoted in these pages, George Washington. In his own province of the artists he paid particular reverence to Palestrina, also to Marcello, the latter little-known except to specializing diggers into the history of Italian music. Likewise, he stood, awed, before the towering achievements of Beethoven, Bach, Haydn and other composers of similar eminence.

In the domain of politics his demigod, as we know, was Cavour. Throughout his venture into what was for him the exotic jungle of international affairs Giuseppe Verdi was hardly more than a yes-man, in a complimentary sense of the term, to the statesman who believed so firmly, as he himself did, in the cause of Italian liberty and unity.

In yet another field, literature, there was also a contemporary of bright fame for whom Verdi felt much the same sincere unquestioning admiration—Alessandro Manzoni, the great Italian novelist, author of that Italian classic, *I Promessi Sposi*.

It was not alone as a literary genius that Verdi revered Manzoni. There was also in the great writer's character and ideals something that appealed to kindred qualities in himself. Of Manzoni he said: "I would have knelt to him if one could worship human beings." And: "I venerated him like a saint."

When Manzoni died, on May 22, 1873, Verdi's grief was again so crushing that it prevented him from reverent attendance at church and cemetery. After the burial, however, he stole away from Sant' Agata without explanations to anybody as to his plans, in order to pay a secret visit to Manzoni's grave. There, after devoting his thoughts through a few moments of silent and solitary homage to the man whom he had so much admired and respected, he resolved to give a practical turn to his devotion by creating something to prove to the world the depth of his admiration and respect for the author of *I Promessi Sposi*. He kept his resolve. And the musical tribute to his dead idol which it led him to create is a landmark in Giuseppe Verdi's musical career.

On the occasion of Rossini's death in 1868, Verdi had wished to commemorate the passing of that renowned composer, by means of a composite Rossini Requiem Mass, of which each of thirteen living Italian composers was to compose a part. Others seconded the idea with enthusiasm. The thirteen composers were duly chosen, the work on the project begun. To Verdi was allotted the composition of the "Libera me."

But the scheme fell through—which, maybe, was just as well, for it is difficult to see how the completed work could have been anything but a distressing crazy quilt. Verdi had already composed the section assigned to him. He played it one day to a friend at Sant' Agata. The friend was swept off his feet by its beauty. "You ought to compose all the rest of a Requiem Mass to go with it!" he told the composer. Just how much that remark had to do with Verdi's resolve after his secret visit to Alessandro Manzoni's grave is not known— it certainly must have had something to do with the plan which began to form in Verdi's brain.

Departing again from Sant' Agata, he took rooms, according to his usual custom, at the Hotel Milan, in the city of that name (or Albergo Milano, as it is called in Italian). From there he sent a message to the Mayor of Milan informing that high official that, since he wished to compose a Requiem Mass in honor of Manzoni—whose death had made an immense impression all over Italy—he would like to enlist the co-operation of the city government in the project.

Having read that message there was no thought in the Mayor of Milan's mind of having Verdi wait on him. Clapping his hat on his head, he hurried to the Albergo Milano, was shown up to the quarters of the composer, and then and there assured the latter that he and the rest of the Milanese municipal authorities would do their utmost on behalf of the contemplated honor to a writer considered by his fellow-countrymen one of the great glories of their native land.

Returning to Sant' Agata, Verdi picked out from a pile of musical manuscripts the "Libera me" which he had intended to include in the projected mass for the glorification of Gioacchino Rossini, and got busy readjusting it to the glorification of Alessandro Manzoni. Little by little, while puttering in his beloved garden, wandering with his dogs over Sant' Agata's pleasant acres, conversing with Giuseppina and the friends of their inner circle, or sitting alone he transmuted his nebulous ideas into concrete musical notes. Considerably before the date set for its first performance the *Requiem* was ready for rehearsals.

After weighing the suitability of several churches suggested the Church of San Marco in Milan was finally selected. The two leading female rôles were entrusted to Teresa Stolz and

Maria Waldmann, respectively the Aïda and Amneris of the
first production at La Scala of *Aïda*, both good singers and
also good friends of Giuseppe and Giuseppina. Two other
prominent operatic singers were chosen for the principal male
parts, the tenor Capponi and the basso Maini. An orchestra
of 150 picked executants was also provided, together with a
chorus of 200. Verdi himself was to conduct.

Except for youthful experiments in the old days at Busseto
and Milan Giuseppe Verdi had avoided composing church
music. Perhaps his veneration for Palestrina made him hesi-
tate to follow in that great master's path. Now, sixty years
old, he asserted again his extraordinary courage and well-
nigh unprecedented capacity for development despite advancing age by presenting himself to the world in a sensationally surprising guise. Undoubtedly, in doing so, he was fully
aware that he would run afoul of critics as hostile to him in
the new field as his implacable London foe, Henry Fothergill
Chorley, had been in the field of opera. But, undaunted, he
marched forth to brave them and their thunders.

On the eve of the first performance Milan's hotels were
filled. Again the music critics had gathered—from Paris, London, Vienna. Seats in the Church of San Marco were greed-
ily snapped up weeks in advance. For some important
journalists from abroad no better place could be found than
the church's organ loft.

Difficulties before production were serious and wearying.
And more than once there was talk of postponement. To this,
however, Verdi interposed vehement objection. Since the
Requiem Mass, he pointed out, had been composed as a
token of the nation's mourning for Alessandro Manzoni, to
present it on any date except the first anniversary of the
novelist's death would rob the tribute of its special significance. Eventually his view prevailed; and, all obstacles having
at last been triumphantly vanquished, the *Requiem* was first

heard on the evening of May 22, 1874, exactly one year after
Manzoni's death.

The big first audience were impressed by the beauty and
power of Verdi's music. The eminent critic Filippi (he who
had gone all the way to Cairo to hear the first Aïda) thought
some parts of it rather un-churchy, but took care to assert in
justification of the composer that successive creators of
Requiem Masses subsequent to Bach (Mozart, Cherubini, et
al.) had introduced into them a steadily progressing note of
human-ness, culminating now in the "unabashed drama" of
Verdi's Requiem.

After a second performance of the work at San Marco,
again under Verdi's direction, the Mass was transferred for
two more auditions to La Scala, with the same singers. Verdi
conducted the first La Scala night but on the second the conductor was Franco Faccio. The migration of the Mass from
church to theater caused the Milanese to throw over whatever restraint the religious surroundings had imposed on the
two initial performances. They now treated it almost as they
would treat any Verdi opera.

In describing next morning the Mass's first night at La
Scala, one of Milan's newspapers, Il Sole, sounded as if the
society editor had pinch-hit for the music critic. "On the left
of the stage was the orchestra, on the right the chorus. The
entrance of the soloists, Stolz in a dress of blue silk trimmed
with white velvet, Waldmann all in pink, was received with
acclaim."

But, with the appearance on the scene of the composer
that reviewer's contribution took on another tone. Verdi
was "as severe as ever, taking his place at the desk in the
middle of the stage. . . . Immediately he gave the signal to
begin. . . . The applause ceased as if by magic." Nevertheless, there were murmurs of approval all through (in the matter of squelching that sort of thing Verdi was no Toscanini).

In fact, the "Offertorium" was actually encored—just as if it were a particularly favored bit of an opera. After the "Agnus Dei," the applause, audible from the very beginning, "changed to roars." All this made it difficult for some of the foreigners present to remember that they were listening not to an operatic performance but to a Mass in honor of a dead man. At the end of the performance a "silver crown on an elegant cushion" was presented to the composer.

For their part in the performance of the *Requiem* in Milan Verdi and all those associated with him received no payment whatsoever. In fact, the Ricordi firm turned over from the receipts a surplus of some 8,000 francs to the municipality of Milan, to help defray unforeseen extra expenses incurred in preliminary preparations.

Immediately after its introduction to Milan the *Requiem* Mass went on tour. And, now, there was no question of something for nothing. The composer, the Ricordis, the musical director, the singers and chorus and orchestra, were all duly paid for their services on a pre-arranged scale. The tour, organized by the Ricordi firm in conjunction with the Escudier brothers, Verdi's agents in Paris, included stops in London, Paris and Vienna.

The London engagement almost fell through because Manager Gye of Covent Garden suggested that the Mass be given at his theater instead of at the Albert Hall, as originally contemplated, owing to the cancellation of several appearances by Adelina Patti which made Covent Garden unexpectedly available. Verdi, infuriated by this suggestion, declared that no work of his, particularly a Mass, could be used as a stop-gap for a prima donna. He threatened to veto the inclusion of London on the tour. Eventually, Gye abandoned the field of battle and the victorious Verdi pitched his tents on it. The *Requiem* was performed at the Albert Hall, with a chorus of

1,200, admirably trained for the occasion by the noted composer-director Barnby.

The tour met with great success. Again there was lavish praise for the beauty, effectiveness and general merits of the music. But—the cleavage of critical opinion regarding it, already noticeable in Milan (and still vocal today), promptly asserted itself. Even some of those who spoke of the *Requiem's* striking craftsmanship and stunning beauty were shocked by what they deemed its worldliness. As for extreme anti-Verdians they damned the whole thing outright.

There was even one critic who declared that the *Requiem* was never intended to be taken seriously, adding: "It is clever and may be taken as another instance of the power of music to excite humorous feelings."

And so it goes to this day.

Early admirers of the *Requiem* were fully as articulate as its early detractors—and, with the passage of time, their voices have tended to muffle to some degree those of their opponents. One London writer called it "the most beautiful music for the church that has been produced since the *Requiem* of Mozart." Another scolded the "puritans" who objected to Verdi's venture for insisting that "all sacred music must conform to accepted English standards."

In religion as well as in ordinary life, as is well known, Italians tend to theatricalism and extremism. Yet, at the same time, they are absolutely sincere. They have no use for the restraints of calmer lands. They have no understanding for the measured methods engendered by colder climates. They are Venice, not London. They are Naples, not New York. They are themselves.

Of this Verdi gives evidence in his *Requiem*. It is not only Verdi, it is Italy. Alive with theatricalism, it is disarming in its sincerity. Rossini once remarked: "There are only two kinds of music: good and bad." He also ridiculed the belief that there was a sharp, clear dividing-line between the music of theaters and the music of churches. Verdi thought the same way. And, thinking thus, he dared assert his beliefs in the Manzoni *Requiem*. That he asserted it with mastery has been attested by many competent critics. And his fellow-Italians see in it what they see in *Aïda* and in its two superb successors and what a growing army of non-Italians see there—a brilliant re-assertion of Italian musical ideals by an Italian composer of genius.

Camille Bellaigue writes:

Remember the first sight that caught Heinrich Heine's attention when he came across the Alps from Germany into Italy. By the side of the road he saw a large Crucifixion, fashioned in wood, and, around the Cross, a vine had grown and blossomed. And, says the poet, it was to him a thing of fearful beauty to see how life thus embraced death, how the luxuriant greenness of the vine twined itself around the bleeding body and crucified limbs of the Savior. Italian music, even in its sacred and funereal forms, likes to resemble that Cross; and . . . along the roads of their country it will always please the music-makers of Italy to see how life embraces death with a dreadful sweetness.

Once again, the music of Verdi's *Requiem* has not forgotten or even attenuated the awfulness of death. It has taken nothing from the sombre crown of the queen of terrors.

When the *Requiem* Mass reached Paris on its tour, one of the many who heard it was a young American girl named Blanche Roosevelt, who was studying singing there and also doing special correspondence for the Chicago *Times* (later included in a book, one of several by her). After sending her Chicago employers a long and enthusiastic description of her impressions of Verdi's venture into church music she proved herself a good reporter by writing to the composer—again much in the headlines—requesting an interview.

Having received an invitation to come and see him (*"il mio Verdi"* was obviously in anything but a bearish temper, though in Paris) Miss Blanche Roosevelt turned up on the appointed day at the Hotel de Bade, where Verdi was staying. She was accompanied by her mother—for those were the days (remoter from us, in a way, than 1492) when young girls traveled around with chaperones, and when chaperones were looked upon as indispensable armor and not as prehistoric monsters.

They found Giuseppe Verdi at breakfast in the drawing room of his hotel suite. At once Blanche Roosevelt started to accumulate personal impressions for transmission to the Chicago of 1875. She wrote:

His personal appearance is not striking; he is small, very broad-shouldered, with a full, generous chest and well-built body. He has large, laughing gray eyes, that flash and change color every instant. The face is strong and shows very few lines for a man of his years. The features are large, the cheek bones high and the lower part of the jaw rather sunken. The chin and side of the face are covered with a short heavy beard, once black, but now slightly mixed with gray. The mouth is large and pleasant, but it is almost totally concealed by a dark moustache which gives the face a very young look. The forehead is very broad and high. . . . The eyebrows are heavy, and also gray and black.

The hair is very long, lying lightly on the forehead; it also is slightly mixed with gray. There are a wonderful firmness and hidden strength in Verdi's countenance, which makes me think of a picture I once saw of Samson.

In one way I was disappointed in his looks: he has the air and figure of anything but an ideal composer. . . . He has the frank social manner of an ordinary individual. . . . I cannot say he lacks dignity. There was an absence of self-consciousness in his bearing, and such a happy, gracious smile on his face that I was charmed. . . .*

---

* Macchetta, Blanche Roosevelt Tucker, *Verdi: Milan and "Othello."* London, Ward & Downey, 1887.

After the young girl and her mother had seated themselves, at Verdi's courteous request, he turned to them and said:

"I haven't taken my coffee yet. Perhaps you will also have a cup. You know, one can always drink coffee in Paris."

Then he asked his young visitor:

"How do you like Paris?"

"Most beautiful city in the world."

"Yes," agreed Verdi. "It is too beautiful. My time is always wasted here. I do nothing. It is far too beautiful for anything but pleasure.

"I never could compose here. I am very fond of city life, but I am more fond of the country—of agriculture, roaming about the fields, through lone forests, where you can be quiet and admire nature with all its many beauties, undisturbed.

"I do all my writing in the country; there, somehow, everything comes to me all at once, quite without effort. And I am contented."

"But," interrupted Miss Roosevelt, "you are going soon to London. How do you like that great city?"

Verdi groaned.

"Don't mention it!" he said. "It is as much too sad as Paris is too gay. I think that, were I to live there three weeks, I should die."

He stirred his coffee vigorously.

"London is a sad, dreary place at all times."

Having learned that Miss Roosevelt was acquainted with Madame Viardot, a famous singer of other days then living in Paris, the composer told this story about himself and her:

"During one of my first visits to Paris, when *Il Trovatore* was to be given at the Théâtre Italien, Madame Alboni was suddenly taken ill. As she was billed to sing the next day I was in despair. I happened to think of Madame Pauline Viardot and I rushed off at once to see her and beg her to undertake the part [Azucena].

"I found her in her music room, at the piano, and I said:

" 'You *must* sing the part—for me. Madame Alboni is ill.'

" '*Il Trovatore!*' screamed Madame Viardot. 'Impossible! I have never even seen the score. And I am very busy.'

" 'Let's look it over,' said I, soothingly.

"That same day, having learned the part in a few hours, she sang it after one rehearsal—superbly."

When his American visitor remarked that some day (she was then about 22) she would sing *Trovatore* for him, he observed:

"Do not be in a hurry. Americans are so ambitious."

"Signor Verdi, when are you going to America?"

"Now don't mention that! I hate the water. And one is so long at sea. Besides, I am getting old now [he was 60]. I must rest. I shall give up composing and traveling. I think that the *Requiem* Mass will be my last work."

"Please don't say that. Never give up writing music."

"But suppose I am tired. Don't you really think that I ought to stop now after so much . . ." (He left the word unsaid, indicating with one slender finger a pile of music near the piano.)

"No, I don't!" exclaimed Miss Blanche Roosevelt. "You are not a bit old. And you look as if you did not mean what you say. Isn't it true that you love composing and will never give it up?"

Verdi bestowed on her a thoughtful smile. Then he remarked, with a tiny French shrug of his shoulders:

"*Que voulez-vous?* I suppose you are right. I am like the others. . . ."

All the while the three of them—Verdi, Miss Roosevelt and her mother-chaperone—had been sitting around the table in the composer's drawing room at the Hotel de Bade, in pleasant, relaxed sociability. And all the while Verdi had been taking little sips from his coffee cup. Finishing it, he pushed cup and tray to one side.

His two guests stood up. Verdi insisted that there was no need for hurry. Then, smiling at mother and daughter—particularly, one may suspect, at daughter—he asked them to come back to see him at any time.

Mother and daughter said their farewells; in another moment they were outside his hotel, on the boulevards. And Miss Roosevelt, turning to her mother, remarked:

"He's a dear!"

VII

MIRACLE

TWENTY-NINE

O N CHRISTMAS EVE in each of a number of successive years in the late 1870's and early 1880's, Giulio Ricordi, head of the famous Ricordi music-publishing firm in Milan to whose universal fame and financial prosperity Giuseppe Verdi had through four decades made mighty contribution (as the firm had to his) used to send to the renowned composer at his winter quarters in Genoa a big cake surmounted by the figure of a little man made of chocolate. Seemingly this present was merely a token of the sincere amity felt by the sender for the recipient. But it had another significance, a very special one.

Supposedly representing Shakespeare's Moor of Venice it was a challenging hint, insistently repeated, that Ricordi, as well as other friends of Verdi, thought it high time for him to turn into reality a rumor, persistent in and out of Italy, that he had decided at last to break his long, self-imposed silence in the operatic field by composing yet another opera— none, it will be recalled, had come from him since *Aïda* in 1871—and that the new work would be based on one of the most celebrated of Shakespearean tragedies, *Othello*.

Ricordi and those other friends of Verdi had long wished ardently that the Grand Old Man would some day set *Othello* to music worthy of the renowned English genius who had created it, the playwright whom Verdi called "the greatest authority on the heart of man." They spoke of their pro-*Othello* propaganda activities as *il projetto di cioccolata*, which, freely translated, means "Operation Chocolate." They

239

hoped that, though long past sixty, Giuseppe Verdi would delight and astound the world by setting *Othello* to music surpassing anything achieved by him so far.

Verdi had often thought about *Othello*—and he had often talked about composing music for it. But nothing concrete had come from thought or talk. Invariably doubts would grip him. One deterring reflection was that, many years before, the great Rossini had tackled the subject. Today, Rossini's *Otello* is almost forgotten. Even in the 1880's it had slipped people's memories. But—Rossini was Rossini. His fame was so immense that Verdi suspected that his presenting another *Otello* might be taken as an impudent challenge to one of Italy's foremost demigods of music.

Always the character of Iago in Shakespeare's drama had fascinated Verdi, so much so that he thought of calling the opera he had in mind, if he ever got around to composing it, not *Otello* but *Iago*. But he soon rejected that idea. For it occurred to him that the substitution of the name of Shakespeare's villain might be taken as a subterfuge on his part to deflect the thoughts of operagoers from the fact that he was impinging on Rossini's domain. And, true to his inner self, he was shocked at such a possibility.

"I prefer," he told Giulio Ricordi, "to have people say, 'He wished to fight a giant and was crushed by him,' than to have them think that I hid behind Iago."

And there was another deterrent:

"Heaven forbid," the old composer would exclaim, "that the operatic public should ever say to me: 'Enough!' " At times, in moments of pessimism, feeling the twinges of advancing age, he would remark: "I am too old. The children of old men are often weak, anemic, rickety." The years remaining to him, he was sure, could not possibly bring him a renewal of youth. (They did, though.)

He had fits of depression. The course of Italian politics

angered him. No governmental set-up pleased him. To his friend the painter Morelli, he wrote: "I feel restless, irritated, bad-tempered. I don't know why."

Morelli wrote back: "When I feel that I cannot work any longer I hum 'Vergine degli angeli' [from Verdi's Forza del Destino]. That makes me feel all right again. It makes me see colors—that song is as expressive as a painting."

But the implied compliment to the composer of the song left Verdi cold. He wrote in reply: "The notes of that song are one thing and I am another. Why should I care if you think about 'Vergine degli angeli?' "

"Health, health!" he groaned in another letter, this time to the Countess Maffei. "Years begin to become too many and I think that life is the stupidest thing, and, worse still, that it is useless. What does one do? What has one done? What will one do? The answer is most humiliating and sad: 'Nothing,' Good-bye, my dear Clarina. Let us avoid and push away such thoughts as long as we can. . . . Friendship still remains."

And he asked the same lady: "Why should I finish Otello? Why? And what then? One is born, one wears away one's health, one reaches the days of aches and ailments, and, after that—Amen."

He was in a bad way.

His world was changing before his eyes. One by one his friends were dropping off. And, with the disappearance forever of each one of them, he felt sadder, lonelier. Not, in the usual sense of the words, gregarious or superficially friendly, he prized highly the chosen few, men and women, to whom he opened up; and they, in turn, prized the friendship that he gave to them, which they knew well was not, as with individuals more accessible, a mere scattering of small change.

One of the most prized among them, the Countess Maffei, died in 1883, when Verdi was seventy years old. Ever since the days of *Nabucco*, forty years back in the past, she and he had been true comrades. Through all those years, ever since she had persuaded him, a bearish young individual, to come to her receptions in Milan, they had often met, and, when separated, exchanged letters. She was lavish with counsel and sympathy and understanding, and his letters to her were remarkable in that he sometimes made them the vehicles of most un-Verdian frankness and bared in them an inner self almost always kept obstinately locked up.

He was at her bedside when she died. So was Giuseppina. For a long time the Maffeis, husband and wife, had formed with the Verdis a quartet cemented together by deep esteem and compatibility and mutual affection.

There have been hints that the bonds uniting Giuseppe Verdi and the Countess Maffei were more than friendship. And the hinters have devoted time and trouble to proving their contentions. But, in their delvings into the relations of the composer and the Countess, as in other delvings into the lives of other women, picked out hopefully as possible heroines of extra-marital affairs with Verdi, hard facts, like the big fish of amateur fishermen's yarns, have shown a striking propensity to elude their nets. However, they can console themselves with the thought that they did their best.

In 1883, Richard Wagner died. Not that he and Verdi were friends. Indeed, the great German almost ignored the great Italian all through his life; and the latter was not a man to seek to break down anybody else's indifference or hostility.

Wagner and Verdi were born in the same year. Both had won shining success; both had encountered furious opposition. Both had been made into symbols of irreconcilable antagonism in music. And both knew well that their beliefs and methods in that art were beyond reconciliation.

Again writing to Giulio Ricordi, after he had read the

announcement of Wagner's death (it had occurred in Venice, physically near the Italian from whom Wagner was otherwise so far) Verdi said: "Sad, sad, sad. When I read the news yesterday I can truthfully say that I was overwhelmed. There is nothing I can say. A great personality has gone from our midst. His is a name that will never be forgotten in the history of music."

When sunk in doubts as to himself, he felt that life was no longer what it had been in those earlier epochs of his opera-making, of his ceaseless, ever re-invigorated dreaming and questing, when the failure of one opera could be dismissed with a shrug and a confident turning to the fashioning of another that might be, that *must* be, a success.

But now things were different. He could take no chances. He stood on his Everest (at least, he *thought* he was standing there). On that highest peak he must stay. Enthroned, acclaimed, fulfilled—so must the world remember him after his death. Return to the old round of trial and error? Impossible! Unthinkable! All very well, that, for youth, with the making of a reputation ahead of it—but, for an old man with all but the dregs of life behind him—suicidal!

In such a mood—and it recurred often after *Aïda*—he would impatiently brush aside dreams of more greatness, greater greatness, thus joining the many in many lands who were lugubriously chanting: "Verdi is through!"—just as he had impatiently brushed aside Temistocle Solera's tempting libretto for *Nabucco* four decades before. And, each time he sank into that state of mind, the Muse of Music would smile at him again, and beckon him onward and upward, as she had in those bright yesterdays, and he would hear again, intoned by siren voices in dreamland:

> *Va, pensiero,*
> *Sull' ali dorate . . .*

and again his blood flowed faster and warmer at the sound of that trumpet call of his youth, and he felt anew the quiver of artistic creation and his dreams sang again. Yes, there he was, musing, impelled by the youthfulness which, in this miracle man of music, was the principal ingredient of his old age—listening, rapt, forgetful of all else—

Go, thought, on wings of gold . . .

It was to encourage such musings on his past for the advantaging of his future, to weaken the attacks of sadness and lack of confidence which came to him after they had passed, that Giulio Ricordi and his fellow-conspirators dispatched to Giuseppe Verdi every year that little brown figure of the Moor of Venice perched on that big Christmas cake. And to their persistence the world owes an immense, unrepayable debt.

Among those hand in glove with Ricordi in Operation Chocolate was Franco Faccio, by now an orchestra leader of steadily rising fame—and, as one would suspect, Giuseppina —in the background, hovering, listening at the door of Verdi's study at Sant 'Agata, or in Genoa (where the Verdis lived no longer at the Palazzo Sauli but at the far more magnificent Palazzo Doria) for musical sounds denoting the throes of composition, hoping, hinting, never prodding.

One day, Ricordi and Faccio, after a bout of concentrated conspiracy, went after the old composer as per pre-arrangement, at a luncheon in Milan to which they had craftily bidden him—just an ordinary luncheon, he thought.

"How about that new Shakespearean opera? What news of your plans for it? When are you going to compose the music for it?" This time they caught Verdi fresh from listening to equally insistent siren voices from dreamland.

"Very well! Done! I *will* compose that new opera!"

They were delighted. Pressing their advantage, Ricordi and

Faccio played another card which they had long had up their sleeves.

They told Verdi that, now that he had decided to do *Otello* —it has become customary, in speaking of the penultimate Verdi opera, to spell its title that way, in order to differentiate it from its parent, Shakespeare's *Othello*—a meeting must be arranged as soon as possible with a certain individual whose help they deemed indispensable in Operation Chocolate.

"Why?" inquired Verdi.

"Because he alone can provide you with the perfect libretto for *Otello*."

"Who is he?"

"Arrigo Boïto."

"All right. Get hold of him."

And thus the stage was set at last for one of the most fruitful collaborations in the history of music.

Arrigo Boïto was born at Padua in Northern Italy in 1842— thus he was 29 years younger than Giuseppe Verdi. His father was an Italian miniature painter, his mother a Polish Countess. The father having abandoned his wife and their two little sons soon after his marriage, the mother courageously did her best to get them educated; and, in 1854, she procured the admission of Arrigo to that Milan Conservatory which many years before had rejected Giuseppe Verdi. Among Arrigo's fellow-students there was Franco Faccio, one of the conspirators at the momentous luncheon at which Operation Chocolate came to a head.

In 1860 the two lads collaborated on a musical work which won them a traveling scholarship. Rushing off to Paris they met Verdi, Victor Hugo, Rossini and Berlioz; and the meeting with Verdi was doubtless responsible for the writing by young Boïto of the words of that *Hymn of the Nations,* al-

ready mentioned, for which Verdi provided the Italian section
of the music. When his funds from the scholarship ran out,
Arrigo Boïto returned to Milan and busied himself with writing and composing. He completed the score of an opera, but,
influenced by the self-criticism which eventually became a
dominant trait in him, he destroyed it, and turned over to
the composer-conductor Luigi Mancinelli the libretto which
he had written for it, on which Mancinelli based his opera
Ero e Leandro.

Boïto soon became a revolutionary reformer both in writing and composing. One piece of musical criticism by him
plunged him into a duel, the result of which caused him to
carry his arm in a sling for quite a while. Work on his opera
Mefistofele was interrupted in 1866 by his joining Garibaldi's
volunteers, with whom he marched into *Italia irredenta*.

In 1868, *Mefistofele*, words and music by Boïto, was produced at La Scala. Before the production violent pro-Boïto
and anti-Boïto factions among the Milanese turned the performance into a wild riot, which, continued furiously in the
streets adjacent to the theater, brought police intervention
and the cancellation by the Chief of Police of further performances of the opera. Produced some years later it was a
success. In New York the great Russian basso Chaliapin did a
memorable job in the star rôle, in which he had already dis-
tinguished himself in Europe.

Boïto wrote and composed still another opera, *Nerone*
(Nero) but self-criticism prevented him from allowing its production during his life-time. After his death in 1918, Arturo
Toscanini, having revised the score, conducted the first performance of the work at La Scala in 1926, amid immense interest all over the musical and literary world. But it failed to
command more than respect from critics and public.

Years before the luncheon shared with Ricordi, Faccio and
Verdi, Arrigo Boïto had disrespectfully tried his hand at turn-

ing *"La donna è mobile"* into a polka. This prank must have
come to Verdi's notice and by no effort of imagination can I
picture him as liking it. Boïto also wrote a bitter diatribe inspired by the unsatisfactory state into which, as he saw it,
Italian opera had fallen, expressing a yearning for the advent
of a composer who should restore the glory of its altar "sullied
like the wall of a brothel." Verdi promptly assumed that this
thrust applied partly to him.

"If I am included," he wrote to Ricordi, "among those
who, as Boïto says, have sullied that altar, let him clean it,
and I shall be the first to light a candle in his honor."

Yet not even this incident definitely alienated the two from
each other. Following the Ricordi-Faccio-Verdi luncheon the
suggested meeting between Verdi and Boïto was brought
about. And so excellently did the two men get along, so
speedily and thoroughly did each probe into the other's ways
of thinking that, within a few weeks, Boïto, who, like Verdi,
had an immense admiration for Shakespeare, submitted to the
composer a complete sketch of his idea for an *Otello* libretto.
And Verdi, he who had so often ruthlessly manhandled the
work of other librettists, found scarcely a flaw in it. If Francesco Piave was listening at some keyhole of the other world
affording a chance to see and hear what was going on in the
world he had left, he must have fallen flat on his face in a
celestial (or infernal) fit.

Still, however, the matter was not definitely settled. Verdi
continued to "stall." But the creative impulse, which was
soon to kick all obstacles out of the way and give *Otello* to
the world, was no longer to be denied. In default of *Otello*, it
led Verdi, in 1879, to turn again to the revision of an opera,
Simon Boccanegra, which, produced without real success, as
I have noted, back in 1857, still stood high in its composer's
affections. Something, he felt, could be done with it. And
here, now, was Arrigo Boïto, to help him do it.

So the two, digging into poor Piave's libretto for the original *Simon Boccanegra*, proceeded to try to pump life into it. Verdi tinkered with this, re-arranged that. Indeed, to crown his repair work, he wrote into the original version the music for an entire new scene, words by Boïto—and that music included some of the best in the whole revamped opera. Meanwhile, in other sections of the original, Boïto administered first aid—and much more—to Piave's text.

One of the most striking defects of the Piave libretto, as Francis Toye caustically puts it, is that "everybody is ignorant of the identity of everybody else and the principal female character even of her own." Such a picture puzzle was enough to baffle anybody. But Arrigo Boïto stuck to his task. Now and then, however, he got restive. Obviously eager to get on with the far more alluring Operation Chocolate, he would grumble to Verdi occasionally about the hopelessness of trying to make over *Simon Boccanegra* into something satisfying. And Verdi would thus admonish him:

"You, with *Otello* in your mind, are aiming at a perfection which is here unattainable. I do not aim so high. I admit that the table is shaky, but by repairing a leg or two I think it can be made to stand up."

Eventually the revised *Simon Boccanegra* was produced in Milan March 24, 1881. The changes were hailed as marked improvements. Yet again it failed to "go over." Verdi was cruelly disappointed.

Like Boïto's *Mefistofele*, *Simon Boccanegra* is still with us. And it still reaps admiration from parts of its audiences. Recently it was revived at New York's Met with flattering results. But, by and large, it remains one of those grand operas to which, though it undoubtedly contains stretches of great merit, genuine success is denied by the operagoing public.

THIRTY

REE of *Boccanegra,* Verdi and Boïto now turned in earnest
to *Otello.* But, at the very beginning of their resumption
of joint work on it, their collaboration almost came to grief.

At a dinner, Boïto, after mentioning how well the creation
of the new opera was progressing, added that he wished that
the music for it, gradually coming into being, was his own.
Verdi, whose blow-hot-blow-cold attitude as to whether he
would ever finish another operatic score had made him very
touchy, promptly got the idea that what his collaborator
meant was that he, Verdi, was incapable at his age of undertak-
ing successfully such a tremendous task as composing the music
for *Otello,* which ought to be the work of a younger man—
i.e., Boïto himself. In his pique he offered to return to his
co-worker the preliminary sketches for the libretto, and leave
the younger man free to set *Otello* to music of his own.

Boïto, by this time a fervent worshiper at the Verdian
shrine, had no difficulty in smoothing the old man's ruffled
feathers. He wrote to the offended maestro:

> Only you can do the music for *Otello.* All the operas com-
> posed by you affirm that truth. If I have been able to grasp in-
> tuitively the great possibilities in transforming Shakespeare's
> tragedy into music—and if I have succeeded in proving this in my
> libretto—it is because I have assimilated the point of view of
> Verdian art—because, in writing my verses, I have felt as you
> would have felt in expressing them in that other language, a
> thousand times more intimate and powerful, the language of
> sound.

That did the trick. Verdi emerged from his huff. The two
went back to their collaboration. And, day by day, the high

mutual regard of Giuseppe Verdi and Arrigo Boïto, thanks
largely to their reverent, subtly understanding grasp of William Shakespeare, grew in depth and solidity and sincerity.
They began spending several hours daily in close conference,
in Milan sometimes, but mostly at Sant' Agata and in Genoa.

In Genoa Giuseppe Verdi was a landmark. The Genoese
were immensely proud of the fact that he had elected to
spend much of each year in their city, and, to show how much
they liked having him around, they used to follow him in
squads wherever he went and stand outside shops into which
he had gone to make purchases, waiting for him to come out,
in order to follow him around some more.

Always without frills or false pride, always feeling himself
a man of the people, Verdi, almost to the end of his long life,
used to go shopping on foot in Genoa; and he thought nothing of carrying home fish and vegetables and other provender
in a basket slung over his shoulder. One day, a fish dealer,
from whom he was making a purchase, remarked that, in his
youth, he had been an opera singer and had once sung the
part of the King of Egypt in *Aïda*.

"Well," remarked the composer of that opera, "I'll bet
you made less money when you wore the crown of Ancient
Egypt on your head than you're going to make from that mess
of fish you're selling me."

One of the many who, as a callow, hero-worshiping youth,
followed Verdi on the street in Genoa was Giulio Gatti-
Casazza, long manager of New York's Metropolitan Opera
House. In later years, he told the great composer how he had
dogged his footsteps. Verdi glowered at him.

"You ought to be ashamed of yourself!" he chided. "At
that age you should not have been following *me*—you should
have been following a pretty Genoese girl."

One night Verdi went to the theater in Genoa with some

friends to see a droll comedian called Ferravilla, who was
making a big local hit. At one point in a comic sketch the
text called for highly laudatory mention of several Italian
composers—Rossini, Bellini, Donizetti. After naming them,
the comedian, turning toward the box in which Verdi was
seated, interpolated: "And Verdi, of course—Peppino, our
dear Peppino."

The house roared with joy. All the spectators stood up,
cheering at the top of their lungs, looking straight at the
great composer. At first he was a bit upset. As always, he had
no desire to strut in the limelight. But, pulling himself together, he bowed his thanks to the audience. Then, yielding
to a sudden and by no means typical impulse, he left the box,
hurried behind the scenes, walked out on the stage, to the
stupefaction of actors and spectators, and, stepping up with
outstretched hand to the comedian, said: "Signor Ferravilla,
Peppino has come to thank you." The ovation that followed
eclipsed the one that had gone before.

That good friend of the Verdis, De Amicis, on a visit to
Sant' Agata, was sitting chatting with Giuseppina in one
room while Verdi and Boïto were manufacturing *Otello* in
another. Suddenly, from the latter, came a succession of piti-
ful cries and savage howls. De Amicis looked up in alarm.
Giuseppina laid a quieting arm on his sleeve.

"Don't worry," she told him. "All that noise simply means
that the ferocious insults of Otello, the anguished protests of
Desdemona and the wicked suggestions of Iago have all
had a collision!"

The arduous duties of housekeeping never made a dent in
Giuseppina's sense of humor. Once, returning, shaking with
laughter, from the kitchen of Sant' Agata to the living room,
where her husband was sitting with a group of guests, she
informed them all:

"You know that new chef of ours? Of all the pompous,

haughty individuals! Just now I walked in on him while he was busy cooking and he never so much as turned around. I didn't like that.

" 'Why don't you say good morning to me?' I inquired coldly.

"Dropping his pots and pans he stood facing me for a moment. Then he replied, all hauteur and pomposity:

" 'Signora, when an officer is on duty he doesn't salute!' "

Famous singers wrote to Verdi beseeching him to include them in the cast of the new opera. He refused to encourage them, even though one of them was the Frenchman Victor Maurel, just about the best dramatic baritone of that era. Maurel had set his heart on being the Iago of the original *Otello* cast. But Verdi refused to commit himself; all his life he hated making promises that he might not be able to fulfill.

To one singer and one only would he vouchsafe anything approaching definiteness. That fortunate songbird was the famous Francesco Tamagno, foremost Italian *tenore robusto* of the 1880's. Tamagno, who happened to be in Spain, was told ("And don't you dare breathe a word, Francesco, to anybody!") to stop off unostentatiously in Genoa on his return for a secret conference with Verdi and Boïto.

Verdi had decided that Tamagno *must* be the first Otello. Unfortunately, the great tenor had defects: for example, he was so slow in learning a part, at grasping its inner meaning (and Verdi and Boïto were stuffing their *Otello*-out-of-*Othello* to the bursting-point with inner meaning) that everything had to be carefully explained to him over and over again. But, once grasped, the explanation stuck. And Tamagno's magnificent voice did the rest.

He was the opposite of Victor Maurel. In a moment, that gifted Frenchman would strike to the core of a rôle, understand it, master it, enact it to perfection. Though Verdi had

refused to commit himself at first regarding Maurel he probably had him in mind for Iago from the beginning.

So Maurel was chosen to portray that highly reprehensible
Shakespearean individual. And what a singularly happy choice
that was!

Otello was discussed in voluble excitement all over Milan
—all over Italy—all over the world. But extremely few of the
multitudinous discussers really knew what they were talking
about. Composer and librettist and everybody else in the
secret had been going around for weeks like so many Sphinxes
in trousers (or skirts), deaf to wheedlings from reporters, musicians, singers, critics, congenital victims of curiosity, etc., etc.

One day word came from Sant' Agata that Verdi would
like to have Giulio Ricordi come to see him there. Eager,
expectant, excited, the publisher hurried away from Milan.
Verdi met him with the laconic announcement:

"It's finished."

Piloting the visitor to his workroom, he sat down at the
piano and played excerpt after excerpt from *Otello*. Verdi
was a good run-of-the-mill pianist, who knew how to make
the keys express his musical ideas.

Ricordi was overwhelmed. He was dazed, snatched out of
this world. Words would not come to his lips. He wept. What
surged through him was not wishful thinking, not unreflecting hero-worship, not insincere, pumped-up admiration, not
vulgar thought of gain for himself and his firm. No!

Giuseppe Verdi had done it again! And he had done it as
he had never done it before—done it as no other Italian creator of opera had ever done it.

At the end of the revelation, the music-publisher, still
thrilled and speechless, noticed Giuseppina, who had been
hovering, as was her habit, just outside the study. Her cheeks,
too, were wet. With tear-stained eyes and shaking voice, she
looked up into Ricordi's face:

"Giulio! Isn't it true? *È ancora bravo il mio Verdi.*"

Meanwhile Milan was *Otello*-mad. Speculators ran up prices
for seats at the La Scala opening to unheard-of peaks. Rumors
were rampant:

"Romilda Pantaleoni [Desdemona] gets 15,000 lire," one
Milanese would tell another, only to have the other counter:

"Pooh! Someone told me—someone, mind you, on the in-
side—a woman related to the sister of the wife of one of the
Ricordis—that she's getting 30,000. Well, let's say, 20,000.
Women exaggerate so."

Boxes were quoted at figures representing to most Italians
small fortunes. Yet they were gobbled up by the dozen.

At the very start Verdi issued a Draconian decree: "No
outsiders at rehearsal!" And he enforced his will on all the
others associated with him, despite grumblings loud and long
right up to and including the dress rehearsal. Dark secrecy
surrounded La Scala for weeks. One local comic journal came
out with a cartoon showing Verdi, Boïto and the Moor of
Venice all huddled together inside a closely-guarded glass
case.

Verdi directed rehearsals. Having assembled the singers on
La Scala's stage, he asked Boïto to read them the whole libretto of *Otello*. "It will do you good," he informed them.

For his convenience, a small flight of steps had been installed leading from the stage to the orchestra pit, to enable
the spry old fellow to run up and down it whenever he had
something special to say to actors or musicians.

At one rehearsal, when he himself was conducting, he suddenly signaled the orchestra to stop playing, and inquired
icily:

"Who is playing so softly that I can't hear him at all?"

An embarrassed 19-year-old 'cellist owned the soft im-
peachment.

"But, maestro," he explained, "the passage is marked *ppp* [usually, on musical scores, the indication for even the least loud notes is *pp*].

Verdi was silent a moment. Then he said:

"You're right. I put in that *ppp* to guide musicians not intelligent enough to realize how very softly that passage ought to be played. If I had put in *pp* they would have played it too loud. You're different. You're intelligent."

Possibly that incident marked the beginning of the veneration felt to this day, nearly seventy years later, by that 'cellist —Arturo Toscanini.

One day Tamagno-Otello failed to show up for rehearsal— he had a cold (he said). So the rôle of the enamored Moor at the end of the first act was played by an obliging volunteer without the slightest bit of previous experience—Giulio Ricordi—and afterward by another with exactly the same qualifications—Giuseppe Verdi.

The composer told the prima donna, Romilda Pantaleoni, acting Desdemona, that he didn't like the way she embraced the man supposed to be her adored adorer (probably La Pantaleoni felt awed at suddenly finding herself in the arms of the most celebrated of Italian composers). Fed up with her hesitations, Verdi abruptly clasped her in a regular bear-hug, which almost squeezed the breath out of her body; and, releasing her with equal abruptness, exclaimed:

"*That* is the way one embraces!"

After Tamagno had returned to rehearsals, Verdi again objected one day to his acting of the final death scene.

"You don't die right," he complained. And he made the big tenor "die" ten times in rapid succession before he told him:

"That's enough for today. You're tired."

But, next day, Tamagno still did not die correctly—according to Verdi. So the composer took over the part of Otello

himself, pretended most realistically to stab himself beside
the bed of Desdemona (whom he was supposed to have
murdered a few minutes before), and capped his performance
by falling flat on his back and rolling down the three steps
from the raised platform on which the bed was placed to the
floor of the stage, where he lay "dead." The entire company
rushed toward him with exclamations of fright and horror.
They thought he had broken his neck. But, picking himself
up with complete nonchalance, he told Tamagno:

"That's the way it's done. Now *you* do it."

Outside the portals of La Scala—so inexorably barred to the
world and his wife during rehearsals—Milan continued to
seethe with anticipation and impatience. And when an Italian city seethes it seethes.

Foreigners gathered in swarms. Hotels were packed from
lobby to garret. In the Galleria, the city's renowned glass-
roofed central thoroughfare, eminent representatives of the
ungentle art of music criticism—British, French, German,
Austrian, American, Scandinavian—exchanged over their Ver-
mouths information, usually inaccurate, allegedly received
straight from behind the scenes.

Milan seemed bereft of interest in all things except *Otello*.
Outside La Scala hundreds of persons stood as if struck to
stone. They just stood. And stood. And stood. Apparently
they had forgotten what to do in order to go away. Very soon,
they knew, the doors of the famous theater would be opened
to admit *Otello's* first audience, those pets of fortune, privi-
leged to pass on the opening night into that hallowed place,
to see and hear the most thought-about, dreamed-about,
guessed-about *première* that had burst on Europe for decades.

Yes, soon those portals would swing wide. . . .

In a week . . .

In three days . . .

Day after tomorrow . . .
Tomorrow . . .
In a few hours . . .

THIRTY-ONE

S HE WAS right there, right on the spot, that American girl
Blanche Roosevelt, who, twelve years before, as a student
of singing and fledgling foreign correspondent in Paris, had
interviewed Giuseppe Verdi over his morning coffee, and,
with bubbling excitement, described her impressions of the
great man to readers of the Chicago *Times*—right there, in
Milan, on the day of the world *première* of Verdi's stento-
rianly heralded, feverishly awaited *Otello*—right on the spot,
itching to tell all about it, this time in a letter to a friend, of
which I give scattered excerpts below, filled with the spirit
of youth alive in that young American, and with the spirit
of madness, of irrepressible, uninhibited hero-worship rampant in the musical capital of Italy—that city, which Blanche
Roosevelt, in her letter, calls, with most felicitous appropriate-
ness to that day of days, not "Milan" but "Otellopolis"—

Otellopolis, February 5th, 1887—
As early as five in the morning everyone was astir. When
Giannetta brought me breakfast she informed me that she had
already been to La Scala. Any number of ladies in the hotel were
having their hair dressed at that unearthly hour. These ladies will
sit all day with bejeweled and elaborately dressed pates and not
dare to lie down or sit back for fear of ruining their puffs, etc.

Before noon I was on the streets. Streets? There were no streets.
Had not the blocks of houses been divided into streets archi-
tecturally everything would have been run together, like honey,
with human beings.

I met Madame M. . . . "Iago's wig fits so badly that not even glue will stick it onto his head. He simply won't sing if . . ."

I turned to look at the square (the Piazza del Duomo). It was alive . . . Men, women and children. Hand organs pealing forth Verdi tunes. *Ernani. Trovatore.* Balconies freighted with excited humanity. Italian-terraced roofs, where people were eating and drinking and shouting. The place was literally black with human forms.

You know, Italian women are fond of bright raiment. They wear hats that would shame a hothouse for brilliancy and their necks are hung with gewgaws and their bodices glow like Oriental chasubles. They looked so happy. Laughing eyes. Glittering teeth. Bodies swaying to the pantomime of anticipated pleasure. And their spirits were so contagious that they seemed to charge the crowd with electricity.

The Piazza della Scala was a sight to see! The cries of *"Viva Verdi! Viva Verdi!"* were so deafening that I longed for cotton wool in my ears. Had he been there he certainly would have been torn to pieces!

We all stood staring at the old theatre. It was the dead of winter—but an Italian doesn't feel cold on an occasion like this. If there had been a change of programme you could not have found a person in Milan courageous enough to put up a notice of the change.

At last, after dinner (I didn't dine, I swallowed food) we started for the theatre. The carriage had to be sent off long before we reached the door. The horses could not make their way through the crowd. I expected my dress would be in rags.

La Scala has never held such an audience. Every seat was occupied. The light murmur of expectant voices issuing from three thousand throats was like night sounds in an enchanted forest. Only in Italy could such a scene take place—for here pride of birth and rank and position give way before the homage which the land of song sows in perpetual laurel at the feet of its great composers.

From pit to dome the immense auditorium was one mass of eager faces, sparkling eyes, brilliant dresses and splendid jewels.

The Italian Court was a rainbow of colors, and Queen Margherita's
ladies of honor looked like a hothouse bouquet of rarest exotics.
The first and second tiers of boxes were so packed with the
Milanese high-bred women, so covered with dazzling jewels and
filmy laces that the house seemed spanned with a river of light
up, up, up to where the last gallery was lost in a dainty cornice
of gold.

The gleam of diamond tiara and corsage bouquet shot oblong
rays on the black-coated background, while the electric lights,
imprisoned in their dead-white globes, shed an unearthly radiance
over the auditorium that made us all look like spectres uprising
from some dead-and-gone rout. . . .

The theatre was packed with officers, certainly the handsomest
men in the world—gorgeous in their varied and brilliant uniforms:
staff officers in full dress and scarred veterans with their whole
record in speaking breast-decorations.

And the women! At the play, they put women of every other
nation in the shade. They are a special embellishment, a part of
the gorgeousness, of the glitter of the performance. They know
just how to dress, just what jewels to wear, how to sit, how to
stand, how to listen at the right moment, and look bored at the
right moment.

But—La Scala's real public is in the upper tiers and pit. There
all the old theatregoers were present, who never miss a first night.

They never need programmes, they know the names of every
living artist. They have heard all the great singers since Catalani
and Pasta, have seen all the dancers since Taglioni. They have
supped with Bellini after success and failure. They know La Scala
and everything pertaining to it by heart. They come to sit in
judgment, to applaud or hiss as they honestly feel, to lend their
presence to the event, to what is to them the entire world.

They have not dined—perhaps not even breakfasted. Their
pockets are full of chestnuts. They were at the theatre hours before the opening of the doors, waiting for a chance to rush pell-
mell to the roof gallery. Many among them have hardly tasted
food for a week; the body may be starved but never the soul. They

consider no sacrifice too great that will enable them to figure at a first night at La Scala.

Hair pomaded, moustache waxed, linen spotless, cravat tied in a perfect knot, flower in the buttonhole, gloves of a sickly white, through having been too often to the cleaner's, they sit down, with a friendly wave of the hand to brother-fossils, as much as to say:

"You see, here I am. Do you think *Otello* could go on were I not present?" *

The audience included members of the Italian royal family; Georges Clemenceau, "the Tiger," already well-known in French politics; Matilda Serao, the famous Italian novelist; Luigi Giacosa, noted writer and friend of the Verdis, who some years later was to collaborate on libretti for Puccini operas; Boldini, the fashionable painter of the day (he did a portrait of Verdi); the critics Filippo Filippi of Milan and Ernest Reyer of Paris, still doing music criticism as they had done it sixteen years earlier when both journeyed to Cairo to attend the *première* of *Aïda*; the prominent French critic and author Camille Bellaigue, a good friend of Giuseppe Verdi.

From the very first part of the first scene there was enthusiastic applause, calls for encores—even demands that the principal persons concerned in the production should drop everything they were doing in the way of singing and acting and directing in order to come to the front of the stage and make a bow.

From the start there were loud shouts for Verdi. The popular craving to get a glimpse of him even thus early in the evening was conveyed to him behind the scenes.

"Not now!" he told the conveyers. "I'm too busy." The great composer, in black tail coat and white waistcoat and white tie, was industriously helping to make the storm over

* Macchetta, *op. cit.*

Cyprus more realistic by banging together two big sheets of metal simulating peals of thunder, obligingly lent him by a stage hand.

As the show progressed, the enthusiasm of the huge audience rose to a frenzied climax. After each act there was an immense ovation. Verdi and Boïto were called before the curtain twenty-odd times. At the end of the performance, says one who was there, "hats and handkerchiefs were waved and the house rose in a body. The emotion was unbounded. Many wept."

When Verdi, his wife and Boïto, after the last curtain, got into their carriage to be driven to the composer's hotel, a great crowd, mad with excitement, unharnessed the horses and dragged the vehicle through the streets, yelling wildly all the way.

Admirable, it seems to me, in the quality of his thinking with regard to *Otello* and in his ability to express his thoughts, is the Frenchman Camille Bellaigue, whom Verdi favored with a degree of esteem accorded by him to very few of those devoted to a calling which he was inclined to hold in contempt. From Bellaigue's book on Verdi I have selected these passages about *Otello*:

In his earlier operas, even in *Rigoletto, Trovatore* and *Traviata,* Verdi, so to speak, only emphasized the culminating points. To be sure, he kindled a flame when he did so; like Apollo, he moved from peak to peak. And this made all the more striking the empty spaces between the summits. This emptiness was filled by *Otello* and *Falstaff.*

In them the truth in the music is not satisfied with flashes, violent blows; it illumines everything, makes everything ring with itself. . . . Verdi's music at first, though it had the brightness of gold, had too much directness and rigidity. But gradually it grew more supple, until, finally, the time came when, without losing any of its brilliancy, it became a more flexible instrument, a more delicate one, with which the composer could penetrate to the centre and core of life. And, with that instrument, he cut through to life's innermost fibres.

Otello's second act consists merely of two long scenes between Otello and Iago, but, in these scenes, a complete musical psychology is developed to which Verdi had never risen before. . . . In that second act two opposed forces act on each other, one expressed through music that is veiled, the other through music in delirium. . . . Such a scene shows the point of development which the Verdian genius has attained. . . .

There are many examples in *Otello* of how Verdi in his final phase became a two-faced Janus among musicians, with one of his faces looking into the future, the other never turned away from his past.*

"The vitality of *Otello* from the first bar to the last . . . would, if it did not exist, be considered incredible in the work of so old a man," says Francis Toye. He points in admiration to "the amazing skill with which Verdi follows every shade of meaning, every change of mood throughout the drama."

[He extols] the flexibility of the dialogue, with the points continually emphasized in an orchestration that is never superfluous, always true to the psychology of the situation; the harmonic invention, as, for instance, in Iago's famous drinking song, where the chromatics suggest in the most subtle manner the Satanic design underlying what appears to be mere boisterous revelry; the ability with which the various personalities are differentiated in the concerted numbers; the lyrical perfection of the opening of the last act . . . the tenderness of that duet between Othello and Desdemona which remains, perhaps, the most satisfactory interpretation of true love, as distinct from passion or lust, in the annals of opera.

And he concludes: "How could a man of over seventy feel these things so acutely as to translate them with such poign-

* Bellaigue, *op. cit.*

ancy into music? . . . *Otello* is the greatest tragic opera of
Italy; it should rank with *Tristan und Isolde* as one of the
two greatest tragic operas of the world." *

Boïto's libretto also came in for an immense amount of
eulogy. Instant recognition went to its succinctness, to the
deft dovetailing of its various sections, to the unvarying respect and comprehension shown by its author for its inspirer,
Shakespeare; to the excellence of the Italian text in which
he appareled the immortal poetry of the original.

A leading ingredient in Boïto's ability was audacity. In
making his libretto for *Otello* he arrived at an audacious decision: to ignore the entire first act of Shakespeare's tragedy.
Salvaging from that act only a few lines, which he adroitly
introduced into subsequent acts at points where he thought
they would do the most good, the daring poet-composer
started off his libretto with the storm on Cyprus. This cavalier treatment of the great Englishman has shocked some
critics. Boïto, they felt, had committed sacrilege in not following the original construction of the classic tragedy, which
they deemed quite dramatic enough for anybody. (Bernard
Shaw, by the way, once remarked that Shakespeare's *Othello*
was practically a ready-made Italian operatic libretto.) But,
to Boïto, suppression of Shakespeare's opening act was im-
perative for his purposes. He was thinking, he pointed out,
primarily from the point of view of grand opera. Sometimes,
he reasoned, what is meat for a dramatist is poison for a
librettist. So he went right ahead with what he considered
an unavoidable surgical operation, refusing to let anyone get
in the way of his knife.

Also, he dared to do something else to Shakespeare which
aroused shock and anger among critics, particularly Anglo-
Saxons: he inserted into his libretto Iago's "Credo," that cynical avowal of depravity, which is not to be found in Shake-

* Toye, *op. cit.*

speare's *Othello*. Boïto, to be sure, used in it some words put into Iago's mouth by Shakespeare. But that does not change the fact that, to all intents and purposes, the "Credo" is not William Shakespeare but Arrigo Boïto.

In self-justification, the audacious Italian, thinking always in terms of drama-with-music, insisted that, for operatic purposes, Iago's wickedness required more explanation than any afforded by Shakespeare in his original play. Playgoers might be satisfied with what is practically self-starting wickedness, but not operagoers. The dramatist, he felt, could explain Iago's inherent badness with a line here and there, but not the librettist. (It may be appropriate to recall here that several Verdi libretti not by Boïto were, according to their detractors, grievously impaired in their effectiveness by the futile endeavors of their authors to convey to the audience, in casual remarks by the actors, important explanations essential to the understanding of the plot.)

In any event, neither the discarding of Shakespeare's first act in *Othello* nor the insertion of Iago's "Credo" into the Boïto libretto have influenced adversely the well-nigh unanimous judgment on it: that, in this branch of writing for the stage, it is one of the two supreme masterpieces.

Verdi, it is said, felt doubts both as to the advisability of the suppression of Shakespeare's Act I and to the introduction of Iago's "Credo" into the opera. If he did, his doubts handicapped not in the slightest the transcendent excellence of the music made necessary by the twin audacities of his collaborator.

Who, having heard Verdi's setting of the storm that opens *Otello*, can ever forget it?—ever wish to forget it? Who, in retrospection, can ever fail to thrill (and shiver) at the memory of it? Those terrific chords, smashing, without the slightest warning, out of a seething orchestra—that fury of tempest compressed into a few cataclysmal moments—that musical thunderclap—that awesome explosion of the elements, recalling in its savagery Amonasro's elemental outburst when he denounces his daughter Aïda—all of these concentrate into compact vivid musical prophecy the coming portrayal of Iago's villainy and Otello's jealousy and Desdemona's doom.

Verdi's music for Iago's "Credo," heard for the first time on that winter evening in 1887 at La Scala, has ever since proved itself a sure-fire hit with audiences. And, like so many other items in opera that become general favorites, it strikes some of the more captious among the multitudes of admirers of the great opera as a bit too much on the hit-you-between-the-eyes side, as lacking to a certain extent the subtlety of most of the rest of *Otello*. That it is extraordinarily effective and searching in its psychology has been acknowledged far and wide. Many who have heard it in opera houses will surely recall vividly how they were galvanized into a bolt upright position merely by the sinister impact of Verdi's prelude to it, one of the best of those unerringly effective *foreshadowing* pieces of music which he knew so well how to write in order to pave the way for the ensuing aria or duet or whatever he had in mind.

In some other opera Iago's "Credo" would have a far better chance of eclipsing what precedes or follows it. But, pitted against the love duet in Act I of *Otello*—against *"Ora e per sempre addio"*—against Iago's subtle poisoning of the Moor's thoughts in their duet in the second act—against *the entire last act*—the "Credo" simply has too much competition in its path.

Yet, as I set down the above observations, the sinister chords of the prelude to the "Credo," merging in my memory with the equally sinister words sung by the Shakespeare-Boïto-Verdi arch-villain and with the doubly sinister notes with which the composer clothed Iago's brazen avowal of wickedness, I am almost inclined to strike out what I have just written, close to high praise though it is.

But I won't. The composer who created *Otello*, must, in relation to the "Credo," pay the penalty for the excellence of the rest of the opera. The love duet dwarfs the "Credo." And how about the final act from beginning to end? How about the divine sweetness of the "Ave Maria"?—and that abrupt, thrilling, literally hair-raising cry from Desdemona after she has bade a last goodnight to Emilia (as fine a musical touch as is to be found in all Verdi)—and the beautiful and terrible poignancy of the repetition in the murder scene of the main theme of the love duet? And how about "*O tu chi sei si pallida*"—and—and—

No! The "Credo" is *not* in the same class with such outpourings of musical genius.

Yet it is magnificent.

The prince of librettists received the high tributes paid him with incredible modesty and self-effacement. Never did he hint that he felt himself even remotely in the same class as either Shakespeare or Verdi. He constantly took pride in avowing that, compared with the composer, he was no more than a devoted disciple.

"The voluntary servitude that I consecrate to that truly great and noble man," he told Camille Bellaigue, "is, of all the acts of my life, the one of which I am proudest."

The importance of Boïto's libretto to *Otello* is well expressed, it seems to me, in this passage from a recent book on musical matters:

He who goes to *Otello* and listens only to the music misses half the opera's greatness. Here is a perfect fusion of music and libretto, and we must think of it as the creation of two miraculously coalesced talents. It is as plainly by Boïto-Verdi as *The Mikado* is by Gilbert-Sullivan. . . . With a superb sense of what was usable on the operatic stage . . . he [Boïto] took just those

relevant parts of *Othello* and really adapted, not merely translated, them for Verdi's use. . . . Verdi accepted the challenge of
a masterly libretto by mating it to a score luminous with precisely
those qualities that many of his otherwise fine early scores con-
spicuously lack—unfaltering good taste, melodic subtlety, expressive harmonic texture. *Otello* moves on as a relentless continuum.
. . . It has no barrel organ tunes, but is instinct with melody of
true dramatic pertinence." *

Ever since *Otello's* first performance in 1887 it has gained
in favor all over the world. Every day more critics praise it,
more operagoers flock to it, more of them wonder why they
did not flock before.

It has not the elements of sensational popular success possessed by *Rigoletto, Trovatore, Traviata* and *Aïda*. It is music
enthusiastically received from the start by the few, which
commands every day more attention and understanding from
the many. Oliver Herford is said to have remarked that the
Waldorf-Astoria (the old one, at Fifth Avenue and 34th
Street in New York) provided "exclusiveness for the masses."
That quip may be applicable one of these days to Verdi's
Otello.

Today, *Otello* is close to 70 years old. Already traditions
are clustering around it—already there are those who wish it
sung and played just so, in accordance with those traditions;
and others who desire to defy custom by changing its pace,
brushing up its traditional scenery, joggling arbitrary notions
handed down from its beginnings.

Once an American tenor was rehearsing the title rôle in
it for the first time. At a certain point he was directed to walk
without any apparent reason from the front of the stage to
the back.

"Why must I do that?" he inquired.

---

* Wallace Brockway and Herbert Weinstock, *Men of Music*. New York,
Simon & Schuster, 1939.

"Because Tamagno always did it."

"Why did Tamagno do it?"

Nobody could enlighten him.

Some time later he met the great Tamagno in Milan, the city where that famous tenor had sung the title part in *Otello* at the opera's opening performance. The American repeated his question. Tamagno sat with knit brows, seeking to remember. Then, all of a sudden, his brow cleared:

"Ah, yes! Of course! Now I remember! At that point in the opera I knew that, in a very few moments, I had to sing a very high and difficult note. So, just before I had to do so, I took advantage of a slight pause and I walked away from the footlights to the rear of the stage in order to spit."

Praise in copious quantities was poured upon Giuseppe Verdi after the first performance of *Otello*—just as it has been poured right up to the present day on his amazingly deep and eloquent score for that great opera. But, immediately after the opening performance, he fell into a melancholy mood. After being hauled in his carriage from La Scala to the Albergo di Milano by a crowd of admirers out of their minds with enthusiasm, he exclaimed, as he threw himself dejectedly into a chair:

"I have fired my last cartridge! I want to go back to the loneliness of Sant' Agata! There's nothing else left for me!"

Those around him tried to cheer him up with glowing comments on his glorious triumph of that night. He cut them short—

"Glory? Glory? Now *Otello* will come no more to Sant' Agata. How I came to love him and Desdemona in the solitude there—out there with me—alone. But now the public, always greedy for novelty, has robbed me of them, left me only the memory of our secret talks, of our dear, dead intimacy."

Sadly he shook his head.

Outside in the street the delirious multitude which had unharnessed the horses from his carriage and dragged him and
Arrigo Boïto and Giuseppina from theater to hotel, still
roared and surged and vociferated *"Evviva Verdi!"* They
wanted him to show himself again on the balcony—"Just once
more, maestro, please!" And, suddenly, a smile flashed over
his face—"that beautiful, severe face," as his friend Bellaigue
called it. And he said:

"My friends, if I were thirty years younger, I would like to
begin work tomorrow on another opera. But—" here he turned
a fleeting glance of deep affection on the man who was de-
servedly sharing with him the glory of that night—"I would
begin work on it only on one condition: that the libretto be
by Arrigo Boïto."

Well, Giuseppe Verdi *was* destined to do another opera.
And the condition made by him that night *was* met. But,
when that opera was produced, the calendar marked a date
indicating that its composer was six years older than on the
opening night of *Otello*.

The calendar was wrong. For that other opera was the
culmination of the miracle of which *Otello* was the prelude.
When it was given for the first time Giuseppe Verdi was, as
he had wished to be, thirty years younger.

THIRTY-TWO

TELL me," said Blanche Roosevelt, as she sat at a formal
dinner in Milan next to Arrigo Boïto, "your impressions
of the opening night of *Otello*."

That young American had been going places since, a dozen
years before, she had talked with Giuseppe Verdi in Paris.
She had lived long in Italy, traveled much there, learned Ital-

ian, met whole squads of Italians high in social-artistic circles. She had renewed her acquaintance with Verdi. As for Boïto, she had found no difficulty in drawing out that taciturn celebrity when she had encountered him at select luncheons and teas and dinners. Blanche had a way with her.

"Wasn't it wonderful?" she remarked. And Arrigo Boïto, one of Italy's leading clams, poured out this:

"I was up in a box with Signora Verdi [Giuseppina] when the maestro sent for us. He turned to me in a half-dazed way. He took my hand." [Boïto's voice when he said this, Blanche Roosevelt recounted later, was trembling and his eyes were half-filled with tears.] "I can never describe to you how he took my hand, his touch—there was something so kind, so paternal, so protecting. And the clasp of his fingers was so thrilling to me that I felt the shock to my heart's core. It was an electric thrill, yet so delicate that I could scarcely realize our hands had come in contact. Ah! Verdi said more to me in that single handclasp than he had said in all our previous intercourse, more than anyone ever will say. I shall never forget it."

"How did you like it when the crowd unharnessed the horses from Verdi's carriage and dragged you and him and his wife to his hotel?"

"It was very disagreeable. There were crowds and crowds and crowds. Signora Verdi got into the carriage. I followed. Finally, the mob let the maestro get in. We had made only a few paces when the yells began: 'Take away the horses!' The difference between Italian crowds and others is that there is no difference between their cries of joy and rage. Their voices sound as threatening when they scream 'Long live Verdi!' as when they're screaming 'Down with the Ministry!' or 'Kill Verdi!' We finally persuaded the maestro to let them unharness the horses. This was done with wild yells.

"It was the most uncomfortable experience that I had ever known. First we were lifted up, up, up—and then, suddenly, without an instant's warning, the vehicle was lowered so that I thought we were going to crash into the paving stones. Then, suddenly, it was lifted quite high up in the air again, then dropped quite as suddenly, shaking us almost as if someone had taken us by the shoulders.

"At last we reached the Hotel Milano and another wild yell broke out that simply curdled my blood. Signora Verdi was as white as a sheet and Verdi was as pale as a ghost.

"We were deposited in front of the hotel entrance. I shall never forget Verdi's face as the carriage door was wrenched open. As he got out he glanced back, with his foot still on the step, with an unsmiling face and an indescribable look, and, giving me a sort of desperate hand-grasp—such a one as a soldier gives his comrade before going into battle—he said to me:

" 'I commend my wife to you!'

"I feared that he would be torn to pieces. The crowd was simply mad, snatching right and left at his garments. But, as you know, he got upstairs whole, and—and—that is all—except that I led Signora Verdi into the hotel." *

That dinner party and the other meetings with Arrigo Boïto gave the young lady from the United States material for this word-sketch of *Otello's* great librettist, which she included in her book about Verdi and Paris and "Otellopolis":

He has the air of a *très grand seigneur* in spite of the artistic life and his to some extent Bohemian surroundings. From his manner you might take him for a prince of the blood, a statesman or ambassador.

In personal appearance Arrigo Boïto is tall, very fair, with clear light blue eyes, light moustache, light hair, and a decidedly Slavic hue of complexion. His countenance has a Slavic cast and his features a decidedly Northern cut. His cheek bones are high, his cheeks very hollow.

All his life he has associated with Bohemian men of letters, musicians, actors, painters, yet he speaks like one who has been brought up at courts. . . . When one speaks to him of operas

* Macchetta, *op. cit.*

or theatres or artists or composers he has all the studied politeness we see in a well-bred continental amateur, but he listens as if he were in the moon, and you, from this globe, were talking the language of earth to him.*

Some days later Blanche Roosevelt paid a farewell call on Giuseppe Verdi at his hotel in Milan.

"I found him," she wrote, "the same old Verdi I had known in Paris, only a little quieter, perhaps a little more staid and a little more gentle than before. Sounds of many voices came to us from the adjoining room. Crowds were in there. . . . I think Verdi is proud enough of it all, but rather tired of it."

At the time of the American's visit Tamagno, the tenor in *Otello's* original cast (that opera had been triumphing nightly at La Scala) was ill, and performances were temporarily suspended. Though La Scala's management had spent lavishly on the production, no understudies had been provided for members of the cast! So there was nothing to do but wait until Tamagno was himself again.

"Is it a case of hoarseness, temper or tenor?" inquired Blanche.

"Tenor, perhaps," answered Verdi.

"It's a thousand pities."

"Well, it is at least *one* pity."

Then the visitor asked:

"Your next opera will also be based on Shakespeare?"

Verdi "smiled all over his face and eyes." But he said nothing.

When she rose to go he accompanied her to the passage outside his hotel suite.

"Au revoir," he said politely.

Still he had vouchsafed nothing about another opera from

* *Ibid.*

him. As they reached the stairway, he came close to his visitor, and remarked:

"Mademoiselle, have you ever seen my birth certificate?"

The specter of old age haunted Giuseppe Verdi. And that did not add to his good humor. Always, his temper was nothing if not peppery, and his giving free rein to it nothing if not frequent. Once a man entirely unknown to him, having sent him a note enclosing a musical composition for criticism, to which the recipient had not replied, wrote him (in May, 1888):

Illustrious Maestro:

Please be so kind as to return to me the piece sent to you by me under date of last August 22d. . . . In my day answering letters was obligatory. At present, it seems to me, we are in an era of retrogression.

To which Verdi countered:

Sir. You take the liberty of giving me a lesson which I refuse to accept. Now, in my turn, I ask you:

Why do you, who are not acquainted with me, send me a sample of your work? And why should I pay any attention to it? Are you aware of how many letters, writings, musical pieces I receive daily from everywhere? Am I obligated to reply to all of them? You say that to do so is my *duty*. But I wish to inform you that to do so would be to bow to a veritable *tyranny*, to acknowledge the necessity on my part of wasting my time by answering all the letters addressed to me, examining all the pieces of writing and music I receive, most of them trivial and worthless!

Verdi's good health and vitality and vigor astounded everybody. But he kept dwelling on how old he was. He thought less and less of doing any more composing. Why not spend his few remaining years at Sant' Agata, among rugged, honest peasants, some of them his tenants, others his nearby neighbors, all of them his admirers and friends.

In city and village, in poverty and affluence, as nonentity and celebrity, he had always been a man of the people. Better to him than opulent hotels, exalted social contacts, laurels and medals and flattery in half a dozen languages, had been always Le Roncole, his tiny birthplace, and, above all, Sant' Agata, the home of his heart, with his acres encompassing it, their crops ripening in the golden Italian sunshine. Why not wander at will for the rest of his life, with his dogs romping and barking around him, over his property—his own, his very own. . . !

In a big carriage, behind a pair of snorting, high-stepping horses, with a liveried coachman enthroned on the box seat, cracking his whip, he had delighted, for years, in driving along the roads, threading the plain of Parma and girt by vineyards and farmland, acknowledging the greetings of the country folk who tilled his fields and paid him rent and supplied his wants—who liked him and understood him.

His people! Kith and kin to him, every one of them, these and their humble counterparts in the big cities. Greeting them, being greeted by them, his thoughts flew far from opera-making, from arguments with fussy impresarios, from headaches brought on by conceited tenors and arrogant prima donnas. Of course, the life of the theater was his element— but never to the exclusion of the countryside—nor to the exclusion of humble city folk who knew nothing of theatrical life. Their world was also his—in some ways more so than the world of La Scala and "La Grande Boutique."

Once, in old age, he had written to Villiers Stanford, the well-known English composer-critic, harking back forty years to a rehearsal of his first success, *Nabucco*, at which he had been deeply impressed by the reactions of some carpenters at work on the stage, to his music for the renowned "Va, pensiero" chorus.

"When the number was finished," he wrote, "they broke into the noisiest applause I had ever heard, crying 'Bravo! Bravo! Viva il maestro!' and beating on the woodwork with their tools. Then I knew what the future had in store for me."

And now he was again among peasants akin to those carpenters, his friends, his comrades. Why ever leave them again? What could the world offer him that was better? And, once more he heard the whisper that he had heard after Aïda nearly twenty years ago: "You are at the top. Relax! Enjoy yourself!"

Filled with such thoughts, he would sit back, musing, in his carriage, and his snorting horses would bear him to the market place at nearby Cremona, and Giuseppe Verdi, farmer, would alight from his carriage, and farming folk, who had been awaiting him, would surround him to bargain with him for the sale of their produce or the purchase of his. And when business was over he would walk into the Albergo del Sole, his Cremona hangout, with smiling peasants and townsfolk shaking his hand; and the smiling innkeeper would show him to his favorite seat at his favorite table.

"Maestro, che cosa prende?"

"What do I want? Don't you know by this time? What I always eat here. Veal cutlet alla Milanese."

Off goes the innkeeper to get it for him. Giuseppe Verdi, composer of Aïda and Otello, dealer in chickens and vegetables, calls him back:

"And, remember, plenty of butter."

"Sì, maestro."

And the cutlet is brought, dripping with good country butter, and Giuseppe Verdi eats it, and washes it down with rough country wine, and smacks his lips, and chats with Cremonese friends. Then—back, behind his prancing horses, through the evening sunset, to Sant' Agata. Who would change such a life for Milan and La Scala, Paris and *"La Grande Boutique"*—

And yet . . .

After a while the old restlessness grips him. Just one more opera? Ha! What was it that old Rossini had said? "Verdi. Such a serious chap. *He* could never write a good comic opera." Indeed? I'll show you, old Rossini! I'll astonish you—peeking sardonically at me from the other world!"

At the dinner table at Sant' Agata Giuseppe Verdi suddenly stops eating. He sits rapt, unseeing, with bent head, oblivious of everything and everybody. The dinner guests are intimate friends, some of them charter members of the Sant' Agata inner circle. Giuseppina catches their eyes with a quick glance, beseeching silence. With her sixth sense she has guessed what is the matter.

Pushing back his chair without a word, her husband walks, as if in a trance, into his study. Giuseppina takes up the interrupted conversation. Nothing is said by anybody about what has just happened. She knows—all the others know—that what has caused the host's behavior is not boorishness nor bearishness—that inspiration is no respecter of etiquette.

For some time he had been turning over in his mind in earnest the idea of doing still another opera. But, as with *Otello*, he had fought hard against getting into harness again—against challenging critics and public once more. He was past 75! What if that additional opera should end his glorious career in disappointment and defeat? ". . . Have you ever thought," he had written to Boïto, "of the enormous number of my years?"

Much of the credit for deflecting Verdi from such defeatism must go to Boïto. Patiently, tirelessly, that good angel of the great composer's old age kept urging him to get to work again.

Credit must also go to Giuseppina. When she realized that *"il mio* Verdi" was indeed thinking of doing another opera, a comic opera this time, she was overjoyed. She knew better than anybody that he could do it. Was she not fully aware how he was mellowing at the end of his long life, how his "great laugh" was ringing out ever more frequently now that his youth and middle age were over and he was younger than ever.

She told Boïto about her belief, about the many years through which she had nurtured it. He was amazed. He asked her:

"Do you mean to say, signora, that you knew this even before I did?" She nodded. He made her a low bow:

"What a miracle of feminine intuition!"

Despite his good health and unbelievable energy, Giuseppe Verdi still had that touch of hypochondria which had been noticeable even in his hale thirties and forties. It still made him worry about himself. Having read somewhere that, if old men worked too hard, they might get cerebral anemia, he abruptly decided that two hours daily must be the maximum he could give to composing. That, of course, slowed things up.

Another thing that contributed to the leisurely pace of his work was the annoyance caused him by the project to make an Italian national celebration out of the fiftieth anniversary of his first work, *Oberto*. As soon as he heard of it he was dead against it. And he made his objections known with typical vehemence to Ricordi and Boïto. So plans for an official celebration were given up.

But he was all in favor of a projected celebration in honor of Beethoven. "That's different," he said.

Even Verdi, however, could not check entirely the over-powering urge among his fellow-countrymen to make the anniversary of *Oberto* a big occasion. On November 15, 1889, fifty years to the day since the date of the production at La Scala by Bartolomeo Merelli of the first Verdi opera, letters of congratulation by the hundred poured in on him. One was from King Humbert of Italy. Another came from Giosuè Carducci, ranked as the most inspired of living Italian poets, extolling in glowing words Verdi's musical genius and patriotism and integrity.

At the time of the original production and subsequent tour of Verdi's Manzoni *Requiem* Mass, it had been bitterly criticized in a German newspaper by Hans von Bülow, the well-known pianist, first husband of Liszt's daughter Cosima, who afterward became the wife of Richard Wagner. Eighteen years later, in 1892, Bülow having completely changed his mind, had the decency to write to Verdi as follows:

Please listen to the confession of a contrite sinner!

Eighteen years ago the undersigned was guilty of a great journalistic brutality. . . . How often has the memory of it caused him repentance and bitter shame! . . . At that time he was blinded by ultra-Wagnerian fanaticism. Seven years later light gradually penetrated into his fanaticism and purified it and transformed it into enthusiasm. . . . In the intellectual and moral world light is equivalent to justice. There is nothing more destructive than injustice, nothing more intolerable than intolerance —as has been already said by that most noble writer, Giacomo Leopardi. . . .

Having studied . . . the *Requiem* Mass . . . I have been moved to tears. . . . And now, Illustrious Maestro, I admire you, I love you! Please forgive me. Please avail yourself of the privilege of monarchs by granting me absolution. Long live Verdi, the Wagner of our dear Allies. [At that time Italy was allied with Germany and Austria-Hungary.]

To this letter Verdi promptly replied:

"You have not committed the shadow of a sin! And there

is no reason whatsoever for your talking about repentance and absolution. If your opinions in other days were different from what they are now you have acted excellently in saying so."

And then came this typically Verdian conclusion:

"As a matter of fact, who knows? Perhaps you were right in the first place!"

One day Arrigo Boïto, in Milan, received in his mail a note from Verdi, who was in Genoa (Sant' Agata had become too cold for Giuseppina).

"Please come to me here," it read.

Dropping everything, Boïto took a train for the maestro's winter home.

There, once more, he and Giuseppe Verdi put their heads together in solemn conference. Soon Boïto submitted again a complete scenario of another libretto. Again, as with *Otello*, Verdi passed it almost without a murmur of dissent—he, so long the arch-harrier and super-worrier of librettists!

The ideal collaboration was functioning again.

The miracle was on its way.

There is a dinner at the home of Giulio Ricordi in Milan, and, among the guests, are Giuseppe Verdi and Arrigo Boïto. Without warning, the latter, having filled his glass with wine, stands up. Everyone expects him to propose a toast to Verdi. Instead, raising his glass, he calls out:

"To Fat-Belly!"

Nobody knows what he means. Neither Ricordi nor any one of his guests is fat. All exchange puzzled glances. Then Ricordi tosses back his head, enlightenment shines in his eyes, and, bringing his fist down on the table, he exclaims:

"*Falstaff!*"

Boïto nods. Verdi smiles. Everyone understands. De-

lighted, all spring to their feet, holding their glasses high, turn
to the Grand Old Man, shout in unison:

"*Falstaff!* To *Falstaff!* Here's to *Falstaff!*"

And that was the first definite announcement that Giuseppe Verdi was bringing to completion another opera, with
Shakespeare again as his inspiration, and Shakespeare's renowned fat-bellied rogue and roisterer, wit and wencher, as
his hero.

THIRTY-THREE

THE LIGHTS go out. There is a murmuring, a whispering in
the darkness. The curtain rises.

The Garter Inn at Windsor. At a table, Sir John Falstaff
(Victor Maurel). Buzzing around him, his henchmen, Bardolph and Pistol (or, rather, Bardolfo and Pistola). Under
the bâton of Maestro Mascheroni music begins to bubble
and chatter and snap and effervesce.

February 9, 1893.

Opening night of Verdi's *Falstaff*. Great multitudes of Italians all over Italy are sighing mournfully at the thought that
they are not among those present. The fortunate few, two or
three thousand of them—in the boxes, fashionably dressed,
bedecked with shining jewels—or above the boxes, in seats
growing progressively humbler up to the humblest far up in
the gallery—or below the boxes, in orchestra stalls, haughty
and conspicuous—are thanking their stars that they are about
to hear an opera rumored to be a miracle by a youth in his
eightieth year.

More wavings of Maestro Mascheroni's bâton. More music.
Music that sounds as if drawn from the Fountain of Youth
itself, as if brought over by Ponce de León from the New

World to the Old. In a few minutes the discerning ones in
Falstaff's first audience, listening, entranced and enchanted,
have learned what they wished to know.

It *is* a miracle.

Through the opera's first audience ran a blend of awe,
wonder and delight. And that same blend has also run
through hundreds of later audiences during the 62 years that
have passed since that opening night, who have also thrilled
to the joy and beauty and fire of the *Falstaff* miracle. Having
heard it as often as he possibly could, that enthusiastic British
pro-Verdi "fan," Francis Toye, in his Verdi book, pulls out
all the stops, goes the limit, hails Verdi's final, culminating
work with every shred of his British calm and caution and
leaning to understatement thrown to the winds.

To him, the concerted number in Act II is "not only one
of the most brilliant things in the opera but one of the most
brilliant things ever written." And the love duet between
Fenton and Nannetta (Shakespeare's Sweet Anne Page) is
"perhaps the only operatic music in which the love of boy and
girl is adequately interpreted in accordance not only with
Latin but with Anglo-Saxon ideals." He calls *"dalle due alle
tre,"* that ultra-delicious bit of mischief and mockery by
which Dame Quickly brazenly bamboozles amorous Sir John,
"an inspiration of genius if ever there was one"; and *"Quand'
ero paggio,"* Falstaff's nostalgic little tribute to himself when
he was light as a feather instead of heavy as a hogshead, "one
of the most exquisite and delicate things ever imagined by
any composer."

He raves over the Fat Knight's famous *"Va, vecchio John,"*
with its "intense physical self-satisfaction embedded in the
gross insistence of the staccato brass, but translated even more
emphatically, perhaps, in the flaring passage for full orchestra
that introduces and closes it, of which both the scoring and
harmony are beyond praise." (When I heard Toscanini con-

duct *Falstaff* in concert form not long ago that "flaring passage" gave me one of the supreme moments of my personal
musical enjoyment. And every time I have heard it since,
with or without Toscanini, it makes me wild with impatience
to hear it again.) To *Falstaff's* final fugue, which some critics
find inappropriate in a comedy-opera and a few "pedantic,"
Toye pays this glowing compliment:

Not only justified but wholly, magnificently right . . . Giuseppina once wrote of his [Verdi's] "great laugh." This is what the
music, bubbling with vitality and humor, expresses. The main
subject is said to have been suggested to the composer by a tune
that a child sang in his garden. Is it too fanciful to imagine the
simplicity of extreme age and extreme youth here joining hands
in instilling into us that sense of divine gaiety which is the best
medicine of the soul. In any case, one is glad that Verdi finished
his operatic career on such a note. Bellaigue most happily illus-
trates the point when he writes that Verdi precisely reversed the
crime of Adam, whom Dante describes as having "changed honest
laughter and sweet playfulness into tears and misery."

Finally, the English critic summarizes the general effect of
Falstaff thus:

From beginning to end the opera resembles a shimmer of light
dancing before the eyes; one incomparable beauty after another
is gone almost before its presence can be noted. . . . *Falstaff* . . .
with its wit, its translucence, remains the most exquisite flower
of Mediterranean musical culture.

A shimmer of light dancing before the eyes.
    That is an extraordinarily apt phrase. If some commentator
on *Falstaff* were to be told that, in describing the score of
that marvelous child of Giuseppe Verdi's miraculous eightieth year, he must confine his description to two words, he
could do no better, it seems to me, than to say: "It shimmers."
Shimmering, if I may be permitted to use a colloquial turn
of American slang, is what *Falstaff* "has the most of."

But if two more words were allowed that commentator he could clinch his description and give it something approaching adequacy by adding: "It crackles."

It shimmers. It crackles.

There you have *Falstaff*—if description of that masterpiece of light and air and fantasy and youth *must* be confined within the nutshell of four words.

The first half of that tantalizingly limited description is particularly appropriate to the Herne's Oak music of the last act—that wonder of thistledown treatment, that jewel of airiness and grace and loveliness, with its elves and fairies tripping through the groves of Windsor Forest, dancing to the "overtones of Shakespeare," which, as somebody felicitously said, can be heard in *Otello* and are still more audible, to my ear at least, in *Falstaff*.

Yes, "it shimmers" suffices in a way to reproduce the key impression left by *Falstaff's* final act. It also suggests admirably the effect of the exquisite music allotted the two young lovers, which, running right through the opera, culminates in Fenton's song of love to his beloved—the opera's only aria. Incredible, isn't it?—*one lone aria* from the man who, frequently in *Aïda*, and, at times, even in *Otello*, was not afraid to halt the action if only slightly in order to revert to the tried method of earlier works which had first brought him renown.

But, for much of the rest of *Falstaff*—though the composer repeatedly sets everything shimmering—I think that "it crackles" is needed to convey with something like completeness the general impression left by Verdi's miraculous score.

"*Va, vecchio John*" crackles. "*Dalle due alle tre*" crackles. Ford's great soliloquy crackles with rage and thirst for vengeance. Every time the Merry Wives come out on the stage, with joy dancing in their sparkling eyes, every note that comes from their sunny lips crackles. The shimmer of the entire opera is overlaid or underpinned, now lightly, now robustly, by a constant crackling of wit and drollery and beauty.

One spectator, beside himself with enthusiasm after *Falstaff*, put his impressions into a nutshell of his own: "The first act is a bottle of Asti Spumante, the second a bottle of Veuve Clicquot, the last a bottle of finest Johannisberger."

Giuseppe Verdi remained to the end of his long life a man of the people. "I am just a peasant," he used to say. "A peasant of Le Roncole." Yet there was also in him a touch—always perfectly natural, never calculatingly assumed—of the aristocrat. His militant integrity, his detestation of sham, his life-long consciousness of the vulgarity inherent in self-advertisement and publicity "stunts"—all these were, as revealed by him, the traits of an aristocrat, in the original and best sense of that badly misused word.

This side of him came out strongly when he was on his country estate. As Squire of Sant' Agata he yielded in manner to no duke—he, the son of a humble innkeeper, whose closest kin were the proletarians at work in the fields surrounding the manor of which he was lord.

And that is why he, among all composers, was the right man in the right place as the creator of the music to express Shakespeare's immortal Fat Knight.

Falstaff was an aristocrat. He was also more than that—and less. He, too, at heart was a man of the people. He appealed not only to the son of England's king but also to Bardolph and Pistol, to Dame Quickly and Doll Tearsheet—and they to him. Many among us, of whose world, sometimes unbeknownst to ourselves, Shakespeare has made Falstaff an integral part, are prone to forget Falstaff's full name—*Sir John* Falstaff.

That *Sir John* made him one of the rulers of aristocracy-ruled England. But it was the less important part of his name, just as the aristocratic prestige inherent in it was the lesser part of the Fat Knight. Falstaff never let it get in his way. To him, the adjective in his nickname was far more to be esteemed than the noun. To himself he was first and foremost not noble Sir John but low, obese, guzzling, gobbling, lecherous Falstaff. He preferred to his aristocratic lineage his fat belly, to the discharging of his obligations as a nobleman his plebeian negation of those obligations as a lusty liver of life.

This Giuseppe Verdi, in the ripe wisdom of his young old age, understood to the full. And his score for *Falstaff* is a towering monument to the fullness of his understanding of Shakespeare's sublime scalawag. Verdi's delineation of that deathless rogue is delicate and robust, ethereal and mundane, aristocratic and earthy. One moment, scaling the heights of intellectual inspiration, it shimmers like sunbeams and dazzles like lightning; the next, abruptly coming down to earth, it warms like an open fire and crackles like popping corn. Yet it was composed by an octogenarian! There you have a miracle if ever there was one!

It has been well said [writes Camille Bellaigue] that, in the 19th century, Italy broke the alliance between music and truth. . . . She acquired a taste for lies. In order to remove all uncertainty as to the resumption of the alliance between the two no less than an *Otello* and a *Falstaff* were required. "Let us turn to the old foundations," Verdi took pleasure in repeating again and again. And, in his old age, he turned to the old masters of Italian music. Pushing aside their descendants, who had proved unfaithful to the truth in music, he ranged himself with their ancestors who loved truth and lived as its servants. . . .

They include the Rossini of *The Barber of Seville* and the Cimarosa of *Il Matrimonio Segreto*. Farther back, they include the Pergolesi of *La Serva Padrona*. . . .

Behold them! The great Italians of the past!—apostles of the truth, champions and guardians of the Latin alliance of truth and music! Too long had that alliance been allowed to lapse! And the supreme glory of *Otello* and *Falstaff* is that they reaffirm this alliance. . . .

The critic Montégut pointed out that the history of Italian poetry and art prove the existence of two Italys, one of them happy and gay, the Italy of Boccaccio and Ariosto, the other tragic and sorrowful, the Italy of Dante and Machiavelli and Michelangelo. For a long time Verdi revealed himself as a true son of the second Italy—for a long time he was obstinately gloomy. As late as his 74th year he produced in *Otello* his ultimate masterpiece in the musical depiction of human suffering.

But, in his 80th year, he gives us *Falstaff*, his sole masterpiece of gaiety. He had raised his ideal to lofty heights, without letting it get lost in the clouds—his own ideal and the ideal of his native land. Instead of coercing and perverting it he had broadened it magnificently.

Erect and triumphant on the pinnacle of his career, the old Verdi could gaze down upon the world surrounding him, conscious that, in climbing to that pinnacle, his feet had touched none but Italian soil; that, in his glorious pilgrimage, the mountain which he had scaled was an entirely Italian mountain.*

The consensus of the world's operatic experts now ranks *Falstaff* with Mozart's *Marriage of Figaro*, Rossini's *Barber of Seville*, and Wagner's *Meistersinger* as one of the four supreme comedy-operas. Some make the total five by adding Richard Strauss's *Rosenkavalier*.

With the shouts of elation and admiration elicited by Verdi's music for *Falstaff* was mingled sincere praise for Boïto's libretto in just and adequate measure. In Italy and other lands, including England, the home of Shakespeare, it was extolled as a masterly piece of intelligent compression, an extraordinarily ingenious and understanding adaption of Shakespearean comedy to operatic purposes.

Again, as in *Otello*, the librettist had shown audacity.

* Bellaigue, *op. cit.*

Though he ventured on nothing quite as drastic as his exclusion of an entire act of *Othello* from *Otello*, or the insertion of a whole scene never imagined by Shakespeare, he, nevertheless, at some points in the *Falstaff* libretto played true to his belief that "the opera's the thing."

In delineating his operatic Sir John Falstaff he confined himself almost entirely to that old rapscallion as he is revealed in *The Merry Wives of Windsor*, with occasional borrowings of illuminating details from the Falstaff of *Henry IV*. These borrowings include the celebrated monologue on honor (with which Verdi did wonders in his music) and the description of Bardolph's lantern-like nose. He also reduced the number of characters in *The Merry Wives* and shuffled those whom he retained into a mixture at which Shakespeare, had he become acquainted with it, would have opened wide eyes.

But, despite all that can be said against it, the world in general thinks that the excellence of Boïto's contribution to the opera enormously outweighs its shortcomings. *Falstaff* is even more fully Boïto-Verdi or Verdi-Boïto than is *Otello*; the Gilbert-and-Sullivan twinship of the two collaborators shines here at its brightest.

Taking into consideration the evolution of tastes in opera since the advent of Verdi's Indispensable Trio in the 1850's and since that of *Falstaff* in the 1890's, it seems correct to state, though the statement is perhaps too sweeping, that, whereas among the operagoers of the world *Rigoletto-Trovatore-Traviata* instantaneously captured the majority without permanently alienating the minority, *Falstaff* instantaneously captured the minority without permanently alienating the majority. And today, when the minority, the intellectuals, tend to regard Verdi's Three Unkillables with increasing favor, *Falstaff* is finding steadily growing favor among the majority—those operagoers who still hanker after catchy melody and uncomplicated vocal and instrumental structure. The

majority have never disliked *Falstaff*; they have merely been
slow to appreciate it.

Deeper understanding of its merits will doubtless bring
greater enjoyment of its delights. The Germans have been the
first to bestow upon Giuseppe Verdi's Miracle Opera the
accolade of genuine popularity; here's hoping that the Americans will not be the last to do so.

One critic, an Italian of much interest to American opera
lovers, could not bring himself to like Falstaff—the character,
I mean, not the opera. That was the late Giulio Gatti-
Casazza, long manager of New York's Metropolitan Opera
House. He found the Fat Knight too gross.

And Arrigo Boïto had his doubts about Sir John's now famous song *"Quand' ero paggio."* He thought it too light for
its context. Verdi, always wont to think over Boïto's suggestions and objections with the most scrupulous care before
discarding them, was of the opinion that its very lightness,
coming as it did in the midst of heavier music, was artistically
exactly right.

Boïto still demurred. Verdi sat in thought for a while. Then
he said:

"I think it best to leave that little song just where it is and
not to change a note of it."

On the first night *"Quand' ero paggio"* was in a way—if
there is such a thing as considering any bit of so closely-knit
an opera as *Falstaff* apart from the rest—the smash hit of the
evening. It brought such joy to the audience that it got two
encores—just as if it were an aria in some earlier Verdi work.
Delighted, the old composer rushed forth to search for Boïto,
whom he found in the front lobby of La Scala.

"Well?" he queried.

"Maestro," said Boïto, "you were right. You are always
right."

✦

So numerous are the bursts of praise for the *Falstaff* score
that the temptation to quote another and still another and
yet another becomes almost irresistible. For good measure, I
shall reprint just two more effusions from critics and then
hold my peace:

"What fun Verdi had with the orchestration!" exclaims
Dyneley Hussey. ". . . *The composer who had made the
greatest popular reputation of his time ended by producing
the musicians' opera;* the romantic had turned pure classicist;
and the master of theatrical effect said farewell to the theatre
in strict fugue."

And that arch-Verdian R. A. Streatfeild, after duly mar-
veling at its having been composed by an octogenarian, says
of *Falstaff*:

. . . He has combined a schoolboy's sense of fun with the grace
and science of a Mozart. . . . The part-writing is often exceed-
ingly elaborate, but the most complicated concerted pieces flow
on as naturally as a ballad. . . .

In the last act Verdi . . . has caught the charm of the sleep-
ing forest with exquisite art. There is an unearthly beauty about
this scene which is new to students of Verdi. . . .

His genius lay not in overturning systems and in exploring paths
hitherto untrodden, but in developing existing materials to the
highest conceivable pitch of beauty and completeness.*

As I have already said, Verdi, after he had finished *Otello*,
was saddened by the thought that the Moor and Desdemona
and their Shakespearean comrades, whose company he had
so keenly enjoyed in the solitude of Sant' Agata, would never
again be with him there. And now it was the same with *Falstaff*—more so, for Verdi was older. Never again would he
commune with that fat ruffian and the Merry Wives and
jealous Ford and enamored Fenton and Sweet Nannetta, with

* R. A. Streatfeild, *The Opera.* Philadelphia, J. B. Lippincott Co., 1902.

whom he had spent uncounted hours in imaginary close companionship. For not even he, unbelievably young in heart and spirit at eighty, could hope for still another spell of such delicious intellectual camaraderie.

This final resignation of the old composer to age and to its unavoidable grim aftermath speaks eloquently from some lines found among his belongings after his death. They are a paraphrase by him of the words of one of the most famous bits in *Falstaff*, "*Va, vecchio John*," the Fat Knight's admiring apostrophe to his strutting self when he thinks (entirely without justification) that he is on the road to amorous conquest:

Tutto e finito—
> *Va, vecchio John,*
> *Cammina per la tua via*
> *Fin che tu puoi—*
> *Divertente tipo di briccone*
> *Eternamente vero,*
> *Sotto maschera diversa,*
> *In ogni tempo, in ogni luogo—*
> > *Va, va!*
> *Cammina, cammina—*
> > *Addio.*

Which, rendered freely into English, means:

All is over—
> Go, go, old John,
> Swagger on your way,
> As long as e'er you can—
> Gay rascal that you are,
> A type forever true,
> Whatever your disguise,
> No matter when and where—
> > Go, go!
> Depart upon your way—
> > Farewell!

Those lines, in Verdi's handwriting, were presented by the wife of the man who discovered them, to that doughty Verdi champion, Francis Toye. Their discoverer was Arturo Toscanini.

The curtain comes down on the last act of *Falstaff* on its opening night at La Scala—on Windsor Forest and the Fat Knight and the assembled company who have just sung the opera's brilliant final fugue.

Giuseppe Verdi has just bowed to the cheering audience. After his first obeisance the applause of the spectators has become so deafening and insistent that all concerned in the initial performance are compelled to come out repeatedly before the curtain, including Verdi.

He bows and smiles and behaves as politely as he can. Naturally, the compliment implied in all this enthusiasm pleases him, but its external manifestations are to him, as always, anathema. (Once, it is said, he went to considerable trouble to contrive a home-made sling which he wore for some time whenever he was exposed to autograph-hunters, in order to be able to say to them, with a perfectly straight face: "Sorry. I can't sign my name for you. I've broken my arm.")

The applause continues. Verdi makes one bow after another. Still the frenzied audience yells for more. Up goes the curtain again. But when those on the stage look around for the composer *he isn't there.*

Amid the riotous excitement he has disappeared. Only too well does he remember that trip six years before, after the *première* of *Otello*, from La Scala to the Albergo di Milano—in a carriage bereft of horses and borne on the shoulders of a mad mob—heaved upward one moment and plunged downward the next, like a rowboat in a rough sea—amid yells which, in Italy (as Arrigo Boïto, a fellow-passenger with Verdi

in that careening vehicle, pointed out to Blanche Roosevelt)
had exactly the same blood-curdling quality whether the yell-
ers had in mind acclamation or assassination.

"Never again!" Giuseppe Verdi had thought to himself
after the first performance of *Falstaff* was over.

So, slipping unobtrusively through a rear door of the theater, he had sidled through Milan's streets, holding his scarf
over his face, and reached his hotel unrecognized—while, at
La Scala, his wild-eyed well-wishers still bellowed:

"*Evviva Verdi!* We want Verdi!"

THIRTY-FOUR

Ended is the long climb—boldly begun, resolutely continued, magnificently completed.

1813, Le Roncole—poverty, obscurity. 1839, *Oberto*—fail-
ure, desolation. 1842, *Nabucco*—first taste of fame. 1853,
Trovatore, Traviata—heady roars of worldwide applause. 1871,
Aïda—dreams come true.

Highest point? Surely it is! Why not stop, relax, enjoy?

Not yet.

1887, *Otello*. First half of the miracle.

1893. The miracle's crowning second half.

Nearly eighty years of working, dreaming, soul-searching.
What a life to look back upon! What a career to re-live in
retrospect, with its heartaches and setbacks, its conquests and
glories—now that, his labors over, vigorous still in mind and
body, Giuseppe Verdi stands on his Everest.

What a development!

That development [wrote H. E. Krehbiel, front-ranker in his
day among New York's music critics] "is one of the miracles of

music. In manner Verdi represents a full century of operatic writing. He began when, in Italy at least, the libretto was a mere stalking-horse on which arias might be hung. . . . Later we see the growth of dramatic characterization in his ensembles and the development of strongly marked and ingeniously differentiated moods in his arias, without departure from the old-fashioned forms. . . .

Then set in the period of reflection. The darling of the public begins to think more of his art and less of his popularity. . . . But the final step necessary to complete his wonderfully progressive march was taken when he associated himself with Boïto . . . poet, dramatist, and musician. No one who has studied *Otello* carefully can fail to see that Verdi owes much to the composer of *Mefistofele*; but the indebtedness is even greater in *Falstaff*. . . . There are no numbers in *Falstaff*; there can be no repetition of a portion of the music without interruption and dislocation of the action. One might as well ask Hamlet to repeat his soliloquy. . . .

The orchestra is bearer of everything . . . it supplies phrases for the singers, supports their voices, comments on their utterances, and gives dramatic color to even the most fleeting idea. . . . It swells the bulk of the Fat Knight until it sounds as if he weighed a ton. . . .*

Before becoming known in Mr. Krehbiel's home town, the metropolis of North America, *Falstaff* had made its bow in the metropolis of South America—the operagoers of Buenos Aires saw it in 1893, only five months after its first performance in Milan, whereas it did not reach New York until February 4, 1895, when it was put on at the Metropolitan Opera House. Victor Maurel, the original Sir John, reappeared in the rôle on which the major part of his fame rests. Others in the cast were Emma Eames, Zélie de Lussan, Sofia Scalchi and Giuseppe Campanari. The conductor was Mancinelli.

* H. E. Krehbiel, *Chapters of Opera*. New York, Henry Holt & Company, 1909.

It was heard again at the Met during the season of 1908-09, with Arturo Toscanini conducting and a cast including Scotti, Emmy Destinn, Frances Alda, Maria Gay and Campanari. And it has since had several revivals at the same opera house, participated in by Louise Homer, Edmond Clément, Antonio Pini-Corsi (the original Ford in Milan), Lucrezia Bori, Kathleen Howard, Beniamino Gigli and Lawrence Tibbett.

Incidentally, long before *Falstaff*, there was a plan afoot to have Giuseppe Verdi visit the United States. He appended to a letter: "Good-bye, good-bye. Yes, yes, we're going to America, but—patience!" Nothing came of the idea. And Gino Monaldi says in his Verdi book:

"This wish to go to America certainly was in his mind. He probably gave it up owing to his invincible dislike of the sea." In another letter Verdi makes an allusion to a place that he calls *Nova Jork*.

In "Nova Jork" and all over the United States his music has always stood high in the regard of a large percentage of Americans. He has held his ground even in the thick of wave after wave of anti-Verdianism in this country. When forced to retreat he has fought tough rearguard actions; and, again and again, he has recovered the lost ground—in fact, particularly during the last few years, he has, in addition, occupied a considerable area beyond it.

From his first bow to an American audience with *Ernani* at New York's Astor Place Theatre in 1847 his vogue in the United States has maintained itself. It has survived some of the most virulent onslaughts ever aimed at a composer. It has outlived fashions, vanquished prejudices.

Much of Verdi's music is forgotten in this country. But among his operas there are four—*Rigoletto, Trovatore, Traviata, Aïda*—which persistently stay on American billboards. As for *Otello* and *Falstaff* they are in this country what they are all over the universe among an increasing army of opera-lovers—peaks of operatic delight, supreme dishes for supreme operatic gourmets. An achievement indeed for a man whose output also includes *Un Giorno di Regno* and *Alzira!*

The durability of his most acclaimed operas is astounding. As the case was put by Edward Johnson, for some years at the head of New York's Metropolitan Opera House: "There is no grand opera without Verdi, Wagner and Puccini." (Please note the order in which he named those Big Three.)

Long before his *Otello-Falstaff* phase Giuseppe Verdi had decided to embark on something of which he used to say mysteriously: "It will be the best of my works." Eventually he disclosed what it was: the establishment in Milan of a home for Aged Musicians—60 men, 40 women. Year by year this pet project progressed toward definite shape in his mind.

Since comparatively early in his career he had been, judged by the standards of the Europe of his era, a rich man. He had never dissipated, never thrown money around wildly. Throughout his life he had cultivated the habits of thrift and prudence of a peasant. Due to his ingrained objection to outside prying into his affairs he had been angered by guesses at the extent of his fortune—what he had or did not have was nobody's business. And he had sought to belittle the affluence brought to him by his operas. "In the old days," he wrote to Ricordi, "when I used to compose many operas I received little for each. Now that I receive a lot of money for each I compose very few."

But, as plans for the foundation and endowment of the Casa di Riposo (House of Rest), the name chosen for his pet charity, matured, facts about the extent of his wealth were bound to come out. It transpired that he was worth around two million dollars—representing far more than the same sum would nowadays. For years he had been accustomed to disburse considerable amounts in charity—and, with typical secretiveness, he had said nothing about them to anyone. Now, with the Casa di Riposo as the prime objective of his last days, he cut down his outlay in unorganized charity—nothing must stand in the way of the prompt construction and future solvency of the Casa di Riposo.

In 1895 he commissioned Camillo Boïto, brother of Arrigo, an able architect, to draw up plans and estimate costs. As with libretti in the epoch of Solera and Piave and Cammarano, he put in his oar at every step in the planning. He wasn't going to allow anybody to play ducks and drakes with his money! When everything had been arranged to his satisfaction he set aside the amount needed for building and equipping his Musicians' Home and willed to it the great bulk of his holdings in order that it might receive after his death a sufficient income to support it adequately and indefinitely. And he enjoined upon those appointed to carry out his wishes one strict stipulation: two persons, after their respective deaths, must be buried inside the Casa di Riposo: Giuseppe Verdi and Giuseppina, his wife.

Falstaff was not Verdi's last musical work. After it, he composed four *Pezzi Sacri* (Sacred Pieces)—an Ave Maria, a Laudi, a Stabat Mater and a Te Deum. They were performed, amid much admiration, in Italy and elsewhere. All have beauty. Among them the Te Deum has earned the most praise. In 1898 at the Turin Exposition they were played under the direction of Arturo Toscanini, already becoming known as a leading conductor in his native country.

The composing of these reverent pieces of church music in his old age throws an interesting light on the basic religiousness of their composer. Always he was a Christian; his indifference to external forms of religion masked an inner core of faith. He felt no scruples about composing a *Requiem* Mass in honor of Alessandro Manzoni; and for Giuseppina, his wife, a devout Catholic, he built a little private chapel on the grounds of Sant' Agata.

Like all of us [said Arrigo Boïto in a letter to Camille Bellaigue, his friend as well as Verdi's], he lost his religious beliefs for a time, but he kept, probably more than the rest of us did, a deep respect throughout his life for those beliefs. He gave evidence of his Christian faith by the solemn beauty of his religious compositions, by the observance of its rites (do you remember his beautiful bowed head in the chapel at Sant' Agata?), by his noble homage to Manzoni, by the instructions for his funeral found when his will was opened—"one priest, one candle, one cross." In the moral and social sense he was a great Christian; but one must take care not to picture him as a Catholic in the political-theological meaning of that word. Nothing would be farther from the truth.

After *Falstaff* Verdi took a trip to Paris. He was 81 years old, but what of that? He gave as the reason for it that he wanted to see whether the French were as crazy as ever. He attended a performance of *Otello* in French at *"La Grande Boutique"* and everybody made a tremendous fuss over him. He took it all with typical wry mellowness—in his old age, the mellowness had been winning out over the wryness.

After *Otello's* triumph in its new Gallic garments President Casimir-Périer of France bestowed upon Verdi the Cross of the Legion of Honor, never before given to a foreign composer.

Playing true to form, Verdi refused to be bowled over by the honor. Turning to a friend after the ceremony, he whispered:

"What do you suppose Giuseppina will say when she sees that the French have drilled a hole in the lapel of my tail coat?" Which recalls what a similarly sardonic Frenchman, Anatole France, said when he was similarly honored: "Good!

With the insignia of the Legion of Honor in one's buttonhole nobody notices grease spots on one's coat. It's as good as cleansing fluid." He and Giuseppe Verdi would have got along well together.

On the eve of the production at the Paris Opéra of *Falstaff* translated into French, Victor Maurel, who had made himself famous in the title rôles of both operas, urged Verdi to visit Paris again. And when the composer called attention to his age—probably a sop to hypochondria, since his health continued to be unbelievably good—Maurel laughed at his objections, and, with the aid of other friends, overcame them. In Paris Verdi was again fêted within an inch of his life. He took it all with wry good humor.

Then—back again to the pleasant rural life at Sant' Agata. Not such long walks in the fields for him now. Not so much puttering in his garden. And, when he drove to Cremona, not so much butter on his cutlet *alla Milanese*. But never for a moment did he allow himself to lapse into inactivity, into what a friend of mine, suffering from an overdose of country life, once called "bucolic imbecility." Not Giuseppe Verdi! Even hypochondria in its most virulent form could not have done that to him.

Friends of the old Sant' Agata inner circle still gathered around him and Giuseppina, as they had gathered ever since the long-past days of *Sturm und Drang*. Arrivabene, to be sure, was no longer there to hear the Verdian "great laugh." And others, too, were never again to "put their feet under the dinner table at six—sharp." But some of the best still remained—Arrigo Boïto, Giulio Ricordi and his wife Giuditta, Teresa Stolz. And there were new additions to the old group, keen to relish the life around the Grand Old Man, to revel in his twilight mellowness of soul, out of which had come *Falstaff*, in his robustness and vigor. One of these newcomers was Giuseppe Giacosa, who, already well-known in his native land for good writing, was destined to acquire reflected worldwide glory as one of the co-librettists of several of Puccini's most famous operas.

Once, on a visit to Sant' Agata, Giacosa happened to mention to his host that he came from Ivrea, a town in the extreme north of Italy, notable neither for size nor importance. After dinner, he, with Boïto and Teresa Stolz, jokingly improvised an informal outdoor performance under the stars in the garden of scenes from Verdi's *Ernani,* to the great delight of the old composer and Giuseppina and their other guests. In later years, Giacosa told how, at a certain point in the "performance," he introduced into his singing a flowery tremolo which he considered the last word in *bel canto.* As he finished he looked toward Verdi, expecting commendation. But all he got was:

"Ah! That, I suppose, is the way they sing in Ivrea."

Around this time a German publishing firm asked Verdi to write his memoirs. He replied:

"After many years of inflicting my notes on the public I'm not going to inflict on it my prose!" And when somebody deferentially inquired what he thought about something or other, he remarked:

"God deliver us from the opinions of old men!"

November 14, 1897.

She had long been ailing. Back in the *Otello* days completion by Verdi of the score of that opera had been delayed because of her illness. And now, not so far behind him in years—she was eighty, he eighty-four—Giuseppina was nearing the end of her long road.

To the last she kept up a courage like that of her husband. She faced and belittled what was coming with Verdian disdain.

That November day he came to her bed-side with a little flower that he had bought for her. She smiled.

"Thank you. I can smell nothing. I have a slight cold."

A few hours later she was dead.

To the last moment of her life she held intact her great love for him. Shortly before the end she had made her will. And she had breathed even into that dry, legalistic, soulless document the fragrance of her love.

"Addio, mio Verdi," she had written just over her signature. "As we were united in life, may God unite us in heaven!"

She had loved him—and he her—in the days of I Lombardi and Ernani, when music was inextricably mixed with patriotism—when Italians mad with the longing for liberty had fought in the streets of Italian cities against the soldiers of hated alien rulers and died singing exultant songs of defiance and hope, composed by the man she loved.

She had known him when Aïda had foreshadowed the true potentialities of his genius. And, when Otello and Falstaff had fully revealed it, she still stood by his side—proud of him, loving him.

And now she lay dead.

He kissed her once. Then, throwing back his head, bracing himself like a man, he walked away to face life without her.

FINALE

H E KEPT his head high. Still his courage remained unshaken. Still he walked over the fields of Sant' Agata—but his walks were ever shorter. Still he drove, behind his prancing horses, over the plain of Parma—but his drives were now to places nearer than Cremona. Light had left him. Even noonday seemed dark.

Still he faced life, looked it straight in the eyes. But, as he faced it, he saw a specter standing beside it, a specter about which he had never bothered before in the fullness of his vigor and vitality and virility.

No surrender.

One by one his loved ones had gone from him. His young wife. His little children. His adored mother. His upright, self-sacrificing father. Antonio Barezzi, his generous benefactor and life-long friend. And other friends—one by one, had vanished. And, now, Giuseppina.

Little by little, despite iron courage and steel-hard will, he grew weaker. His step grew slower. The walks over his fields were given up. The carriage drives became too tiring. Instead, a wheel chair, a shawl over his shoulders when Sant' Agata winds grew too keen—as in the days when Giuseppina had shivered in their blasts and longed for Genoa.

At Sant' Agata and Genoa he was lovingly cared for by his cousin Maria Verdi-Carrara, daughter-in-law of his old friend, Doctor Carrara of Busseto. But—if only Giuseppina were there to adjust the shawl with a smile and a joke! And, at that thought, Giuseppe Verdi bows his head and pain darts across his face—his "beautiful, severe face."

Friends still live, true friends. And there are still dogs to play with, dogs that romp around his wheel chair, sticking out their paws, like Lulu and Black in the past, to wheedle caresses from him, while they gaze, with faithful eagerness, into his dimming eyes.

No surrender.

Three months after his 87th birthday he is in Milan. At the Albergo di Milano his old rooms have been reserved for him, the rooms to which his carriage, robbed of its horses, had been pushed and pulled by wildly yelling Milanese crowds after the glorious first night of *Otello*. There are business matters to be attended to, friends with whom to lunch and dine and chat—the Casa di Riposo to inspect. . . .

Life as usual. The calendar be damned. Old age be doubly damned.

Rising from his bed at the Albergo di Milano on a morning late in January, 1901, he starts to dress in order to resume his everyday round. He is putting a collar button into his shirt when, eluding his fingers, it slips to the floor. He stoops to pick it up.

And that was the last move made in life by Giuseppe Verdi that had anything to do with volition on his part. A short time later they found him stretched on the floor, speechless and motionless.

No surrender. That day and the next and the next he fights. Around him, heart-broken, stand Arrigo Boïto, Teresa Stolz, Maria Carrara, Giulio Ricordi and Giuditta, his wife, Giuseppe Giacosa, Monsignor Cadena, a priest, who is another good friend—Giuseppe Verdi's little world.

After long hours of unconsciousness the dying man suddenly opens his eyes. Those around him, sobbing, draw nearer. Monsignor Cadena holds out his hand. Giuseppe Verdi takes

it, presses it—and over his face spreads a beautiful smile. Then
he closes his eyes, never to open them again. "That smile,"
says the priest to the others, "will suffice for getting him into
heaven."

January 27, 1901.

The maestro is dead [wrote Arrigo Boïto]. He carried away with
him a great quantity of light and vital warmth. We had all basked
in the sun of his magnificent old age. He died magnificently, like
a fighter, redoubtable and mute. The silence of death fell on him
a week before he died. With his head bent, his eyebrows set, he
seemed to measure with half-shut eyes an unknown and formidable adversary, calculating in his mind the strength that he
could summon up in opposition. . . . The breathing of his great
chest sustained him for four days and three nights; on the fourth
night the sound of his breathing still filled the room, but what
a struggle, poor maestro! How magnificently he fought up to the
last moment. In my life I have lost persons whom I idolized. . . .
But never have I felt such a hate for death, such a loathing for its
mysterious, blind, stupid, triumphant, infamous power.

And now, forever mute, Giuseppe Verdi lay in state. Before his body filed the people of Milan, tearful and reverent
—the people of the city of his triumphs and sorrows—where
he had sown in youth and reaped in maturity and found con-
tentment in old age—where he had strode forth, in the vanguard of Italian patriotism, to do battle against Italy's foes,
his weapon not a sword but a song. When, after a few days,
his body was taken to a temporary grave, the funeral, in deference to the maestro's wish, was of the simplest. One priest,
one candle, one cross. So he had wished and so his wish was
carried out.

But when, one month later, he was taken to the Casa di
Riposo, the Old Musicians' Home created by his generosity,

chosen by the dead man as his final place of sepulture, the people of Milan, having shown respect once for his wish, felt now that it was their wish that must be respected.

So—with all business halted in their city—with its buildings shrouded in black—the Milanese stood in solid masses waiting for the funeral cortège. After a solemn funeral service, at which 900 singers sang under Arturo Toscanini's direction, the horses drawing the hearse came into sight. And there arose from the throats of those massed multitudes a great sound of song—the poignant notes of "*Va, pensiero*," the famous chant of lamentation from *Nabucco*, which Toscanini had just conducted at the funeral rites. To the strains of that moving and lovely melody, between crowds in the grip of genuine grief— heads bowed, tears pouring from their eyes, shaking, sobbing, on their knees—the cortège paced majestically on its way, until it stopped before the Casa di Riposo.

There—by the side, in death as in life, of Giuseppina Strepponi—in the midst of comrades to whom devoted service to music had not meant, as it had to their benefactor, wealth and glory but pain and want—lies Giuseppe Verdi, master of melody, lover of liberty, symbol of a nation's soul.

LIST OF OPERAS
AND OTHER PRINCIPAL MUSICAL WORKS
BOOKS CONSULTED

LIST OF OPERAS
AND OTHER PRINCIPAL MUSICAL WORKS
BY GIUSEPPE VERDI

OPERAS

WORK	FIRST PRODUCED	PLACE
Oberto	November 17, 1839	Milan
Un Giorno di Regno	September 5, 1840	Milan
Nabucco	March 9, 1842	Milan
I Lombardi	February 11, 1843	Milan
(French version, called Jérusalem, produced in Paris, November 26, 1847)		
Ernani	March 9, 1844	Venice
I Due Foscari	November 3, 1844	Rome
Giovanna d'Arco	February 15, 1845	Milan
Alzira	August 12, 1845	Naples
Attila	March 17, 1846	Venice
Macbeth	March 14, 1847	Florence
I Masnadieri	July 22, 1847	London
Il Corsaro	October 25, 1848	Trieste
La Battaglia di Legnano	January 27, 1849	Rome
Luisa Miller	December 8, 1849	Naples
Stiffelio	November 16, 1850	Trieste
Rigoletto	March 11, 1851	Venice
Il Trovatore	January 19, 1853	Rome
La Traviata	March 6, 1853	Venice
Les Vêpres Siciliennes	June 13, 1855	Paris
Simon Boccanegra	March 12, 1857	Venice
Aroldo	August 16, 1857	Rimini
(Revised version of Stiffelio)		
Un Ballo in Maschera	February 17, 1859	Rome
La Forza del Destino	November 10, 1862	St. Petersburg
Macbeth (revision)	April 21, 1865	Paris
Don Carlo	March 11, 1867	Paris
Aïda	December 24, 1871	Cairo
Simon Boccanegra (revision)	March 24, 1881	Milan
Otello	February 5, 1887	Milan
Falstaff	February 9, 1893	Milan

OTHER WORKS

Hymn of the Nations	May 24, 1862	London
String Quartet in E Minor	April 1, 1873	Naples
Manzoni Requiem Mass	May 22, 1874	Milan
Four Sacred Pieces	April 7, 1898	Paris

BOOKS CONSULTED

Bellaigue, Camille, *Verdi*, Henri Laurens, Paris, 1912.

Biancolli, Louis, *The Opera Reader*, McGraw-Hill, New York, 1953.

Bonavia, Ferruccio, *Verdi*, Dennis Dobson, London, 1947.

Botti, Ferruccio, *Giuseppe Verdi*, Istituto Missionario Pia Società San Paolo, 1941.

Brockway, Wallace, and Weinstock, Herbert, *Men of Music*, Simon & Schuster, New York, 1939.

Colles, H. C., *Oxford History of Music*, Macmillan, New York, 1910.

Colonna, E. D., *Giuseppe Verdi, Biografia Annedotica*, Casa Editoriale Salvatore Biondo, Palermo, 1902.

Copialettere di Giuseppe Verdi, edited by Cesari, Gaetano, e Luzio, Alessandro, Milano, 1913. (Published by the Italian government in centenary year of Verdi's death.)

Crowest, Frederick J., *Verdi, Man and Musician*, Scribner, New York, 1897.

Dannreuther, Edward, *The Oxford History of Music*, Oxford University Press, New York, 1932.

Erskine, John, editor, *A Musical Companion*, Alfred A. Knopf, New York, 1935.

Garibaldi, Franco Temistocle, *Giuseppe Verdi*, B. Bemporad & Figlio, Firenze (Milano-Roma), 1904.

Gascó Contell, Emilio, *Verdi*, Casa Editoriale Franco-Ibero-Americana, Paris, 1927.

Gatti, Carlo, *Verdi*, Arnoldo Mondadori Editore, Milan, 1951.

————, *Revisioni e Rivalutazioni Verdiani*, Edizione Radio Italia, 1951.

Gerigk, Herbert, *Giuseppe Verdi*, Akademische Verlagsgesellschaft Athenaion, Potsdam, 1932.

Gianoli, Luigi, *Verdi*, La Scuola Editrice, Brescia, 1951.

Grout, Donald Jay, *A Short History of Opera*, Columbia University Press, New York, 1947.

Grove, Sir George, *Dictionary of Music and Musicians*, Macmillan, New York, 1952.

Holl, Karl, *Giuseppe Verdi*, Verlagsbuchhandlung Franz Perneder, Wien, 1942.

Huneker, James, *Overtones*, Scribner, New York, 1909.

Hussey, Dyneley, *Verdi*, E. P. Dutton, New York, 1940.

Kolodin, Irving H., *The Story of the Metropolitan Opera House*, Alfred A. Knopf, New York, 1953.

Krehbiel, H. E., *Chapters of Opera*, Henry Holt, New York, 1908.

——, *More Chapters of Opera*, Henry Holt, New York, 1919.

Lambert, Constant, *Music Ho!*, Scribner, New York, 1934.

Lang, Paul Henry, *Music in Western Civilization*, W. W. Norton, New York, 1941.

Lumley, Benjamin, *Reminiscences of the Opera*, Hurst and Blackett, London, 1864.

Luzio, Alessandro, "Il Pensiero Artistico e Politico di Giuseppe Verdi," nelle sue Lettere Inedite al Conte Opprandino Arrivabene, *La Lettura*, 1921.

Macchetta, Mrs. Blanche Roosevelt Tucker, *Verdi, Milan and "Othello*," Ward & Downey, London, 1887.

Monaldi, Gino, *Verdi*, Fratelli Bocca, Torino, 1926.

Morazzoni, G., *Le Opere Verdiane, Lettere Inedite*, Fratelli Bocca, Torino, 1926.

Mundula, Mercede, *La Moglie di Verdi*, Garzanti, Milano, 1941.

Oberdorfer, Aldo, *Autobiografia delle Lettere*, Rizzoli Editore, Milano, 1951.

Pompée, Hélène, *Peppino: ou l'enfance et jeunesse di Giuseppe Verdi*, Editions Correa, Paris, 1940.

Pougin, Arthur, *Verdi*, Calmann-Levy, Paris, 1886; English translation, Scribner & Welford, New York, 1887.

Pratt, Waldo Selden, *The History of Music*, H. Schirmer, New York, 1908.

Streatfeild, R. A., *The Opera*, J. B. Lippincott, Philadelphia, 1902.

Taylor, Deems, *Of Men and Music*, Simon & Schuster, New York, 1937.

Toye, Francis, *Giuseppe Verdi, His Life and Works*, Alfred A. Knopf, New York, 1946.

Weissmann, Adolf, *Verdi*, Deutsche Verlags-Anstalt vereinigt mit Schuster und Loeffler, Stuttgart-Berlin, 1922.

Werfel, Franz, *Giuseppe Verdis Briefe*, herausgegeben und eingeleitet von Franz Werfel, ubersetzt von Paul Stefan, Paul Zsolnay Verlag, Berlin-Wien-Leipzig, 1926.